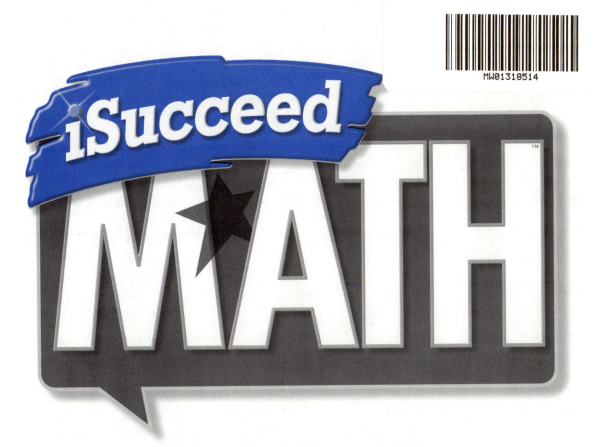

TEACHER'S GUIDE

Volume II: Decimals, Fractions, and Other Rational Numbers

A Division of Houghton Mifflin Company

Acknowledgments

We gratefully acknowledge the teachers and supervisors who reviewed the lessons in the *iSucceed Math*™ Teacher's Guides.

Stephanie Auld
Fourth Grade Teacher
Emma W. Shuey School
Rosemead, California

Keith Case
Teacher, Owens Elementary School
Cypress-Fairbanks ISD
Houston, Texas

Judy Chambers
Math Consultant
Fayetteville, Georgia

Janie Coburn
SES Specialist
Palm Beach Schools
West Palm Beach, Florida

Rosalie Fazio
Elementary Mathematics District Trainer
Broward County Schools
Fort Lauderdale, Florida

Denise Finney
Staff Development Resource Trainer
Chula Vista Elementary School District, Chula Vista, California

Caroline Goodnight
Teacher
Elk Grove Unified School District
Elk Grove, California

Sharon Greenwald
Elementary Mathematics District Trainer
Broward County Schools
Fort Lauderdale, Florida

Jerilynn Lawless
Staff Developer
District 31
New York City, New York

Nigel Nisbet
Professional Development Facilitator
Los Angeles USD
Los Angeles, California

Mary Esther Reynosa
Instructional Specialist for Elementary Mathematics
Northside ISD
San Antonio, Texas

Kay Seabolt
Math Coordinator (retired)
Fayette County Schools
Fayetteville, Georgia

Margaret B. Silva
Teacher
San Diego USD
San Diego, California

Bre Welch
Math Teacher/Department Chair
Pioneer Middle School
Tustin, California

Writing: *Concept Builder and Skill Builder Lessons:* Kane Publishing Services, Inc.; *Unit Openers:* Carol DeBold; *Supporting English Learners introduction:* Miriam A. Leiva; *Active Practice:* Patsy Kanter
Design/Production: Taurins Design
Electronic Art: Deborah Brouwer/Taurins Design
Cover and Package Design: Kristen Davis/Great Source
Editorial: Carol DeBold, Kathy Kellman, Marianne Knowles

Copyright © 2008 by Great Source Education Group, a division of Houghton Mifflin Company. All rights reserved.

Permission is hereby granted to the teacher who has purchased Great Source iSucceed MATH™ (ISBN 978-0-669-00624-7) to reprint or photocopy in quantities for classroom use the Active Practice Recording Sheets and Copymasters in this book, provided that each copy made shows the copyright notice. Such copies may not be sold and further distribution is expressly prohibited. Except as authorized above, prior written permission must be obtained from Great Source Education Group to reproduce or transmit this work or portions thereof in any other form, or by any other electronic or mechanical means, including any information storage or retrieval system, unless expressly permitted by federal copyright law. Address inquiries to Permissions, Great Source Education Group, 181 Ballardvale Street, Wilmington, MA 01887

Printed in the United States of America

Great Source® and Great Source iSucceed MATH™ are registered trademarks of Houghton Mifflin Company.

International Standard Book Number: 978-0-669-00509-7

2 3 4 5 6 7 8 9 10–MA–12 11 10 09 08 07

Contents

INTRODUCTION
How to Use This Book.. vi
Volume II Overview viii

CONCEPT-BUILDER AND SKILL-BUILDER LESSONS

Lessons for planning and leading whole-class and small-group discussions on key concepts and skills related to decimals, fractions, and other rational numbers

Getting Ready 2

Details on preparing to use the lessons in this volume

Develop Math Vocabulary.. 4

Decimals 8

1. Decimal Numbers (Grade 3)* 10
2. Relate Decimal Numbers to Money (Grade 3) 14
3. Compare and Order Decimal Numbers (Grade 4) 18
4. Add Decimal Numbers (Grade 4) 22
5. Subtract Decimal Numbers (Grade 4) 26
6. Check Decimal Sums and Differences (Grade 4) 30
7. Multiply Decimal Numbers (Grade 5) 34
8. Check Decimal Products (Grade 5) 38
9. Divide Decimal Numbers (Grade 5) 42
10. Decimal Divisors (Grade 5) 46
11. Check Decimal Quotients (Grade 5) 50

*Indicates grade level at which topic is typically introduced; your curriculum may differ.

Fractions 54

12 Fractions: Parts of a Set (Grade 2)* 56
13 Fractions: Parts of a Whole (Grade 2) 60
14 Fractions: The Division Model (Grade 4) 64
15 Equivalent Fractions (Grade 5) 68
16 Simplest Form (Grade 5) 72
17 Relate Fractions to Decimal Numbers (Grade 3) 76
18 Compare and Order Fractions (Grade 5) 80
19 Model Adding Fractions (Grade 4) 84
20 Model Subtracting Fractions (Grade 4) 88
21 Model Multiplying Fractions (Grade 5) 92
22 Reciprocals (Grade 5) 96
23 Model Dividing Fractions (Grade 5) 100
24 Mixed Numbers (Grade 5) 104
25 Add Mixed Numbers (Grade 5) 108
26 Subtract Mixed Numbers (Grade 5) 112
27 Multiply Mixed Numbers (Grade 5) 116
28 Divide Mixed Numbers (Grade 5) 120
29 Use a Calculator Appropriately (Grade 3) 124

Positive and Negative Numbers 128

30 Integers (Grade 5) 130
31 Add Integers (Grade 5) 134
32 Subtract Integers (Grade 5) 138
33 Multiply Integers (Grade 6) 142
34 Divide Integers (Grade 6) 146
35 Rational Numbers (Grade 7) 150
36 Compare and Order Rational Numbers (Grade 7) 154
37 Add and Subtract Rational Numbers (Grade 7) 158
38 Multiply and Divide Rational Numbers (Grade 7) 162

*Indicates grade level at which topic is typically introduced; your curriculum may differ.

ACTIVE PRACTICE INTRODUCTION

Lessons that model, monitor, and reteach Active Practice games 166

Active Practice Model Lessons

1. Fill In 1 Whole (Grade 3)* 168
2. Order Decimal Numbers (Grade 4) 170
3. Draw To Add Decimals (Grade 4) 172
4. Draw to Multiply Decimals (Grade 5) 174
5. Order Fractions (Grade 5) 176
6. Giant Inch (Grade 5) 178
7. Draw To Add Fractions (Grade 4) 180
8. Integers (Grade 5) 182

Active Practice Recording Sheets

Copymasters; also provided on CD-ROM for Volume II

1. Fill in 1 Hole Recording Sheet 184
2. Order Decimal Numbers Recording Sheet 185
3. Draw to Add Decimals Recording Sheet 186
4. Draw to Multiply Decimals Recording Sheet 187
5. Order Fractions Recording Sheet 188
6. Giant Inch Recording Sheet 189
7. Draw to Add Fractions Recording Sheet 190
8. Integers Recording Sheet 191

COPYMASTERS

Use with Concept-Builder and Skill-Builder lessons; also provided on CD-ROM for Volume II

- M1 Place-Value Charts 192
- M2 Number Lines 193
- M3 Place-Value Models 194
- M4 Place-Value Addition and Subtraction 195
- M5 Grid Paper 196
- M6 Hundred Charts 197

INDEX 198

*Indicates grade level at which topic is typically introduced; your curriculum may differ.

How to Use This Book

Introduction

This Teacher's Guide is part of Volume II of the five volumes that make up the *iSucceed MATH*™ program. Mathematical concepts in Volume II range in skill level from grade 3 through grade 7. Resources in this Teacher's Guide and in the rest of Volume II help students to develop a thorough understanding of rational numbers, from simple fraction and decimal concepts through computing with negative numbers. For a complete explanation of how this Teacher's Guide fits within the entire *iSucceed MATH*™ program, see the Program Overview in your kit.

Concept-Builder and Skill-Builder Lessons

Each Concept-Builder and Skill-Builder lesson in the Teacher's Guide is meant to be used with intervention students in a small- or large-group setting. Struggling students talk about mathematical concepts, developing important vocabulary as well as understanding concepts. Discussions are at a level basic enough that all students should profit from and be able to participate in them. These discussions help assure that students have the vocabulary and background mathematical skills to successfully complete their courseware assignments and Practice Sheets, and to benefit from the rich and varied practice provided by the Active Practice. In Concept-Builder lessons, discussions revolve around core mathematical concepts. In Skill-Builder lessons, discussions include hands-on activities to help students use mathematical tools.

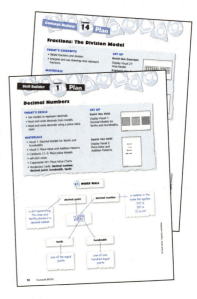

Active Practice

There are eight Active Practice games associated with Volume II. In your Volume II kit, you will find Active Practice cards that provide instructions for each partner activity, as well as examples of appropriate play. Lessons that model how to play each game, and copymasters for the student Recording Sheets, are found in this Teacher's Guide. (The Recording Sheets are also available on the Teacher's Resource CD-ROM in the Volume II kit.) After an Active Practice first appears in the Lesson Support popup for a courseware lesson that a student has completed, it becomes an appropriate review and reinforcement activity for that student at any time.

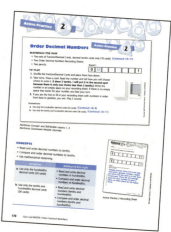

Deciding Which Lessons to Teach

Your curriculum and the requirements of your Intervention students will help you to decide which Concept- and Skill-Builder Lessons to use. Look at your students' courseware assignments. Find the lowest-level assignment, and look at the Lesson Support popup for that lesson. Start your discussions with the first Concept- or Skill-Builder listed there. Choose further Concept- and Skill-Builder lessons based on students' needs and the Intervention curriculum in your district. To see how independent courseware assignments are made, see the Program Overview in your kit, the User's Guide, or the Courseware.

Program Components for iSucceed MATH™

Program Overview
- Orientation to the program
- Implementation Plans
- Professional Papers
- Scope and Sequence

Guide for using the program

Teacher's Guide
- Concept-Builder and Skill-Builder lessons
- Active Practice model lessons

Whole- and small-group instruction

related components:
- consumable Lesson Visuals, 2 per lesson (11 in. × 17 in.) also on Teacher's Resource CD-ROM
- Vocabulary Cards
- Cardstock

Courseware
- Web-based lessons and assessments
- Practice Sheets and Family Activity Letters
- Student Lesson Reports and Lesson Support

Individualized instruction

related components:
- Diagnostic Placement Tests
- Practice Sheets and Family Activity Letters also on Teacher's Resource CD-ROM

Active Practice
- Math games on cards
- Models in Teacher's Guide

Small-group and paired practice

related components:
- number cubes
- Cardstock
- Active Practice Recording Sheets (in Teacher's Guide and on CD-ROM)

Tutoring Plans
- Lesson plan book

One-on-one remedial instruction

related components:
- *Math to Know*
- *Math at Hand*
- *Math on Call*
- Cardstock

Fact Fluency*
- Student Edition with flash cards
- Annotated Teacher's Edition

Active and independent practice for mastery

*Volume I only

Teacher's Resource CD-ROM

Resources for instruction and practice, to print out or to project on interactive whiteboards

Volume II • Decimals, Fractions, and other Rational Numbers

Volume II Overview

This volume, Decimals, Fractions, and Other Rational Numbers, includes guidance and materials to help the teacher lead 39 basic-skills discussions and eight introductions to multi-use Active Practice games. Volume I of *iSucceed MATH*™ covers the basic facts of mathematics and how to use them in whole-number situations. Volume II takes those basic facts, skills, and concepts and shows students how to use, combine, and extend them to the numbers between whole numbers and the numbers less than zero.

nits

Getting Ready
Unit 1 Decimals
Unit 2 Fractions
Unit 3 Positive and Negative Numbers
Active Practice

Research

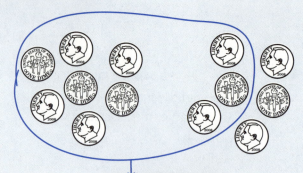

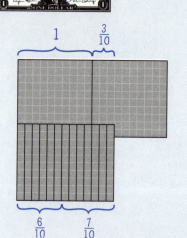

In order to successfully function in our world, we need to know facts, to know how to use these facts, and to understand how to combine these facts into more useful knowledge. This applies to mathematics students as well as to citizens of the wider world.

Example: A student knows whole-number addition facts, but cannot make the transition to correctly placing the decimal point when adding simple decimal numbers whose sum is greater than one. Research suggests that demonstrating the procedure with manipulatives, such as dimes and dollars or place-value models, then helping the student to use simple diagrams to simulate the physical manipulation of these objects will help the student understand that adding decimal numbers requires just one small additional step beyond adding whole numbers: placing the decimal point in the sum directly below the decimal point in the addends in a properly set-up example.

oncept Trace

Prior Knowledge	Instruction	Future Instruction
• place value • compare and order whole numbers • basic whole-number facts • properties of addition and multiplication	• decimal place value • rational numbers • compare and order rational numbers	• evaluate expressions and solve equations • collect and analyze data • find ratios, rates, and percents

Supporting English Learners

Knowing with understanding the relationships and connections among fractions, decimals, percents, and ratios is key to the application of mathematics in the real world. When students leave school, this knowledge will be most useful in their daily life—even when many do not recognize it as mathematics!

If students have not yet encountered fractions, decimal numbers, and other rational numbers in school, they still live in a world where such numbers are part of the social dialog, so you will have natural starting places for your discussions. Here are a few examples they will have encountered that require knowledge and decision making such as, "Can I afford it?"

- Gas costs $2.35 per gallon.
- The car can drive 40 miles per gallon.
- The rent on the apartment is $\frac{3}{4}$ of your monthly salary.
- The recipe needs a $1\frac{1}{4}$ quarts of milk.
- The area of the rug is 100 square meters.

Help students to explain their thinking by scaffolding the teaching and learning. When you scaffold, you are not giving away the answers, but using smart questioning to lead them to understanding. This is particularly useful when teaching students who have fallen behind or who have a language barrier, such as second language learners.

Example: Display the picture of the rectangle divided into 4 squares, and ask students to pair up, discuss, and write three statements that describe the picture. Some possible answers for which you might prompt, depending on grade level, are:

- $\frac{1}{4}$ is shaded.
- 0.25 (twenty-five hundredths) is shaded.
- $\frac{3}{4}$ is white.
- 3 out of 4 squares are white.
- If there were eight squares, two of them would be shaded to keep the same relationship.

Push on the language and math skills related to per hundred: 25% and 75%. Remind students that math is a language that may have several names for the same concept.

Examples: Make further connections to enhance students' academic and mathematical language:

- $\frac{1}{4}$ of the dollar is a quarter or 25 cents or $\frac{25}{100}$ of a dollar.
- $\frac{1}{4}$ of a gallon is a quart or $\frac{25}{100}$ of the gallon.
- On a clock, you read a quarter to and a quarter after the hour.
- Note words that begin with "qua-" and direct students to come up with other such words or similar: quadrilateral, quadruplets, and so on.

BIBLIOGRAPHY

Hasselbring, Ted S., Alan C. Lott, and Janet M. Zydney, *Technology-Supported Math Instruction for Students with Disabilities: Two Decades of Research and Development* in LDOnline, 2006

McCloskey, Michael and Paul Macaruso, *Representing and Using Numerical Information*, in American Psychologist Vol. 50 No. 5, 1995

Willis, Gordon B. and Karen C. Fuson, *Teaching Children to Use Schematic Drawings to Solve Addition and Subtraction Word Problems* in Journal of Educational Psychology Vol. 80 No. 2, 1998

Getting Ready

Prepare Materials

WORD WALLS

Review the Word Walls on the first page of each lesson; prepare examples and definitions. Keep the Vocabulary Cards together, in alphabetical order, as they are often reused. Place the other materials (including push pins, yarn, and examples) for each Word Wall in its own labeled bag, so posting the Word Wall either before or during the lesson will proceed efficiently.

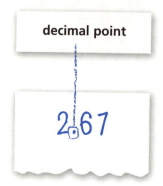

PERSONAL GLOSSARIES

If you haven't already done so, decide on the format for students' personal glossaries and have materials ready: loose-leaf binders, spiral-bound notebooks, folders, or index cards. See page 6 for more complete directions for preparing personal glossaries.

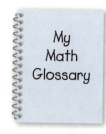

CONCEPT- AND SKILL-BUILDER LESSONS

- Punch out and place in plastic bags Cardstock C1-C3: Place-Value Models, C4: Paper Money, C5: Coins, C6–C7: Fraction Models, C8–C11 Fraction/Decimal Cards, and C12: Digit Cards.
- Make enough copies for all students of Copymasters M1: Place-Value Charts, M2: Number Lines, M3: Place-Value Models, M4: Place-Value Addition and Subtraction, and M5: Grid Paper.
- Cut in half about 20 small and 10 large self-stick notes.
- Make an adding-machine tape number line from 0–26.
- Collect and have available: push pins, yarn, teacher-scissors, colored pencils, and #2 pencils.
- If you will teach Skill Builder 29, it will help to have some calculators.

ACTIVE PRACTICE

- Make copies of Recording Sheets for Active Practice 1–8 and Copymasters 2 and 5.
- Punch out and bag Fraction/Decimal Cards and Digit Cards. A full set of Digit Cards is one each, 0–9.
- Separate the Active Practice Student Cards.
- Prepare the number cubes for Active Practice according to this table:

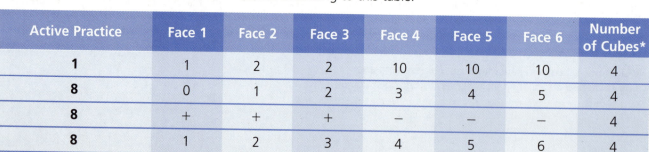

Active Practice	Face 1	Face 2	Face 3	Face 4	Face 5	Face 6	Number of Cubes*
1	1	2	2	10	10	10	4
8	0	1	2	3	4	5	4
8	+	+	+	−	−	−	4
8	1	2	3	4	5	6	4

*Assumes four pairs of students working on the same activity at the same time.

Make four bags of materials for each Active Practice Game. The table describes the contents of one bag for each Active Practice. There are enough student cards for four bags.

Active Practice	Contents of One Bag
1: Fill In 1 Whole	1 Active 1 Practice Student Card 1 number cube (1, 2, 2, 10 10, 10) 8 copies Active Practice 1 Recording Sheet
2: Order Decimal Numbers	1 Active Practice 2 Student Card 2 sets of Fraction/Decimal Cards 8 copies Active Practice 2 Recording Sheet
3: Draw to Add Decimals	1 Active Practice 3 Student Card 2 sets of Digit Cards without 1s or 2s (16 cards) 8 copies Active Practice 3 Recording Sheet
4: Draw to Multiply Decimals	1 Active Practice 4 Student Card 2 sets of Digit Cards (20 cards) 8 copies Active Practice 4 Recording Sheet
5: Order Fractions	1 Active Practice 5 Student Card 2 sets Fraction/Decimal Cards 8 copies Active Practice 5 Recording Sheet
6: Giant Inch	1 Active Practice 6 Student Card 1 coin 8 copies Active Practice 6 Recording Sheet
7: Draw to Add Fractions	1 Active Practice 7 Student Card 2 sets of Digit Cards without zeros (18 cards) 8 copies Active Practice 7 Recording Sheet
8: Integers	1 Active Practice 8 Student Card 3 number cubes (0–5, +/−, and 1–6) 8 copies Active Practice 8 Recording Sheet

Develop Math Vocabulary

If you have already used another volume of *iSucceed MATH*™, then you may not need to conduct the discussion in the following lesson, Develop Math Vocabulary. This lesson deals with using a graphic organizer, the Word Wall, to encourage careful and accurate use of mathematical terms. It also guides students in creating their personal glossaries.

Skill Builder Plan

Develop Math Vocabulary

TODAY'S SKILLS
- Participate in whole-class discussion.
- Discuss vocabulary.
- Use a graphic organizer to relate math terms.
- Create a personal journal and glossary.

MATERIALS
- Visual i: Make a Personal Glossary
- Visual ii: Look It Up!
- Cardstock label: Word Wall
- Vocabulary Cards: **geometry**, **mathematics**, **operation**, **whole number**
- yarn, pushpins, and scissors
- Great Source math handbook
- loose-leaf or spiral-bound notebooks, or folders
- paper and pencils

SET UP
Build the Skill
- Visual i: Make a Personal Glossary
- Find wall space or a bulletin board to use for your Word Wall. The display on this wall will change for each new Concept Builder or Skill Builder lesson.

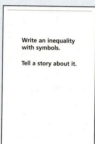

Apply the Skill

Display Visual ii: Look It Up!

WORD WALL

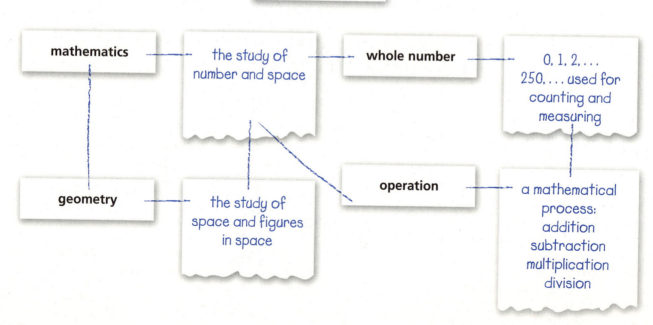

iSucceed MATH

PROFESSIONAL DEVELOPMENT

Graphic Organizers A graphic organizer is a diagram that shows how ideas or vocabulary terms are related. The Word Wall uses Vocabulary Cards and hand-made descriptions, examples, or definitions, connected by yarn or string to show relationships.

Connect to Vocabulary In this program, we suggest that you create a graphic organizer for every Concept Builder and Skill Builder lesson. You may copy the sample Word Wall shown on the first page of every lesson, or you may work with students during the day's discussion to create the organizer in a way that's special for them.

Problem Solving The Draw a Diagram problem-solving strategy is a good example of the way graphic organizers can help students to make sense of mathematics. There are several ways students can use graphic organizers to solve problems. See Figure 1 and Figure 2 for examples.

Figure 1

Maria xxxxxxxxxxxxxxx Armand

In a race, Maria finished second. Armand finished fifteenth. How many runners finished between Maria and Armand? (This problem is tricky: the answer is not 13. A diagram will help students to see the characteristics of the problem. There are 12 runners between Maria and Armand.)

Figure 2

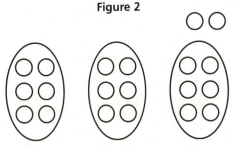

Three girls share 20 grapes equally. How many does each girl get, and how many are left over? (Students who do not have a good grasp of division can solve this problem with a good diagram. Each girl gets six grapes and there are two grapes left over.)

Teach

BUILD THE SKILL

Display Visual 1: Make a Personal Glossary. Distribute materials for making Personal Glossaries. Your goal in this discussion is to help students become responsible for correctly using math vocabulary.

- Show students the collection of Vocabulary Cards from your kit. *Whenever we have a new vocabulary term, we will work together to define it and post it on our Word Wall.*
- Show students the handbooks from your kit and demonstrate the use of their glossaries.
- *Whenever we use a new math term, we will talk about what it means and how it is used. I will ask you to record the term in your Personal Glossary.* Read the sample entry on the Visual.
- Help students to create a notebook for their personal glossaries. A separate section of the book may be used for journal entries.
- *How can you organize your Glossaries?* (See right.)
  1. Label several pages with each letter of the alphabet.
  2. Write the word, a definition, an example, and/or a diagram.
  3. Since new words will not be added in alphabetical order, just keep all of each letter together.
  4. Leave room to add to the entry at a later time.
- Based on the Vocabulary Cards for the entire program, we recommend allocating at least pages six pages for most letters of the alphabet. Also assign pages for symbols and formulas.

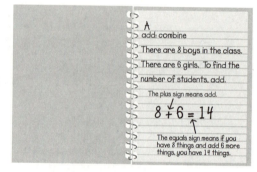

This is one way to organize a spiral notebook as a Personal Glossary. Other set-ups are possible, depending on the materials you have.

EXPLORE THE SKILL

- Post the **mathematics** Vocabulary Card on your Word Wall. Ask volunteers to share their definitions of mathematics. (Mathematics is the study of number and space. "Math" is a short way to say "mathematics.")
- Listen to all suggestions. Work with the class to write a definition, example, or description. Use yarn or string to connect the card to your definition and to related cards.
- *How is geometry related to mathematics?* (It is one part of mathematics.) Discuss the definition of geometry (the study of space and figures in space), post the card and the definition or example, then show this relationship with your yarn.

Connect to Vocabulary Discuss and display the Vocabulary Cards for **whole number** (any of the numbers 0, 1, 2, 3, 4, 5, and so on) and **operation** (a mathematical process that uses at least two numbers to produce another number) in the same way.

Wrap Up *What are the ways you can make sure that you know the meanings of math terms or other words?* (Look in a handbook glossary, look at the Word Wall, use the class dictionary.)

Reteach Choose any four words from the Vocabulary Cards and work with students to make a Word Wall.

How can you find the definition of the math term, obtuse? (To find it in the handbook, turn to the O section of the glossary, and find the word.)

APPLY THE SKILL
Problem-Solving Skill: Find Information You Need

Present the Problem Display Visual 2: Look It Up! Ask a volunteer to read the problem: *Write an inequality with symbols. Tell a story about it.*

- *Do you know what to do to solve this problem?* (It's likely that some, if not all, students will not have a clear definition for inequality.)
- *What can you do to help the class understand the problem?* (Students can either go through the Vocabulary Card set, or use the handbook glossary to look up inequality: a mathematical sentence that compares two amounts using the symbols $\neq$, $<$, or $>$.)
- Discuss how the example in the handbook can help them understand the inequality symbols $<$, and $>$. (By studying the example, $4 + 2 > 4$, they should figure out that $>$ means *greater than*.) Help them to remember that the symbol always points to the number that is less.
- After you are satisfied that everyone knows the definition of inequality, and how to use the $<$ and $>$ symbols, ask students to write at least one inequality on a piece of paper.
- **EL** Help students to see that the prefix *in-* is like the prefix *un-*: it is a negative. In any <u>in</u>equality, the numbers are <u>not</u> equal.

Discuss the Solution Have students share their inequalities. Record as many as you can. Then, encourage every student to tell a story about one of the inequalities. (Sample story: Joey has 5 brothers and sisters. I have 4 brothers and sisters. Joey has more brothers and sisters than I do; $5 > 4$.) Make sure that all students participate and help them find pleasant, constructive ways to prompt, correct, and question others.

REFLECT

What are three ways to find out what math words mean? (Look at the Word Wall; use a handbook glossary; use a dictionary or other reference book.)

How will you find definitions of math terms that are new to you or that you have forgotten? (Look them up in handbooks, dictionary, math textbook, Word Wall, or Personal Glossary.)

How can you write an inequality to compare the number of boys to the number of girls in this class? (Be sure that students can both write and say the inequality.)

UNIT 1

Decimal Numbers

Lessons

1 **Decimal Numbers** (Grade 3)* 10

2 **Relate Decimal Numbers to Money** (Grade 3) 14

3 **Compare and Order Decimal Numbers** (Grade 4) 18

4 **Add Decimal Numbers** (Grade 4) 22

5 **Subtract Decimal Numbers** (Grade 4) 26

6 **Check Decimal Sums and Differences** (Grade 4) 30

7 **Multiply Decimal Numbers** (Grade 5) 34

8 **Check Decimal Products** (Grade 5) 38

9 **Divide Decimal Numbers** (Grade 5) 42

10 **Decimal Divisors** (Grade 5) 46

11 **Check Decimal Quotients** (Grade 5) 50

*Indicates grade level at which topic is typically introduced; your curriculum may differ.

MATERIALS

- Volume II Unit 1 Lesson Visuals 1–22
- Volume II Cardstock: Place-Value Models, Paper Money, Coins
- Copymasters: M1 Place-Value Charts, M2 Number Lines, M3 Place-Value Models, M5 Grid Paper
- adding machine tape
- small self-stick notes in three colors
- colored pencils

VOCABULARY CARDS

< (is less than), = (is equal to), > (is greater than), ≈, addend, compatible numbers, decimal number, decimal point, difference, dividend, divisor, dollar sign, estimate, factor, hundredth, nearest whole number, product, quotient, regroup, round, sum, tenth

Introduction

This unit applies basic place-value and computation concepts to decimal numbers. The focus of the unit is on using decimal numbers to name, compare, and compute with numbers between whole numbers. A recurring theme is: The rules for whole numbers and decimal numbers are exactly the same. You just need to keep track of the decimal point.

Two keys to working successfully with decimal numbers are place value and number sense.

Common Errors

Example: Find the product of 6.32 and 5.

Error: The student writes 3.16.

Intervention: This student misplaced the decimal point in the product. Help the student to estimate the product by rounding 6.32 to the nearest whole number. Since $6 \times 5 = 30$. then 6.32×5 must be near 30. The correct product is 31.6 or 31.60.

Division with decimal numbers can be confusing, especially when the divisor is a decimal number. Patterns are good way to demonstrate why the algorithm works.

Example: Find the quotient: $7.2 \div 1.2$.

Error: The student writes 0.6.

Intervention: This student remembered to move the decimal point in the divisor to turn it into a whole number, then divided 7.2 by 12. The student, however, forgot the rule, "Whatever you do to the divisor, you must also do to the dividend." Start with simple patterns until the rule becomes clear to the student, then go back to find the correct quotient of $7.2 \div 1.2$. (6)

Sample Pattern: $30 \div 5 = 6$

$30.0. \div 5.0. = 6$

$3.0. \div 0.5. = 6$

Skill Builder Lesson 1 Plan

Decimal Numbers

TODAY'S SKILLS
- Use models to represent decimals.
- Read and write decimals from models.
- Read and write decimals using a place-value chart.

MATERIALS
- Visual 1: Decimal Models for Tenths and Hundredths
- Visual 2: Place-Value and Addition Patterns
- Cardstock C1–3: Place-Value Models
- self-stick notes
- Copymaster M1: Place-Value Charts
- Vocabulary Cards: **decimal number, decimal point, hundredth, tenth**

SET UP

Build the Skill
Display Visual 1: Decimal Models for Tenths and Hundredths.

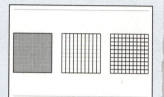

Apply the Skill
Display Visual 2: Place-Value and Addition Patterns.

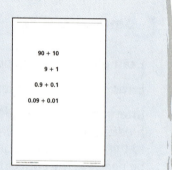

EL WORD WALL

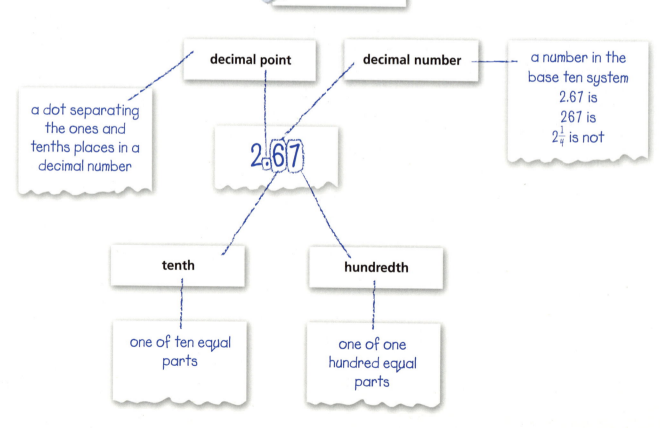

- **decimal point**: a dot separating the ones and tenths places in a decimal number
- **decimal number**: a number in the base ten system
  - 2.67 is
  - 267 is
  - $2\frac{1}{4}$ is not
- **tenth**: one of ten equal parts
- **hundredth**: one of one hundred equal parts

2.67

10 iSucceed MATH

PROFESSIONAL DEVELOPMENT

Math Background The decimal number system is a place-value system based on powers of 10. Numbers are expressed as sequences of the digits 0–9. Each successive digit to the right or left of the units (ones) position indicates a multiple of a power of 10. In other words, numbers in the hundreds place are multiples of 10^2. Similarly, numbers in the tens place are multiples of 10^1, or 10, and numbers in the ones place are multiples of 10^0, or 1. The pattern continues to the right of the ones place. Numbers in the tenths place are multiples of 10^{-1}, or 0.1, and numbers in the hundredths place are multiples of 10^{-2}, or 0.01. Although students will not encounter the powers of ten notation until later, it is important that they understand the place-value pattern used in the decimal system.

Decimal Models When students are introduced to decimal numbers, they may think that hundredths are greater than tenths because hundreds are greater than tens. In the transition from place-value models showing ones, tens, and hundreds to models showing ones, tenths, and hundredths, the filled-in model now represents 1. The tenths models have full columns filled in. The hundredths models have single cells filled in. The decimal part of any decimal number is less than the whole-number part of the number. This comparison works the same as with whole numbers.

Example:

In 5.9, $5 > 0.9$.

In 59, $50 > 9$.

Using Decimal Models Have self-stick notes readily available to hang the decimal models.

Place-Value Charts Writing decimals in place-value charts can make recording and reading decimal numbers easier. Understanding these numbers is easier if you and your students use their fraction names.

Write: 5.4

Say: *Five and four tenths*

Don't say: *Five point four*

Courseware Connections

Module: Decimals

Decimals: Tenths and Hundredths

GET REAL: Go Cart Race

Fold a self-stick note so that both outside faces have glue on them. Stick to both the cardstock and the Visual or the board.

one   one tenth   one hundredth

Lesson 1 Teach

BUILD THE SKILL

Display Visual 1: Decimal Models for Tenths and Hundredths. Your goal in this discussion is to help students understand how to recognize, read, and write decimal numbers using models.

- Remind students that they have used models to show ones, tens, and hundreds. *Now you are going to use the same models to represent numbers that are 1 or less.* Explain how the models show 1, 0.1, and 0.01.

- *Decimal numbers are numbers that are written using place value. Whole numbers are decimal numbers: the same digit in each place in a decimal number has ten times the value of that digit in the next place to the right. Use a decimal point to separate the digit in the ones place from the digit in the tenths place.*

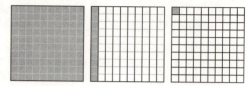

The whole is 1. Divide the whole into ten equal parts. Each of the ten equal parts is one tenth, or 0.1. Divide each tenth into ten equal parts. Each of these parts is one hundredth, or 0.01.

Connect to Vocabulary Help students to see how the new terms are related. Present a variety of decimal models and have students identify the digit in the tenths or hundredths place. Demonstrate how to write the numbers from the models.

- Add the new Vocabulary Cards **decimal number, decimal point, tenth,** and **hundredth** to the Word Wall.

- **EL** Point out that the "th" in tenth and hundredth means their value is less than one.

EXPLORE THE SKILL

- Now have students read numbers from models. Display a variety of models (C1–3). Demonstrate how to write the number in a Place-Value Chart (M1) to help students read the number in words. *If the number is less than one, first read the number as if the decimal point is not there. Then, add on the word tenths or hundredths to name the least place of the decimal number.*

- When students can read tenths and hundreds correctly, add ones models.

Wrap Up Write 9.3 on the board. *How can you read this number and use decimal models to show it?* (Read the number as "nine and three tenths." Show 9 ones and 3 tenths.)

Reteach Use Cardstock C4–5: Paper Money and Coins to develop the relationship between place value and decimals. Use dollars for ones, dimes for tenths, and cents for hundredths. Have students read and write decimal numbers for different amounts of money.

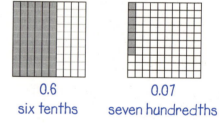

0.6   0.07
six tenths   seven hundredths

Because the number shown in each model is less than one, the digit in the ones place is 0.

Tens	Ones	Tenths	Hundredths
	0	6	7

Write: 0.67
Say: sixty-seven hundredths

Assess

How does writing a decimal number in a place-value chart help you read the number? (It shows the value of each place. The least place tells what decimal word to say.)

12   iSucceed MATH: Decimal Numbers

APPLY THE SKILL
Problem-Solving Strategy: Look for a Pattern

Present the Problem Display Visual 2: Place-Value and Addition Patterns. Have cardstock models available (C1–3). Read the problem set-up and instructions:

- *How do the numbers change in each sum?*
- *Work with a partner to describe the pattern.*

Discuss the Solution After students have had time to solve the problem, help the class discuss their solutions.

- *What is each sum?* (100, 10, 1, 0.1) *How are the sums related?* (Each value is ten times the value of the sum below it.)
- *Describe the pattern.* (When the place starts with a 9 in it and you add 1 more in that place, you must take the 10 from that place and add 1 in the next greater place.)

REFLECT
Discuss why you want students to use place-value names when they read decimal numbers. There are a number of good reasons:

- The place-value names make clear how numbers compare to one another.
- The place-value names leave no room for doubt about the number.
- Later, using place-value names will help students to compute.

Vocabulary
- Direct students' attention to the Word Wall.
- Discuss how to define the terms before asking students to record their definitions in their personal glossaries along with a diagram and/or an example for each.

90 + 10 = 100

9 + 1 = 10

0.9 + 0.1 = 1.0

0.09 + 0.01 = 0.10

How does the place-value change?

Journal Prompt

Why can you use the same models for hundredths, tenths, and ones as you use for ones, tens and hundreds? (Students should recognize that the number system is based on tens and that the value of each place is ten times the value of the place to its right. This means that the same models can be used for different places.)

Assess

How is adding 10 to 90 like adding 0.1 to 0.9? (In both cases the number jumps to the next greater place value.)

Concept Builder — Lesson 2 Plan

Relate Decimal Numbers to Money

TODAY'S CONCEPTS
- Relate decimals to money.
- Apply place value to money.

MATERIALS
- Visual 3: Decimal Place-Value Chart
- Visual 4: Coin Purse
- Cardstock C4: Paper Money (dollars only)
- Cardstock C5: Coins
- small self-stick notes
- Vocabulary Cards: **decimal point, dollar sign, hundredth, tenth**

SET UP
Build the Concept
Display Visual 3: Decimal Place-Value Chart.

Tens	Ones	Tenths	Hundredths

Apply the Concept
Display Visual 4: Coin Purse.

$0.35

EL WORD WALL

tenth — dime — **$35.72** — penny — hundredth

dollar sign $: a symbol that denotes the basic unit of U.S. currency

decimal point : a dot separating the ones and tenths places in a decimal number

14 iSucceed MATH

PD PROFESSIONAL DEVELOPMENT

Money provides a natural transition to decimal numbers because most students are already familiar with money notation, as well as with reading and writing money amounts.

Place Value Decimal numbers follow the same place-value pattern as whole numbers. In fact, whole numbers are decimal numbers; we just don't write the decimal point unless the number has a part less than one. No matter which place you are looking at, the value of a digit is ten times the value of the same digit one place to its right. The decimal point separates the whole number part of a number from the decimal part of the number. Place-value charts can help students to understand the value of each digit in a decimal number as well as how to read the number.

EL Decimal Point In the United States, the decimal point is represented by a period. In Britain, a raised period is used, while in continental Europe a decimal comma is used.

Examples of equivalent decimal representations:

United States and Mexico	Britain	Continental Europe and Cuba
2.53	2·53	2,53

Sources: Weisstein, Eric W. "Decimal Point." From MathWorld—A Wolfram Web Resource, and WordReference.com Language Forums. Retrieved December, 2006

Reading Decimal Numbers Read decimal numbers as you read equivalent mixed numbers.

Write: 7.3

Say: *7 and 3 tenths*

Don't say: *7 point 3*

Emphasize that you say "and" for the decimal point. In fact, indicating the decimal point is the only time "and" should be used when reading a number.

Example:

One hundred and twenty-four thousandths means 100.024

One hundred twenty-four thousandths means 0.124

Fractions and Decimals If your students are already comfortable with fractions, then connect the way you read decimals and fractions to fraction notation. $0.3 = \frac{3}{10} =$ three tenths.

Courseware Connections

Module: Decimals
Introduction to Money
Counting Money
Making Change

Lesson 2 Teach

BUILD THE CONCEPT

Display Visual 3: Decimal Place-Value Chart. Your goal is to help students understand the place value of decimal numbers.

- Use C4 and C5: Paper Money and Coins. Stick a $1-bill, 3 dimes, and 4 pennies on the board. Discuss how to count, record, and read the amount. ($1.34)

- Follow the same procedure and have students count, record, and read several other amounts. Include at least one example with no dollars, such as 3 quarters. ($0.75)

Connect to Vocabulary Help students relate the dollar sign and decimal point in money notation. Post **dollar sign** and **decimal point** on the Word Wall.

- *What symbols do we use to record money amounts?* (dollar sign and decimal point) *How do the symbols help you read the money amounts?* (Sample answer: Read the amount before the decimal point as a whole number. Say "dollars." Say "and" for the decimal point. Read the amount after the decimal point as a whole number. Say "cents.")

EXPLORE THE CONCEPT

- Use self stick notes to place 0.6 in the place-value chart. *There are no ones in this decimal number. To read the number, read as if it were a whole number, "six." Say the name of the last place in the number, "tenths."*

Connect to Vocabulary Post on the Word Wall and discuss: **tenth** and **hundredth**.

- Connect the tenths to dimes, and the hundredths to cents.
- Post on the Visual and work with students to read a variety of decimal numbers, such as 3.5, 1.07, 2.45, and 0.81. Stress the importance of reading "and" for the decimal point.

Wrap Up Write the number 124 on the board. *Should I read this number as one hundred and twenty four? Why or why not?* (No, the "and" means there should be a decimal point between the one hundred and the next number you read. The number is one hundred twenty-four.) Write 1.24. *How do you read this number?* (one and twenty-four hundredths)

Reteach Make a class-size poster to show the relationship between place-value and money amounts. Have students make their own chart that they can use as a reference.

Fold a self-stick note so that both outside faces have glue on them. Stick to both a coin or dollar and the board.

Say: one dollar and thirty-four cents
Write: $1.34

Tens	Ones	Tenths	Hundredths
	0	6	

Say: six tenths

$10	$1	$0.10	$0.01
Tens	Ones	Tenths	Hundredths

Use a chart to relate place-value and money.

How can you use a place-value chart to help you read decimal numbers? (Possible answer: The place-value chart shows you how to read the whole-number and decimal parts of the number by naming the places.)

APPLY THE CONCEPT

Problem-Solving Strategy: Make a List

Present the Problem Display Visual 4: Coin Purse. Allow students access to Cardstock C5: Coins. Read the problem set-up and instructions:

- There is $0.35 in the coin purse. What are all the possible ways to make the amount of money in the coin purse using pennies, nickels, and dimes?
- Work with a partner. Make a list to help keep track of the possible ways to make $0.35 using the coins.

Discuss the Solution After students have had time to solve the problem, help the class discuss their solutions. If students are struggling, you may wish to start this discussion before everyone has solved the problem.

- *How did you use a list to keep track of the coins?* (Sample answer: We wrote different combinations of coins to make the amount.)
- *How do you know you found all the possible ways to make $0.35?* (Sample answer: We kept track of all the ways to make $0.35 by increasing the other coins as the number of pennies decreased.)

Pennies	35	30	25	25	20	20	15	15	15	10	10	10	5	5	5	5	0	0	0	0
Nickels	0	1	2	0	3	1	4	2	0	5	3	1	6	4	2	0	7	5	3	1
Dimes	0	0	0	1	0	1	0	1	2	0	1	2	0	1	2	3	0	1	2	3

Organize the list by decreasing pennies as other coins increase. There are 20 possible ways to make $0.35.

REFLECT

Vocabulary

- **EL** Discuss the importance of "th" when reading decimal numbers. The "th" denotes a new set of places in the place value chart. Tenths have a different value than tens and hundredths have a different value than hundreds.
- Direct students' attention to the Word Wall. Discuss various ways to define the terms before asking students to record new definitions and examples in their personal glossaries.

Journal Prompt

Explain how money and decimal numbers are related. (Sample answers: Both representations use a decimal point. Tenths are like dimes, and hundredths are like pennies. Both ways read "and" for the decimal point. The cents amounts are less than one dollar as the decimal amounts are less than one.)

Assess

How does understanding place value help you understand decimal numbers and money amounts? (Sample answer: The numbers to the right of the decimal point follow the same pattern as the numbers to the left of the decimal point. A digit in a place has 10 times the value of the same digit one place to its right. The same is true for money.)

Concept Builder — **Lesson 3** — **Plan**

Compare and Order Decimal Numbers

TODAY'S CONCEPTS
- Compare and order decimal numbers using decimal models and number lines.
- Read decimal numbers aloud to identify and compare their place values.

MATERIALS
- Visual 5: Decimal Models 1
- Visual 6: Money Line
- Copymaster M2: Number Lines
- Vocabulary Cards: < (is less than), = (is equal to), > (is greater than)

SET UP

Build the Concept
Display Visual 5: Decimal Models 1.

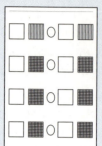

Apply the Concept
Display Visual 6: Money Line.

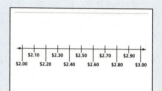

 WORD WALL

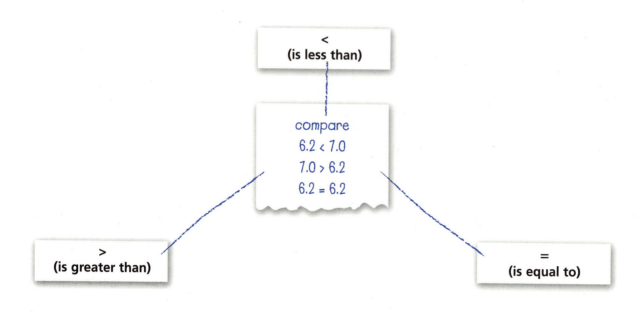

18   iSucceed MATH

PROFESSIONAL DEVELOPMENT

Math Background Some students may say the word "and" when reading whole numbers. For example, a student might read 825 incorrectly as *eight hundred and twenty-five* (rather than *eight hundred twenty-five*). This can lead to confusion when students begin to read decimals. When reading numbers, say the word "and" only at the decimal point.

Write: 0.825

Say: *eight hundred twenty-five thousandths*

Don't say: *eight hundred and twenty-five thousandths* (which is written 800.025).

Compare Decimals Students will eventually learn to compare numbers by lining up their ones places or decimal points and comparing the digits from left to right. For now, students should simply know that if two numbers have different whole number parts, they don't need to compare the decimal parts. The decimal number with the greater whole number part is greater, regardless of its decimal part.

7.1 > 6.9 because 7 > 6

Word Problems *Greater* doesn't always mean *best*. For example, if a problem asks students to find the winner of a foot race, the answer will be the runner with the least time. If a problem asks students to find the baseball player with the best batting average, the answer will be the player with the greatest average.

Organize for Learning The tens pattern of place value continues in the decimal part of a number. A digit in a number has a value ten times the value of the same digit in the place to its right. In later lessons, students will learn to use this pattern as a mental-math way to multiply and divide by powers of ten (10; 100; 1,000; and so on).

Example:

Since 0.1 is ten times as great as 0.01,

Then, 10 × 0.01 = 0.1

and, 0.1 ÷ 10 = 0.01.

Courseware Connections

Module: Decimals

Comparing and Ordering Decimals Through Hundredths

Comparing and Ordering Decimals Through Thousandths

Lesson 3 Teach

BUILD THE CONCEPT

Display Visual 5: Decimal Models 1. Your goal in this discussion is to show students how to use decimal models to compare decimal numbers. Students will also learn how to compare decimal numbers by reading them aloud.

- Tell the class that you want to compare two decimal numbers: 1.8 and 1.6 (*one and eight tenths, and one and six tenths*). Write 1.8 under the first pair of squares and 1.6 under the second pair of squares. Shade the first pair of squares to show 1.8 and the second pair to show 1.6.
- *In which model is the shaded part bigger?* (the first) *Which decimal number is greater?* (1.8) Write 1.8 > 1.6.
- Remind students that, when they read decimals, they should say "and" at the decimal point. Have volunteers read 1.8 and 1.6. (one and eight tenths; one and six tenths).

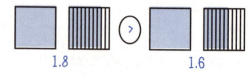

1.8 is greater than 1.6

Connect to Vocabulary Post and discuss the Vocabulary Cards, **< (is less than), = (is equal to),** and **> (is greater than)**. Make sure that students understand the meaning of each symbol.

- Help students think of ways to remember the difference between < and >. (The arrow points to the number that is less; the big end faces the greater number; or some other mnemonic device.)
- Repeat the discussion with different decimal numbers to give students opportunities to use the vocabulary.

EXPLORE THE CONCEPT

- Write 1.35 and 1.37 under the second pair of models and shade the appropriate regions. *In which model is the shaded region smaller?* (the first) *Compare the decimal numbers.* (1 and 35 hundredths is less than 1 and 37 hundredths) Write 1.35 < 1.37.
- Repeat with 1.8 and 1.08. (1.8 > 1.08)
- **EL** Discuss the differences in spelling and pronunciation between the words *tens* and *tenths* and between *hundreds* and *hundredths*. Help students identify digits in the tens, tenths, hundreds, and hundredths places on the Visual.

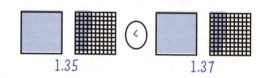

1.35 is less than 1.37

Wrap Up Write 1.5 on the Visual and fill in 1.5 squares. *This number is one and five tenths.* Label the second pair of squares 1.50. *How shall I shade the squares to represent one and fifty hundredths?* (The shading will be the same as for 1.5.) *Why?* (One tenth equals ten hundredths, so 5 tenths = 50 hundredths.) *How do you compare 1.5 and 1.50?* (Use the equals sign.)

Reteach Make a number line with the adding machine tape in your kit. Write pairs of decimals (such as 1.3 and 1.7) on a number line that extends from 1 to 2. Have volunteers read them aloud, point to the greater decimal number, and state the comparison.

How do you tell which is greater, one and eight tenths or one and nine tenths? (Since eight tenths is one less tenth than nine tenths, eight tenths is less than nine tenths.) Which is greater, one and seventy-seven hundredths or one and sixty-three hundredths? (1.77)

APPLY THE CONCEPT
Problem-Solving Strategy: Draw a Picture

Present the Problem Display Visual 6: Money Line. Make sure everyone understands that 1¢ is one hundredth of a dollar, or $0.01, and that 10¢ is one tenth of a dollar, or $0.10. Make available copies of Copymaster M2: Number Lines. Read the problem set-up and instructions:

- *Carlos bought four baseball cards for the following prices: $2.66, $2.59, $2.57, and $2.70. He wants to display the cards in order, from least expensive to most expensive. To do this, he needs to order the four costs from least to greatest.*

- *Work with a partner. Make your own number line that shows dollars and cents. Mark the price of each baseball card on the number line, and write the prices in order, from least expensive to most expensive.*

Discuss the Solution After students have had time to solve the problem, help the class discuss their solutions.

- Remind students that they have used number lines to compare whole numbers.

You can also use number lines to compare decimal numbers.

- Have volunteers read the prices in order. ($2.57, $2.59, $2.66, $2.70)

REFLECT

How is a decimal number line like other number lines you have used? Discuss how the idea of equal intervals is constant, no matter whether they're modeling whole numbers or decimal numbers.

Vocabulary

- Direct students' attention to the Word Wall. Have volunteers point out each symbol and tell what it means. Have other volunteers name decimal numbers to go on the left side of each symbol. Finally, have others name decimal numbers to go on the right side of each symbol, making the inequality or equality true.
- Ask students to add decimal comparisons to their personal glossaries, using the appropriate symbols.

Journal Prompt

Tell how you know that 1.25 is greater than 1.2. (1.25 has the same number of ones and tenths, but 5 more hundredths than 1.2)

Assess

Show a decimal model and a number line model for comparing 1.4 to 1.5. Tell which model you like better and why. (Students may choose either model for different reasons. The number line is generally faster.)

Concept Builder • Lesson 3 • Teach

Concept Builder — Lesson 4 Plan

Add Decimal Numbers

TODAY'S CONCEPTS
- Compare adding decimal numbers to adding whole numbers.
- Add decimal numbers.

MATERIALS
- Visual 7: Decimal Models 2
- Visual 8: Book Fair Sale
- Cardstock C1–3: Place-Value Models
- Copymaster M3: Place-Value Models
- Vocabulary Cards: **addend**, **hundredth**, **sum**, **tenth**

SET UP
Build the Concept
Display Visual 7: Decimal Models 2.

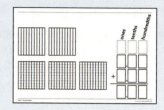

Apply the Concept
Display Visual 8: Book Fair Sale.

EL WORD WALL

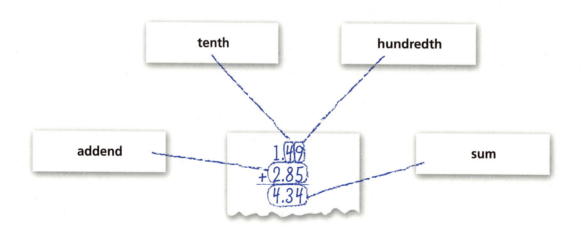

22 iSucceed MATH

PROFESSIONAL DEVELOPMENT

Math Background Because we add like place values, adding decimal numbers is essentially the same as adding whole numbers. The key elements are: pay close attention to place value, add in each place, and regroup when needed. When using the algorithm to add both whole and decimal numbers, align the addends on the ones place. Doing so will line up the decimal points, too.

Annexing Zeros in Decimal Numbers Some students may find it easier to annex zeros so that all the addends have the same number of places when adding decimals. Although doing this is not necessary, students may do so if it makes the computation easier. This can only be done in decimal places to the right of the non-zero digits.

Example:

0.1 is one tenth

0.10 is one tenth and no hundredths

0.100 is one tenth, no hundredths, and no thousandths

In all of these numbers, the place value of the significant digit (1) stays the same, so they all have the same value.

Error Analysis Regrouping decimal numbers is the same as regrouping whole numbers. Students must regroup when the digits in a column total 10 or more. Have students refer to models if they become confused with regrouping decimal numbers. If place-value models are confusing, then use money models.

9¢ = 0.09

10¢ = 0.10 or   10¢ = 0.1

$\frac{9}{100} = 0.09$, $\frac{10}{100} = \frac{1}{10} = 0.1$ or 0.10

Courseware Connections

Module: Adding and Subtracting Decimals

Adding and Subtracting Money

Adding Decimals Through Hundredths

Adding Decimals (Adding Zeros)

Adding More Than Two Decimals

Adding Decimals Through Thousandths

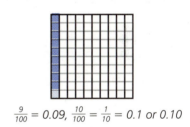

$\frac{9}{100} = 0.09$, $\frac{10}{100} = \frac{1}{10} = 0.1$ or 0.10

Lesson 4 Teach

BUILD THE CONCEPT

Display Visual 7: Decimal Models 2. You may also wish to post a copy of Copymaster M3: Place-Value Models. Your goal is to help students understand how to add decimal numbers.

- *You can use models to add decimals.* Write 0.6 + 0.7. *Why did I write a zero in the ones place when I wrote each of these addends?* (Neither number has any ones. Both decimal numbers are less than 1 whole.)

- Fill in 6 tenths, then 7 more tenths on the Visual as shown. *Will the sum be greater than or less than 1?* (greater) *What is the sum?* (1.3)

- *You can also use place value to add.* First, line up the ones digits in each addend. Doing this also lines up the decimal points. Regroup when the sum of digits in a column is 10 or greater. Demonstrate by writing on small self-stick notes on the Visual.

- Repeat the discussion for 1.49 + 1.25 = 2.74. Provide additional examples as needed.

Connect to Vocabulary Post on the Word Wall and discuss: **addend**, **hundredth**, **sum**, **tenth**.

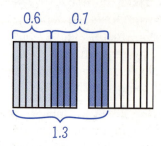

Add 0.6 + 0.7
Think: 6 tenths + 7 tenths = 13 tenths or 1.3

Adding decimals is like adding whole numbers. Add from least to greatest place value and regroup as needed.

Add the tenths first. Regroup. Add the ones. Write the decimal point in the sum.

EXPLORE THE CONCEPT

- Sometimes, when you line up the ones digits and the decimal points, the right side of the addends may look uneven, or ragged. To make computing easier, you can give all of your decimals the same number of places by tacking on zeros.

$$35 + 0.28 \rightarrow \begin{array}{r} 35.00 \\ +0.28 \\ \hline 35.28 \end{array}$$

Remember, a whole number can be written with a decimal point. For example, 35 = 35.00 because 35.00 has three tens, five ones, no tenths, and no hundredths.

- Work through several more sums, such as 2.9 + 4 (6.9) and 1.3 + 0.64 (1.94).

Wrap Up *Can you always tack on zeros to the right of numbers so that all the addends have the same number of digits? Explain.* (No, you can only tack on zeros to write equivalent decimal numbers. You cannot tack on zeros before the decimal point.)

Example: 1 = 1.0, but 1 ≠ 10

Reteach Have students use the Cardstock C1–3: Place-Value Models to find sums of decimal numbers.

How can you use place value to add 3.1 + 0.48 + 2? (Sample answer: Line up the ones digits and write equivalent decimals. Then add like places.
3.10 + 0.48 + 2.00 = 5.58)

24 iSucceed MATH: Add Decimal Numbers

APPLY THE CONCEPT

Problem-Solving Skill: Choose an Estimate or Exact Amount

Present the Problem Display Visual 8: Book Fair Sale. Read the problem set-up and instructions:

- *Lucia has 1 quarter, 3 dimes, and 4 nickels in her pocket. Does she have enough money to buy two bookmarks?*
- *Her father has two $10-bills, one $5-dollar bill, and three nickels in his pocket. Does he have enough money to buy a hardcover book and a paperback book?*
- *Work with a partner. Choose an estimate or an exact answer to solve each problem. Explain which method you chose and how it helped you solve the problem.*

Discuss the Solution After students have had time to solve the problems, help the class discuss their solutions.

- *Did you use an exact answer or an estimate to decide whether Lucia has enough money? Explain.* (Sample answer: Find an exact answer because she only has $0.75; $0.35 + $0.35 = $0.70 and $0.70 < $0.75, so she does have enough money.)
- *Did you use an exact answer or an estimate to decide whether Lucia's father has enough money? Explain.* (Sample answer: Use an estimate because Lucia's father has so much more money in his pocket. He has $25.15. Both books cost less than $5.00, so he has enough money.)

REFLECT

Does the decimal part matter when you compare numbers such as 25.15 and 0.75? Explain. (No, the whole number part is greater, so you do not have to worry about the decimal part in the comparison.)

Vocabulary

- Direct students' attention to the Word Wall. Review the connection between decimal numbers and place value.
- Encourage students to add definitions and examples to their personal glossaries.

Journal Prompt

How is adding decimal numbers like adding whole numbers? (Sample answer: Add decimals the same way you add whole numbers by adding like places. Regroup when needed. Line up the ones digits to keep like places together. Write the decimal point in the sum.)

Assess

Can the sum of two decimal numbers be a whole number? Explain and give an example. (Yes, when you regroup, there may be no tenths or hundredths in the sum. For example, 1.5 + 1.5 = 3.0 or 3.)

Concept Builder — Lesson 5 Plan

Subtract Decimal Numbers

TODAY'S CONCEPTS
- Compare subtracting decimal numbers to subtracting whole numbers.
- Subtract decimal numbers.

MATERIALS
- Visual 9: Decimal Models 3
- Visual 10: Lunch Cart Menu
- Copymaster M4: Place-Value Addition and Subtraction
- Copymaster M3: Place-Value Models
- small self-stick notes
- Vocabulary Cards: **difference**, **regroup**

SET UP
Build the Concept
Display Visual 9: Decimal Models 3.

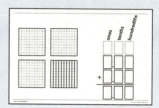

Apply the Concept
Display Visual 10: Lunch Cart Menu.

EL WORD WALL

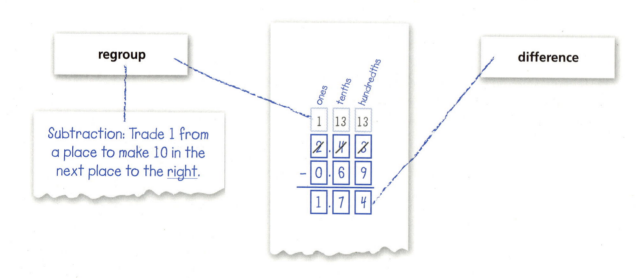

regroup
Subtraction: Trade 1 from a place to make 10 in the next place to the right.

difference

26   iSucceed MATH

PROFESSIONAL DEVELOPMENT

Math Background Just as adding decimal numbers is like adding whole numbers, subtracting decimal numbers is essentially the same as subtracting whole numbers. Students may be comforted by knowing that they are not learning anything really new. The key elements are still: pay close attention to place value, regroup when needed, and subtract in each place right to left. As with addition, the ones digits must be lined up in order to subtract decimal numbers. This also lines up the decimal points.

Annexing Zeros in Decimal Numbers While annexing zeros so that decimal place values match up in addition is not necessary, it is much more critical in subtraction. While students may be able to subtract 3.25 − 1.6 without writing 1.60 for 1.6, they may struggle to subtract 3.2 − 1.65 without writing the equivalent decimal 3.20 for 3.2 before they try to regroup.

More than One Regrouping All regrouping for subtraction can be done before starting to subtract. For struggling students, this is an especially good idea. Keeping things neat and readable may be a problem. If it is, make multiple copies of Copymaster M4: Place-Value Addition and Subtraction and encourage them to do all of their paper-and-pencil subtraction on these charts.

Courseware Connections

Module: Adding and Subtracting Decimals

Subtracting Decimals Through Hundredths

Subtracting Decimals (Regrouping)

Adding and Subtracting Decimals Through Thousandths

GET REAL: At the Grocery Store

GET REAL: At the Gas Station

Lesson 5 Teach

BUILD THE CONCEPT

Display Visual 9: Decimal Models 3. You may also wish to post a copy of Copymaster M2: Place-Value Models. Your goal is to help students understand how to subtract decimal numbers.

- *You can use models to subtract decimals, such as 3.2 − 1.8.*
- Using the model shown, work through the problem with students.
- *Regroup 1 one as 10 tenths.* Darken the tenths rules on the third model to show the regrouping. *Now how many tenths do we have to subtract 0.8 from?* (12) *What is the difference?* (1.4)
- *You can also use place value to subtract. First, line up the ones digits in each number. This means the decimal points line up. Regroup when there are not enough to subtract from. Subtract in each column from right to left. Remember to write the decimal point in the difference.* Demonstrate by writing on self-stick notes on the Visual.
- Repeat the discussion for 2.43 − 0.69 = 1.74. Provide additional examples as needed, helping students regroup the tenths and hundredths.

Connect to Vocabulary Post on the Word Wall and discuss: **difference, regroup.**

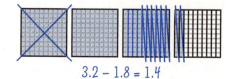

3.2 − 1.8 = 1.4

Think: 0.2 < 0.8, so you need more tenths.

Subtracting decimals is like subtracting whole numbers. Subtract from least to greatest place value and regroup as needed.

There are not enough tenths to subtract 8 tenths. Regroup 1 one. Regroup 1 one to 10 tenths. Now you have 12 tenths. Subtract the tenths: 12 tenths − 8 tenths = 4 tenths. Subtract the ones. Write the decimal point in the difference.

EXPLORE THE CONCEPT

- *Sometimes, you need to tack on zeros in order to subtract. When you line up the ones digits and the decimal points, the right side may be uneven. To make all the decimal numbers have the same number of places, tack on zeros in places that do not already contain digits.* Demonstrate with a money example: 2 dimes = 20 cents, so 0.2 = 0.20.
- Compare finding the differences of 0.42 − 0.2 and 0.2 − 0.02.

Subtract. 0.42 − 0.2

```
  0.42
 −0.20
  ————
  0.22
```

0.2 − 0.02

```
   1 10
  0.2̸0̸
 −0.02
  ————
  0.18
```

Write equivalent decimal numbers so that both numbers have the same number of decimal places.

Wrap Up Work through several more examples, such as 4.63 − 1 = 3.63 and 1 − 0.37 = 0.63.

- Is it always necessary to tack on zeros to subtract when the number of decimal places is different? (no)
- How does tacking on the zeros make it easier to subtract? (It may make it easier to keep track of each place.)

Reteach Provide students with their own copies of Copymaster M4: Place-Value Addition and Subtraction to find differences of decimal numbers.

Describe and demonstrate how to subtract 1 − 0.6. What is the difference? (There are no tenths to subtract from, so you have to regroup 1 one as 10 tenths. There are 0 ones left. The difference is 0.4.)

28 iSucceed MATH: Subtract Decimal Numbers

APPLY THE CONCEPT
Problem-Solving Skill: Choose an Estimate or Exact Amount

Present the Problem Display Visual 10: Lunch Cart Menu. Read the problem set-up and instructions:

- *Joey has $5. He buys a turkey sandwich. How much money does he have left to buy a drink?*
- *Crystal also has $5. She buys a ham sandwich. Does she have enough money left to buy a cheese sandwich?*
- *Work with a partner. Choose an estimate or an exact answer to solve each problem. Explain which method you chose to solve the problem.*

Discuss the Solution After students have had time to solve the problems, help the class discuss their solutions.

- *Did you use an exact answer or an estimate to find how much money Joey has left to buy a drink? Explain.* (Sample answer: Use an exact answer since the problem asks for a specific amount. $5.00 − $3.80 = $1.20)
- *Did you use an exact answer or an estimate to decide whether Crystal has enough money left to buy a cheese sandwich? Explain.* (Sample answer: Use an estimate since exact amounts are not required. The ham sandwich is about $3.50. Crystal has about $1.50 left, not enough to buy the cheese sandwich, which costs about $3.00.)

REFLECT

How is subtracting decimal numbers like subtracting whole numbers? (Sample answer: Subtract decimal numbers the same way you subtract whole numbers, by subtracting like places. Regroup when needed. Line up the ones digits to keep like places together and write the decimal point in the difference.)

Vocabulary

Direct students' attention to the Word Wall. Ask volunteers to define the vocabulary terms in their own words. Have students add definitions and/or examples to their personal glossaries as needed.

Journal Prompt

How do you decide whether you need an estimate or an exact number? (Responses should include reference to the question asked in the problem and the numbers involved.)

Assess

Can the difference of two decimal numbers be a whole number? Explain and give an example. (Yes, there may be no decimal parts left after you subtract. For example, 4.56 − 1.56 = 3.00 = 3)

Concept Builder — Lesson 6 Plan

Check Decimal Sums and Differences

TODAY'S CONCEPTS
- Use inverse operations to check decimal sums and differences.
- Round decimal numbers to the nearest whole number.

MATERIALS
- Visual 11: Crooked Number Lines
- Visual 12: Skateboard Ad
- Vocabulary Cards: **estimate**, **round**, ≈

SET UP
Build the Concept
Display Visual 11: Crooked Number Lines.

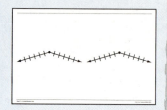

Apply the Concept
Display Visual 12: Skateboard Ad.

EL WORD WALL

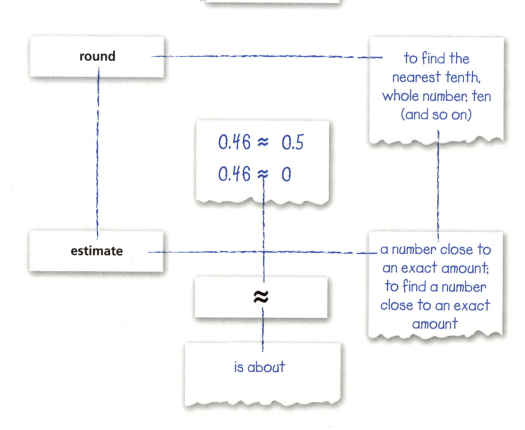

- **round** — to find the nearest tenth, whole number, ten (and so on)
- **estimate** — a number close to an exact amount; to find a number close to an exact amount
- **≈** — is about

$0.46 \approx 0.5$
$0.46 \approx 0$

PROFESSIONAL DEVELOPMENT

Math Background Addition and subtraction are inverse (opposite) operations. This relationship between the operations is useful when checking any sum or difference. Checking by using the inverse operation should yield an exact amount that corresponds to a number in the original problem. If not, something is wrong in one of the calculations.

Rounding Decimals To round decimal numbers, follow the rules used to round whole numbers because decimal numbers follow the same place-value system as whole numbers. It is conceivable that a pair of decimal numbers will both round, to the nearest whole number, to zero. When this is the case, the sum or difference will always be less than 1.

Example:

   0.42
+ 0.49
   0.91

Both addends are less than 0.5. They round, to the nearest whole number, to 0. The sum must be less than 1.

Estimating with Decimals Because money is represented by decimal numbers, it is very important for students to be both comfortable with and competent in estimating decimal sums and differences. For example, students should be able to estimate sums to compare money amounts and differences to estimate change.

Courseware Connections

Module: Adding and Subtracting Decimals

Adding and Subtracting Money

Subtracting Decimals (Regrouping)

Lesson 6 Teach

BUILD THE CONCEPT

Display Visual 11: Crooked Number Lines. Your goal is to help students use at least two methods to check decimal sums and differences.

- *Why is checking the sum or difference when computing with decimal numbers an especially good idea?* (The decimal numbers may have different places and by checking you may catch errors, such as not writing equivalent decimals or not lining up the ones digits.)

- Have the class add 4.3 + 1.78. (6.08) *Addition and subtraction are opposite operations. How can you subtract to check that the sum is correct?* (6.08 − 1.78 = 4.30 = 4.3 or 6.08 − 4.3 = 1.78)

- Now have the class subtract 2 − 0.93. (1.07) *What operation is the opposite of subtraction?* (addition) *How can you add to check that the difference is correct?* (1.07 + 0.93 = 2.00 = 2)

EXPLORE THE CONCEPT

- *When you use the opposite operation to check a sum or difference, you probably will not use mental math. What if you want to quickly check that a sum or difference is reasonable?* (Use an estimate.)

- *You can round decimal numbers to the nearest whole number to estimate sums and differences. Follow the same rules you use to round whole numbers. Round to the nearest one.* Review how to label and use the crooked number lines to estimate.

- Have students round to the nearest whole number to estimate the sum, 8.26 + 3.74. (estimate: 12; exact: 12.00) Repeat with 8.26 − 3.74. (estimate: 4; exact: 4.52)

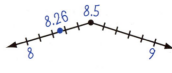

Round each addend to the nearest whole number. (Round 8.26 down to 8; round 3.74 up to 4.)
8 + 4 = 12, so 8.26 + 3.74 ≈ 12
8 − 4 = 4, so 8.26 − 3.74 ≈ 4

Connect to Vocabulary Post on the Word Wall and discuss ≈, **estimate**, and **round**.

Wrap Up *How can you use an estimate to check a sum or difference of decimal numbers?* (One way: Round each number to the nearest whole number. Then, add or subtract. The result should be close to the computed sum or difference. If not, recalculate.)

Reteach Introduce another way to check decimal sums or differences. Estimate the sum or difference using the whole number part of the decimals. Then check to see whether the last digit in the sum or difference is correct. For example, the difference of 4.2 − 1.05 should have its last digit in the hundredths place.

How can you use rounding to estimate 7.1 − 2.39? (Round 7.1 down to 7 and 2.39 down to 2. The difference is about 7 − 2, or 5.)

APPLY THE CONCEPT
Problem-Solving Skill: Is the Answer Reasonable?

Present the Problem Display Visual 12: Skateboard Ad. Read the problem set-up and instructions:

- *Giorgio and Natsumi each want to buy a skateboard. Giorgio has four $10-bills, four $1-bills, 7 quarters, and 12 dimes. Natsumi has four $10-bills, three $5-bills, 2 quarters, and 8 nickels.*
- *They think they have enough money to buy the skateboards they want. Work with a partner to decide whether they do.*

Discuss the Solution After students have had time to solve the problem, help the class discuss their solutions.

- *What did you do to help you make your decision?* (Add all the money each person has.) *How do you know your sums were correct?* Review checking methods: add in a different order; subtract; estimate.
- *Does Giorgio have enough money to buy the Arrow skateboard? How do you know?* (Yes: he has $46.95 which is greater than $45.50.)
- *Does Natsumi have enough money to buy the Eagle skateboard? How do you know?* (No: she has $55.90 which is less than $59.29. However, she has enough to buy the Arrow skateboard.)

REFLECT
Will you always use the same method to check addition or subtraction? Discuss when recalculating in a different order, using opposite operations, and estimating might be most useful. Remind students that, if one way works best for them, then they should use that method regardless of the method their friends are using.

Vocabulary
Direct students' attention to the Word Wall. Ask volunteers to define the terms in their own words and use them in sentences. If they have additions to make to their personal glossaries, they should make them now.

Skateboard Sale

| Arrow | $45.50 |
| Eagle | $59.29 |

Giorgio wants to buy the Arrow Skateboard and Natsumi wants to buy the Eagle Skateboard.

Journal Prompt
Write two decimal numbers between 3 and 4. Find the sum of the numbers and then explain how to use an estimate to check the sum. (Sample answer: Round each number to the nearest whole number and add. Then, compare the estimate to the exact sum for reasonableness.)

Assess
What are three decimal numbers that round to 1? Does each number round up or down? (Sample answers: 0.7, up; 0.82, up; 1.3, down)

Concept Builder — Lesson 7 Plan

Multiply Decimal Numbers

TODAY'S CONCEPTS
- Multiply with whole numbers.
- Multiply with decimal numbers.

MATERIALS
- Visual 13: Compare Factors
- Visual 14: Blue Route
- small self-stick notes in 3 colors cut in half
- Vocabulary Cards: **factor**, **product**

SET UP

Build the Concept

Display Visual 13: Compare Factors.

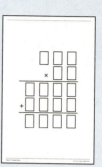

Apply the Concept

Display Visual 14: Blue Route.

Blue Route	
Stops	Distance (miles)
Main to Elm	4.6
Elm to Poplar	3.7
Poplar to Oak	5.8

EL WORD WALL

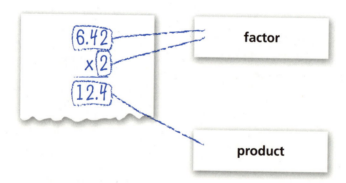

factor

product

34 iSucceed MATH

PROFESSIONAL DEVELOPMENT

Math Background Finding the product of one or more decimal factors draws upon the prior skill of multiplying whole numbers. Decimal factors are initially treated as whole numbers. After finding the product, a decimal point is inserted. There are at least two ways to do this.

1. Estimate the product and place the decimal point accordingly. This technique has the advantage of making sense of the rule.

   Since $6 \times 2 = 12$

   Then, $6.4 \times 2 = 12.8$

2. Use the rule: Count the number of decimal places in the factors, then count that same number of places from the right before placing the decimal point in the product.

Aligning Decimal Factors In addition and subtraction, decimal numbers must be aligned by their decimal points. However, decimal factors are treated as whole number factors. They are best aligned by their terminal digits.

Problem Solving The *Look for a Pattern* problem-solving strategy will help students recognize the rule for placement of a decimal point in a product. Having students color code whole-number digits and decimal digits in factors will help them to identify the pattern.

Courseware Connections

Module: Whole-Number Multiplication

Multiplying by One-Digit Numbers with Regrouping

Multiplying by Two-Digit Numbers

Module: Multiplying Decimals

Multiplying Decimals by 10, 100, and 1,000

Multiplying Decimals by Whole Numbers

Multiplying Money

Multiplying Decimals Through Hundredths

Multiplying Decimals with Zeros in the Product

Multiplying Decimals Through Thousandths

$$\begin{array}{r} 4.62 \\ \times\ 1.3 \\ \hline 6.006 \end{array}$$

Color-coding decimal digits also helps students check the reasonableness of a product. The visual differentiation allows them to scan their work to see whether the total number of color-coded digits in the factors matches the number of digits to the right of the decimal point in the product.

Lesson 7 Teach

BUILD THE CONCEPT

Display Visual 13: Compare Factors. Your goal in this lesson is to help students compare multiplication of whole numbers and multiplication of decimal numbers.

- Write 312 × 24 on self-stick notes on the Visual. *The numbers being multiplied are called factors. Find the product.* Work with students to find the product as shown. (7,488)

- Refer again to the Visual. Place small pieces of a different-colored self-stick note as decimal points to show 3.12 × 2.4. Replace the 3 and 2 on different-colored notes.

- *What is the product of 3 and 2?* (6) *What is a good estimate of the product of 3.12 and 2.4?* (a little more than 6)

- *We do not need to change our computation, because we are multiplying the same digits in the same order. Where shall I place the decimal point in the product?* (between the 7 and the 4 because we know the product is near 6.)

Connect to Vocabulary Use the multiplication sentences 312 × 24 = 7,488 and 3.12 × 2.4 = 7.488 to help students review the new terms factors and product.

- **EL** Produce and product belong to the same word family. Explain that produce is a verb that means "to make or create something," while product is a noun that means "anything that is made or created."

- Add the Vocabulary Cards **factors** and **product** to the Word Wall.

EXPLORE THE CONCEPT

- Repeat the procedure in Build the Concept with 3.57 × 1.2 (4.284) and 6.5 × 4 (26.0).

- *Compare the products of decimal factors. What pattern do you see in the number of decimal digits in the factors and the product?* (The number of decimal places in the product equals the total number of decimal places in the factors.)

Wrap Up Write 4.6 × 5.3 on the board. *What is a good estimate of the product?* (between 20 and 25) *How many decimal places will the product of these factors contain?* (2) Then, have students multiply to find the product. (24.38)

Reteach Provide students with different multiplication sentences involving whole numbers and decimal numbers. Have them estimate each product, then write an addition sentence that shows the number of decimal places in each product. For 5.69 × 3.7, the addition sentence would be:
2 decimal places + 1 decimal place = 3 decimal places.

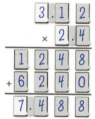

Begin by multiplying the top factor by the ones digit of the bottom factor. Then multiply the top factor by the tens digit of the bottom factor. Add the partial products to find the final product.

The decimal numbers are made up of the same digits as the whole-number factors. The product is made up of the same digits as the product of the whole-number factors.

Assess

How are the products of 17.4 × 3.2 and 1.74 × 0.32 alike? How do they differ? (Both pairs of factors produce decimal products containing the same digits. The products differ in the location of the decimal point. Because 1.74 is about 2 and 0.34 is about $\frac{1}{2}$, the second product must be very small compared to the first.

APPLY THE CONCEPT
Problem-Solving Strategy: Write an Equation

Present the Problem Display Visual 14: Blue Route. Read the problem set-up and instructions:

- *The table shows the distances between stops on a bus route. On Monday, the bus had traveled 0.6 of the distance from Poplar to Oak when it broke down. How far from Poplar was the bus? How far from Oak?*
- *Work with a partner to make a plan to solve the problem. Follow your plan and answer the question.*

Discuss the Solution After students have had time to solve the problem, help them discuss their solutions.

- *Is the distance the bus traveled greater or less than 5.8 miles?* (less) *How do you know?* (Since 0.6 is less than 1, the bus traveled less than the whole 5.8 miles.)
- *What do you know?* (the distances between bus stops)
- *What do you need to find out?* (0.6 of the distance from Poplar to Oak, and the distance from that point on to Oak) *What word sentences help you to organize the information for the first question?* (total distance × 0.6 = distance from Poplar)
- *How did you find the distance from Oak?* Discuss several strategies students might have used. (total distance × 0.4 = distance from Oak; or total distance − distance from Poplar = distance from Oak)
- *How far from Poplar was the bus?* (3.48 miles) *From Oak?* (2.32 miles)

REFLECT

- *How else can you check whether the product of two decimal factors seems reasonable?* (estimate)
- *How can you use a pattern to check whether the product of two decimal factors is reasonable?* (Find the total number of decimal places in the factors. Check to see that the number of decimal places in the product is the same.)

Vocabulary

- Direct students' attention to the Word Wall. Ask volunteers to define the vocabulary terms in their own words. Have other volunteers provide examples.
- Ask students to add to the definitions and examples in their personal glossaries.

Journal Prompt

If you know that 213 × 14 = 2,982, can you find the product of 2.13 × 1.4 without actually multiplying? Explain why or why not. (Yes. The digits in both multiplication sentences are the same. As a result, the digits in their products will be the same. However, the product of the second sentence will contain a decimal point because it has decimal factors. Since 2 × 1 = 2, then the decimal point goes between the first 2 and the 9.)

Assess

I estimate a product to be about 10. Where shall I place the decimal point if the digits are 9416? (between the 9 and the 4)

Concept Builder — Lesson 8 Plan

Check Decimal Products

TODAY'S CONCEPTS
- Round to the nearest whole number.
- Estimate decimal products.

MATERIALS
- Visual 15: Number Lines
- Visual 16: Average August Rainfall
- Vocabulary Cards: **nearest whole number, round**

SET UP
Build the Concept
Display Visual 15: Number Lines.

Apply the Concept
Display Visual 16: Average August Rainfall.

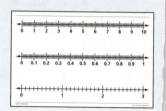

EL WORD WALL

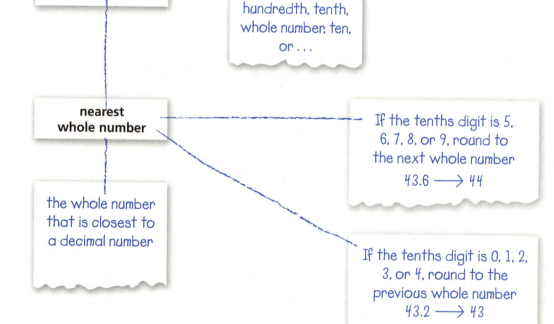

round — Find the nearest hundredth, tenth, whole number, ten, or . . .

nearest whole number — the whole number that is closest to a decimal number

If the tenths digit is 5, 6, 7, 8, or 9, round to the next whole number
43.6 ⟶ 44

If the tenths digit is 0, 1, 2, 3, or 4, round to the previous whole number
43.2 ⟶ 43

38 iSucceed MATH

PD PROFESSIONAL DEVELOPMENT

Math Background Estimating decimal products is a strategy for checking the reasonableness of a calculated result.

Rounding One way to estimate a decimal product is to round the factors.

1. Round the decimal factors to the nearest whole number.
2. Find the product of the rounded factors.
3. Compare this estimated product with the calculated product to decide whether this product is reasonable.

Rounding often requires paper and pencil computation, so it may not be the most efficient way to check products.

Examples:

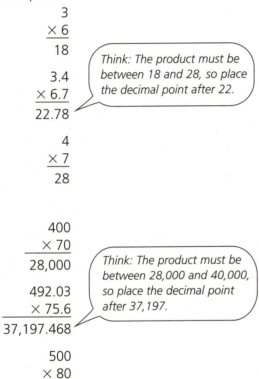

Courseware Connections

Module: Decimals
 Rounding Decimals Through Hundredths
 Rounding Decimals Through Thousandths

Module: Multiplying Decimals
 Multiplying Money
 Multiplying Decimals by Whole Numbers
 Multiplying Decimals Through Hundredths
 Multiplying Decimals with Zeros in the Product
 Multiplying Decimals Through Thousandths

Estimates If students round to a given place before estimating, their results will all be the same. However, estimates using another technique (compatible numbers, front-end, rounding to any place instead of a given place) may vary.

High Stakes Tests Many adults and students do not consider it worth their time to check that the results of computation are reasonable. However, this quick procedure can find easy-to-fix computational errors in high-stakes environments. Encourage your students to take their time and to check their work, regardless of the speed with which others appear to finish their work.

Concept Builder • Lesson 8 • Plan

Lesson 8 Teach

BUILD THE CONCEPT

Display Visual 15: Number Lines. Your goal is to help students estimate the product of two decimal numbers.

- *We are going to estimate the product of 3.4 and 7.5. First, have students help you to mark and label 3.4 on the first number line. What whole number is closest to 3.4?* (3) *Yes, 3.4 rounds to 3.*
- Repeat with 7.5. *What whole number is closest to 7.5?* (7.5 is halfway between 7 and 8) *How do you round a number that is halfway between?* (Halfway numbers round up.)
- *Now find the product of our rounded numbers. Since 8 × 3 = 24, 24 is a good estimate of the actual product.*

Use a number line to round the decimal factors. What whole number is closest to 3.4? (3) Round 3.4 down to 3.

CONNECT TO VOCABULARY

- Add **round** and **nearest whole number** to the Word Wall.
- **EL** Discuss the meanings of the homonyms "hole" and "whole." Consider placing "whole number" on the class difficult-words list.

EXPLORE THE CONCEPT

- Write 0.42 and 0.48. Demonstrate on the second number line as you work. *If we round these to the nearest whole number, what will be our estimated product?* (0) *Is that useful?* (maybe not)
- *We can use 0, 0.5, and 1 to estimate. Is 0.42 closer to 0, 0.5, or 1?* (0.5) *What about 0.48?* (0.5) *If we use 0.5 for both factors, what is our estimated product?* (0.25).
- *In order, the digits of the product of 0.42 and 0.48 are 2, 0, 1, 6. Where does the decimal point go?* (at the far left; the product is 0.2016)
- Repeat with 1.45 × 0.78 on the third number line. (1.131)
- **EL** Compare "estimate" (noun) and "to estimate" (verb). Explain that the words are related; an "estimate" is an approximate answer while "to estimate" is to calculate about how much or how many.

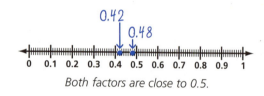

Both factors are close to 0.5.

Wrap Up Discuss underestimates and overestimates. *If you round both factors down, will your estimate be less than or greater than the exact answer?* (less than) *If you round both factors up, will your estimate be less than or greater than the exact answer?* (greater than)

Reteach Use the adding machine tape in your kit or Copymaster M2 to make a number line 4–9 marked in tenths. Have students circle all decimal numbers that round to 5 and underline all decimal numbers that round to 8. Have them refer to the number line to write multiplication sentences involving different pairs of decimal factors that have an estimated product of 40. (Sample answers: 4.9 × 7.7, 5.4 × 8.3, 4.6 × 7.5)

Estimate 2.5 × 9.8 by rounding. How can you tell whether your estimate is less than or greater than the exact product? (The estimate, 30, is greater than the exact answer because both decimal factors are rounded up.)

APPLY THE CONCEPT
Problem-Solving Skill: Check for Reasonableness

Present the Problem Display Visual 16: Average August Rainfall. Read the problem set-up and instructions:

- *The table shows the average amount of rain that fell on four cities during the month of August. The average August rainfall in City E, was 3.2 times the rainfall in City A. What is a reasonable estimate of the amount of rain that fell on City E?*
- *Work with a partner to make a plan to solve the problem. Follow your plan and answer the question.*

Discuss the Solution After students have had time to solve the problem, help the class discuss their solutions.

- *What operation did you use?* (multiplication)
- *What factors did you multiply to find your estimate?* (Most will use 2 × 3.)
- *About how much rain fell in City E during the month of August?* (more than 6 inches)
- *Is your answer an overestimate or an underestimate?* (If both factors were rounded down, as in the sample, it is an underestimate.)
- Extend the discussion by comparing rainfall in Cities B, C, and D with that in City E.

REFLECT

Describe a situation in which you might estimate a decimal product using the next greatest whole number for each factor, regardless of the tenths digits (Probe for situations in which students want to make sure they have enough of an item, such as determining the amount of money needed for a purchase or the amount of ingredients needed for multiple batches of a recipe.)

Vocabulary

- Direct students' attention to the Word Wall. Ask volunteers to define the new vocabulary terms in their own words. Have other volunteers provide examples.
- Encourage students to add to the definitions and examples in their personal glossaries.

Journal Prompt

Why is it a good idea to estimate a product? (Answers should reflect the need to check reasonableness of results.)

Assess

How can you estimate the product of 4.7 × 5.9? (Round each decimal number to the nearest whole number. Round 4.7 to 5 and 5.9 to 6. Then, find the product of the rounded numbers. 5 × 6 = 30. The product of 4.7 × 5.9 is about 30.)

Concept Builder Lesson 9 Plan

Divide Decimal Numbers

TODAY'S CONCEPTS
- Divide whole numbers.
- Divide decimal numbers.

MATERIALS
- Visual 17: Compare Division
- Visual 18: Salary Guide
- colored pencils
- Vocabulary Cards: **dividend**, **divisor**, **quotient**

SET UP

Build the Concept
Display Visual 17: Compare Division.

Apply the Concept
Display Visual 18: Salary Guide.

EL WORD WALL

quotient

divisor) dividend

dividend ÷ divisor = quotient

and

$$\frac{dividend}{divisor} = quotient$$

42   iSucceed MATH

PD PROFESSIONAL DEVELOPMENT

Math Background This lesson focuses on dividing a whole or decimal number by a whole number. The division continues instead of writing a whole-number quotient and a remainder. This process is similar to division of whole numbers, which is a skill students have already explored. Since the lesson deals with whole number divisors, there is no need to multiply dividend and divisor by a power of 10 to move the decimal point before dividing.

Common Error Alert Students must take care to write each partial quotient directly above the corresponding digit in the dividend.

Example:

```
       2.1
   7)14.7
    −14 0
        7
      − 7
        0
```

Failure to align these digits can result in a quotient with a misplaced decimal point. If students have difficulty aligning digits, have them use grid paper or turn a sheet of lined paper horizontally. The rules form columns that can be used to align digits.

Zero in the Quotient Every time a digit from the dividend is used, a corresponding digit must be inserted in the quotient. If two digits must be used in order to divide, then a zero must be inserted in quotient above the first of those two digits.

Example:

```
       2.02                    2.02
   7)14.14                 7)14.14
    −1400         or       −14↓
       14                      1
     − 14                   − 0↓
        0                     14
                           − 14
                              0
```

Check with Multiplication The solution to every division problem can be checked through multiplication. If the product of the divisor and the quotient is the dividend, then the solution is correct.

Courseware Connections

Module: Dividing Decimals

Dividing Decimals by 10, 100, and 1,000

Dividing Decimals by Whole Numbers

More on Dividing Decimals by Whole Numbers

GET REAL: Ice Cream Consumption

Lesson 9 Teach

BUILD THE CONCEPT

Display Visual 17: Compare Division. Your goal is to help students divide decimal numbers.

- Write 6,436 ÷ 8 in the first division housing on the Visual.
- Model the division. Emphasize what you are doing at each step: estimate, multiply, subtract. Stop when you get a remainder. *Who can tell me how 6,436 compares to 6,436.0?* (They are equivalent.) *If I write a decimal point and a zero in the dividend, I can keep dividing, but I need to remember that the rest of my quotient is to the right of the ones place. How do I show that?* (Put a decimal point in the quotient above the one in the dividend.)
- Complete the division. (804.5)

```
        8 0 4
    8)6 4 3 6
     -6 4 0 0
         3 6
        -3 2
           4
```

There is a remainder, but you can keep dividing.

Connect to Vocabulary Add the Vocabulary Cards **dividend**, **divisor**, and **quotient** to the Word Wall.

EXPLORE THE CONCEPT

- Write 643.6 ÷ 8 in the second division housing on the Visual.
- Model the division with students. *How is this quotient similar to the earlier problem?* (Both are made up of the same digits.) *How do they differ?* (The dividend and quotient in the second are less than in the first; decimal points are in different places.)
- Write 6.436 ÷ 8 on the board. Have volunteers explain how to proceed with the division (0.8045).
- *How is this quotient similar to the earlier quotients?* (All are made up of the same digits.) *How do they differ?* (The decimal dividends yielded decimal quotients.)

```
        8 0 . 4 5
    8)6 4 3 . 6 0
     -6 4 0 0
         3 6
        -3 2
           4 0
          -4 0
             0
```

Place a decimal point in the quotient directly above the decimal point in the dividend. Then divide as with whole numbers.

Wrap Up Write 5.463 ÷ 9 on the board. Have students divide to find the quotient. (0.607) *How will the quotient change if I move the decimal point in the dividend?* (The decimal point in the quotient will move in the same way.)

Reteach Have students estimate quotients for 49.7 ÷ 7, 81.18 ÷ 9, and 13.89 ÷ 6. (7, 9, 2) Then, ask them to ignore the decimal point in the dividend, tack on as many zeros as needed, and divide until there's no remainder. They then place the decimal point in the quotient according to their estimates. (7.1, 9.02, 2.315)

Assess

How are the quotients of 3.66 ÷ 4, 36.6 ÷ 4, and 0.366 ÷ 4 alike? How do they differ? What causes this difference? (All quotients contain the same digits. The quotients differ in the number of decimal places they contain. The difference is caused by a varying number of decimal places in each dividend.)

APPLY THE CONCEPT
Problem-Solving Skill: Solve in More Than One Way

Present the Problem Display Visual 18: Salary Guide. Read the problem set-up and instructions:

- *Workers at Packaging Plus work 8 hours each day. The table shows the amount workers at Packaging Plus earn for a 5-day week. What is a manager's hourly wage?*
- *Work with a partner to make a plan to solve the problem. Then follow your plan and answer the question.*

Discuss the Solution After students have had time to solve the problem, help the class discuss their solutions.

- *How did you solve the problem?* Some students may be able to divide by 40. Some will break up the problem into easier steps. They might divide by 8, then by 5; or by 5, then by 8. Model all of the students' solution methods.
- *How did you decide where to place a decimal point in your quotient?* (Most students will place the decimal point in the quotient directly above the decimal point in the dividend in their long division set-up.)
- *How much does a manager earn per hour?* ($18.97)
- Extend the problem by computing the hourly wages of the Delivery Person and the Sales Clerk. ($14.12, $8.54)

REFLECT

An odd number is divided by 2. What do you know about the quotient? You may need to define "odd number" before discussing the question. Give a few examples, like 3 ÷ 2 = 1.5, 13 ÷ 2 = 6.5, 15 ÷ 2 = 7.5, to help students see that the quotient will always be some whole number and five tenths.

Vocabulary

- Write the division sentences 6.432 ÷ 8 = 0.804 and 643.2 ÷ 8 = 80.4 on the board. Make sure students understand that a division sentence written in this format lists the dividend, then the divisor, and finally the quotient.
- Reinforce the concept by writing Dividend ÷ Divisor = Quotient beneath the sentence.
- **EL** Point out to students that division, divisor, and dividend belong to the same word family. If they have trouble distinguishing among them, consider adding them to the class difficult-word list.
- Encourage students to add or extend definitions and examples for today's terms in their personal glossaries.

Journal Prompt

If you know that 645 ÷ 5 = 129, can you find the quotient of 6.45 ÷ 5 without actually dividing? Explain why or why not. (Yes; the digits in both division sentences are the same. The digits in their quotients will be the same. The quotient of the second sentence will contain two decimal places.)

Assess

Which quotient will be greater, 804 ÷ 8 or 80.4 ÷ 8? (The first will be greater than the second.)

Concept Builder Lesson 10 **Plan**

Decimal Divisors

TODAY'S CONCEPTS
- Divide whole numbers by decimal numbers.
- Divide decimal numbers by decimal numbers.

MATERIALS
- Visual 19: Divide by a Decimal
- Visual 20: Earl's Change
- Vocabulary Cards: **dividend**, **divisor**, **quotient**

SET UP
Build the Concept
Display Visual 19: Divide by a Decimal.

$4.00 ÷ $0.25 = ☐

25)400   0.25)4   0.3)1.89

Apply the Concept
Display Visual 20: Earl's Change.

Earl's change: $4.95
3 dimes
___ nickels

EL WORD WALL

quotient

divisor) dividend

16.
0.25.)4.00.

46 iSucceed MATH

PROFESSIONAL DEVELOPMENT

Math Background The algorithm for dividing with decimal numbers is essentially the same as for dividing with whole numbers. To divide by a decimal number, multiply the divisor and the dividend by the power of ten that turns the divisor into a whole number. Then divide. In practice, move the decimal point of the divisor the number of places needed to make the divisor a whole number. Move the decimal point in the dividend the same number of places. Sometimes the extra places in the dividend will have to be filled in with zeros. Students should understand that after the dividend and divisor have been adjusted, the division is the same long division that they have already mastered.

Equivalent Fractions Multiplying the divisor and the dividend by the power of ten that turns the divisor into a whole number does not change the relationship between the divisor and the dividend because they are actually equivalent fractions. Think of the division definition of a fraction and write an equivalent fraction to understand why the expressions are equivalent.

Example: $6 \div 0.3 = \frac{6}{0.3} = \frac{6 \times 10^1}{0.3 \times 10^1} = \frac{60}{3} = 60 \div 3$

Place Value For students who still have difficulty multiplying by 10, 100, or 1,000, revisit place value and the base ten number system. Review the fact that each digit in the decimal system has ten times the value of the same digit one place to its left. Moving the decimal point in a number one place to the right has the same result as multiplying the number by 10; moving it two places to the right has the same result as multiplying by 100, and moving it three places to the right has the same result as multiplying by 1,000.

Estimation Encourage students to look back to check that their quotients are reasonable. They can estimate using compatible numbers or they can check using multiplication if an estimate is not easy.

Courseware Connections

Module: Dividing Decimals
Finding Decimal Quotients
Dividing Decimals Through Hundredths

Lesson 10 Teach

BUILD THE CONCEPT

Display Visual 19: Divide by a Decimal. Your goal in this discussion is to help students understand how to divide by a decimal number.

- Have students use mental math to divide $4.00 by $0.25. Remind them to think of money as they divide. (There are four quarters in a dollar, so there are 16 quarters in four dollars.) Record the work and the quotient on the board.

- Have students divide 400 by 25. Record the work and the quotient on the Visual. (16) *What do you notice about the two quotients?* (They are the same.)

- *What is the product if we multiply 0.25 by 100?* (25) *When we multiply 4 by 100, what is the product?* (400) *This suggests a way to find the quotient of 4 ÷ 0.25. Multiply the dividend and the divisor by 100 and then divide.*

Connect to Vocabulary Post on the Word Wall an discuss: **dividend**, **divisor**, and **quotient**. Check that students understand how the divisor and the dividend change when the divisor is a decimal number.

EXPLORE THE CONCEPT

- Model 4 ÷ 0.25 on the Visual. Demonstrate how to move the decimal point in the divisor. Elicit that the decimal point moves when 0.25 is multiplied by 100. The decimal point in the dividend moves the same number of places. Complete the division.

- Work through the last problem on the Visual. Have volunteers explain how to divide 1.89 ÷ 0.3. *By what number do we multiply the divisor to make it a whole number?* (10)

- Check that students understand how to move the decimal point in both the divisor and the dividend. *What is the equivalent division expression we need to solve?* (18.9 ÷ 3) *What is the quotient?* (6.3) *How can we check the quotient?* (Multiply: 0.3 × 6.3 = 1.89.)

Wrap Up *How is dividing by a decimal divisor different from dividing by a whole number divisor? How is it similar?* (To divide by a decimal divisor, move the decimal point in the decimal divisor to make a whole number and move the decimal point in the dividend the same number of places. Then divide the same way as with a whole number divisor.)

Reteach Use cardstock bills and coins (C4–5) to model dividing decimals.

$$0.25{\overline{\smash{\big)}\,4.00}} = 16$$

Multiply the divisor and dividend by 100 to write 4 ÷ 0.25 as 400 ÷ 25.

Assess

Explain how to find the quotient of 3.36 ÷ 2.4.
(3.36 ÷ 2.4 → 33.6 ÷ 24 = 1.4)

48   iSucceed MATH: Decimal Divisors

APPLY THE CONCEPT
Problem-Solving Strategy: Solve Multi-Step Problems

Present the Problem Display Visual 20: Earl's Change. Read the problem set-up and instructions:

- *Earl has been saving nickels. He also has 3 dimes. If his total amount of change is $4.95, how many nickels does Earl have?*
- *Work with a partner to solve the problem.*

Discuss the Solution After students have had time to solve the problem, help the class discuss their solutions.

- *What do you know?* (Earl has some nickels and 3 dimes that are worth $4.95.)
- *What do you need to find out?* (How many nickels does Earl have?)
- *How did you start?* (Most students should see that taking the dimes out of the mix simplifies the problem.)
- *What number sentence tells what you did next?* (Since $4.95 − $0.30 = $4.65, $4.65 ÷ $0.05 = nickels.)
- Some students may use the Guess, Check, and Revise strategy. Others may know how to write and solve the equation ($4.95 − $0.30) ÷ $0.05 = *n*. If either strategy comes up in discussion, take time to demonstrate it.
- Have students explain how they moved the decimal point in the divisor and the dividend to complete the division. *How many nickels does Earl have?* (93 nickels)
- Discuss how to check the answer.

REFLECT

Discuss the reason for moving the decimal point in the divisor to divide by a decimal.

Vocabulary

Refer students to the Word Wall. Discuss examples, then ask students to add to the definitions and examples in their personal glossaries.

Journal Prompt

Which values change before you divide by a decimal number? Explain. (Answers should include multiplying the dividend and the divisor by the same power of ten to make the divisor a whole number.)

Assess

What is the quotient of 9.1 ÷ 0.35? Explain. (9.1 ÷ 0.35 = 910 ÷ 35 = 26) Check students' explanations.

Concept Builder — Lesson 11 Plan

Check Decimal Quotients

TODAY'S CONCEPT
- Estimate decimal quotients.

MATERIALS
- Visual 21: Estimate and Divide
- Visual 22: Rock Samples
- small self-stick notes, some cut in half
- Vocabulary Card: **compatible numbers**

SET UP
Build the Concept
Display Visual 21: Estimate and Divide.

Apply the Concept
Display Visual 22: Rock Samples

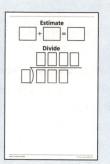

EL WORD WALL

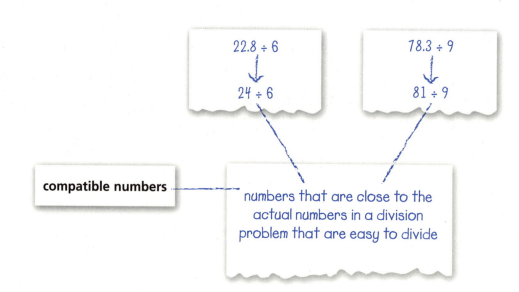

compatible numbers — numbers that are close to the actual numbers in a division problem that are easy to divide

$22.8 \div 6 \rightarrow 24 \div 6$

$78.3 \div 9 \rightarrow 81 \div 9$

50 iSucceed MATH

PROFESSIONAL DEVELOPMENT

Compatible Numbers You can use compatible numbers to check the reasonableness of a decimal quotient. First, identify whole numbers close to the dividend and divisor that are easy to divide. If the divisor is one digit, look for facts or near-facts with that number. Compare the whole-number quotient to the computed decimal quotient.

Example:
16.8 ÷ 6 = 2.8   computed quotient
18 ÷ 6 = 3   estimated quotient

Since 2.8 is close to 3, it is a reasonable result. The point of using compatible numbers is to be able to use mental math.

Check by Rounding Rounding is another way of checking the reasonableness of a decimal quotient, but this often precludes using mental math to estimate. Round the dividend and divisor to the nearest whole number. Divide and compare quotients.

Example:
14.8 ÷ 4 = 3.7
15 ÷ 4 = 3.75

Since the quotients are close, the computed result is reasonable.

Check Decimal Places Estimates should help students to make sure that the decimal point is correctly placed in the quotient.

Courseware Connections

Module: Dividing Decimals
  Finding Decimal Quotients
  More on Dividing Decimals by Whole Numbers
  Dividing Decimals Through Hundredths

Lesson 11 Teach

BUILD THE CONCEPT

Display Visual 21: Estimate and Divide. Your goal is to show students how to use compatible numbers to check a decimal quotient.

- Write 60.8 ÷ 8 on self-stick notes on the Visual. Have students draw upon their previous knowledge to work through the problem. *What is the quotient?* (7.6)
- *We can use compatible numbers to see whether our quotient is reasonable.*
- *What whole number is close to 60.8 and divisible by 8?* (64 or 56) Show the estimate on self-stick notes on the Visual.

Connect to Vocabulary Add **compatible numbers** to the Word Wall.

 Explain to students that people who get along with each other and work well together are said to be *compatible*.

EXPLORE THE CONCEPT

- Change the problem on the Visual to 73.8 ÷ 8. *What compatible numbers can we use to estimate the quotient?* (72 and 8 or 70 and 10)
- *What is the quotient of 72 ÷ 8?* (9) *Will the exact quotient be less than or greater than the estimated quotient? How can you tell?* (Greater than; the compatible number 72 is less than the exact dividend of 73.8.)
- *How can you decide where to place the decimal point in the quotient if I tell you that its digits, in order, are 9, 2, 2, 5?* (The quotient must be a little greater than 9, so the decimal point is to the right of the ones place: 9.225.)

Wrap Up Write 37.8 ÷ 9 = 0.42. *Is this quotient reasonable? Why or why not?* (No. Using compatible numbers of 36 and 9 shows that the actual quotient should be close to 4. *What mistake was likely made?* (The decimal point was put in the wrong place. The correct quotient is 4.2.)

Reteach Write 25.8 ÷ 3. Have students name a whole number close to but less than 25.8 and divisible by 3. (24) Then have them name a whole number close to but greater than 25.8 and divisible by 3. (27) Write 24 ÷ 3 = 8 and 27 ÷ 3 = 9. Explain that using two sets of compatible numbers can provide a range for the actual quotient. Have students solve the original problem. Then have them use a number line (Copymaster M2) to decide whether their computed quotient falls within the range.

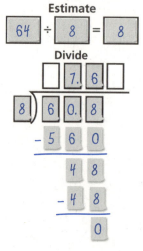

The compatible numbers 64 and 8 give an estimated quotient of 8. The computed quotient, 7.6, makes sense.

How can you use compatible numbers to check the reasonableness of a decimal quotient? (Express the decimal dividend and divisor as whole numbers close to the actual numbers. Find the quotient of the compatible numbers. Compare the quotient with the exact quotient.)

52 iSucceed MATH: Check Decimal Quotients

APPLY THE CONCEPT
Problem-Solving Skill: Check for Reasonableness
Problem-Solving Strategy: Solve Multi-Step Problems

Present the Problem Display Visual 22: Rock Samples. Read the problem set-up and instructions:

- *For three weeks, a group of scientists gathered rock samples near a volcano. The samples were then shipped to a lab. The samples were divided evenly among 8 containers. How many pounds of rock samples did each container hold?*
- *Work with a partner to make a plan to solve the problem. Follow your plan and answer the question.*

Discuss the Solution After students have had time to solve the problem, help the class discuss their solutions.

- *What did you do first to solve this multi-step problem?* (Add to find the total weight of the samples.)
- *What was your next step?* (Divide the total of 157.2 pounds by 8.)
- *How did you check the reasonableness of your quotient?* (Some students will use compatible numbers, some will multiply, some will divide twice.)
- *How many pounds of rocks were in each container?* (19.65 pounds)

REFLECT

- *Why might two classmates come up with different estimated quotients for 26.4 ÷ 6?* (One person might use 24 ÷ 6 = 4, and the other person might use 30 ÷ 6 = 5)
- *Without computing, tell how these estimates compare to the exact answer.* (The exact answer is between 4 and 5 because 24 < 26.4 and 30 > 26.4.)

Vocabulary

- Direct students' attention to the Word Wall. Ask volunteers to define compatible numbers in their own words. Have other volunteers provide examples.
- Ask students to record their definitions and examples in their personal glossaries.

Journal Prompt

Danye used the compatible numbers 30 ÷ 6 = 5 to estimate a quotient. Seth also used these compatible numbers to estimate a quotient. Does this necessarily mean that Danye and Seth were trying to solve the same problem? Give Examples. (No, they also could be solving different problems with numbers that are close to 30 and 6. For example, Danye could be solving 29.2 ÷ 6 while Seth is solving 33.7 ÷ 6.)

Assess

How do you prefer to check quotients? (Some students will use compatible numbers to estimate, some will multiply, some will divide twice.)

UNIT 2

Fractions

Lessons

12	Fractions: Parts of a Set (Grade 2)*	56
13	Fractions: Parts of a Whole (Grade 2)	60
14	Fractions: The Division Model (Grade 4)	64
15	Equivalent Fractions (Grade 5)	68
16	Simplest Form (Grade 5)	72
17	Relate Fractions to Decimal Numbers (Grade 3)	76
18	Compare and Order Fractions (Grade 5)	80
19	Model Adding Fractions (Grade 4)	84
20	Model Subtracting Fractions (Grade 4)	88
21	Model Multiplying Fractions (Grade 5)	92
22	Reciprocals (Grade 5)	96
23	Model Dividing Fractions (Grade 5)	100
24	Mixed Numbers (Grade 5)	104
25	Add Mixed Numbers (Grade 5)	108
26	Subtract Mixed Numbers (Grade 5)	112
27	Multiply Mixed Numbers (Grade 5)	116
28	Divide Mixed Numbers (Grade 5)	120
29	Use a Calculator Appropriately (Grade 3)	124

*Indicates grade level at which topic is typically introduced; your curriculum may differ.

MATERIALS

- Volume II Unit 2 Lesson Visuals 23–58
- Volume II Cardstock: Coins, Fraction/Decimal Cards, Fraction Models
- Copymasters: M2: Number Lines, M4: Grid Paper
- counters
- adding machine tape
- small and large self-stick notes

VOCABULARY CARDS

addend, calculator, computation method, decimal number, common denominators, denominator, difference, divide, dividend, division, divisor, equivalent fractions, factor, fourth, fraction, greatest common factor (GCF), half, mental math, missing addend, mixed number, numerator, paper and pencil, product, quotient, reciprocals, regroup, rename, simplest form, subtract, sum, third, whole number, = (is equal to), > (is greater than), < (is less than)

Introduction

Unit 1 focused on ways to use decimals to name, compare, and compute with numbers that lie between whole numbers. Unit 2 features ways to use fractions to name, compare, and compute with numbers that lie between whole numbers. Fractions compare part to all of a set or whole. With decimal numbers, the equal parts of the whole are always multiples of 10. With fractions, there can be any number of equal parts of the whole. With decimal numbers, the rules for computing follow the rules for computing with whole numbers. With fractions, the rules are different.

Adding and subtracting fractions may be counter-intuitive for some students, and is often more difficult for them than multiplying fractions. In fact, a common error is for students to assume that the algorithm for multiplying fractions (multiply numerators, then multiply denominators) must transfer to other operations with fractions.

Common Errors

▶ **Example:** Find the sum of $\frac{1}{4}$ and $\frac{5}{8}$.

Error: The student writes $\frac{6}{12}$.

Intervention: Use fraction models to help the student to see that eighths and fourths are not equivalent and so cannot be added until he or she finds a way to name them with the same denominator. Divide a unit square into equal fourths. Shade one of the fourths. Then, divide each fourth into two equal parts so that the student sees the equivalence of $\frac{1}{4}$ and $\frac{2}{8}$. Return to the sum and show that $\frac{1}{4} + \frac{5}{8} = \frac{7}{8}$.

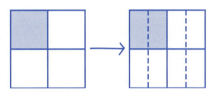

One fourth is equivalent to two eighths.

The algorithm for dividing fractions includes a commonly-forgotten step: find the reciprocal of the divisor, then multiply.

▶ **Example:** Find the quotient: $\frac{1}{4} \div \frac{5}{8}$.

Error: The student writes $\frac{5}{32}$.

Intervention: This student remembered to multiply, but forgot to find the reciprocal of $\frac{5}{8}$ first. After you are sure that the student can use models to compute, help him or her to differentiate among all of the fraction-computation algorithms. Consider devising mnemonics to help keep track of when to use which set of rules. Here are some samples:

- To <u>a</u>dd or <u>s</u>ubtract, find a <u>c</u>ommon <u>d</u>enominator, then compute with the numerators and keep the denominator. *<u>A</u>fter <u>s</u>upper <u>c</u>all the <u>d</u>og.*

- To multiply, multiply numerators, then multiply denominators. *Multiply everything.*

- To divide, multiply by the reciprocal of the divisor. *Do not multiply right away.*

Unit 2 • Fractions

Concept Builder **Lesson 12** **Plan**

Fractions: Parts of a Set

TODAY'S CONCEPTS
- Understand fractions as part of a set.
- Read fractions.

MATERIALS
- Visual 23: Fraction Mat
- Visual 24: Marble Collection
- counters (12 of each of 3 colors)
- large self-stick notes, some cut in half
- Vocabulary Cards: **denominator**, **fourth**, **fraction**, **half**, **numerator**, **third**

SET UP
Build the Concept
Display Visual 23: Fraction Mat.

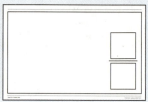

Apply the Concept
Display Visual 24: Marble Collection.

WORD WALL

Look at page 60 to see how this Word Wall will change for Concept Builder 13.

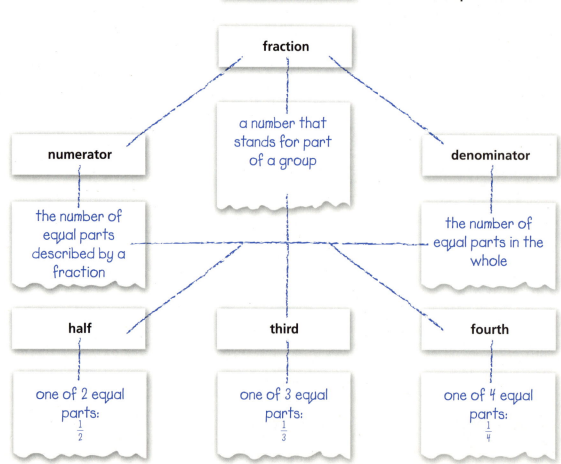

56 iSucceed MATH

PD PROFESSIONAL DEVELOPMENT

Math Background A fraction is like a decimal number in that it is a number that stands for part of something. A fraction can name a part of a set (collection of things) or a part of a whole. Students will examine each way to identify a fraction in separate lessons. Whether a fraction is standing for part of a set or for part of a whole, it is essentially functioning in the same way.

Reading Fractions When reading a fraction, say the number in the numerator first. In English, starting with fourths, the denominator of a fraction is read by adding "th" to the number name. This pattern makes it easy to read fractions and works except for halves, thirds, and most other numbers that end in 2 or 3.

Write: $\frac{5}{6}$

Say: *five sixths*

EL Fractions in Other Languages If students know fraction names in their first language, they might benefit from making and posting a chart that equates the fractions and their names in English with their names in the students' first language.

Error Alert Although students will not compare fractions until a later lesson, they should understand that fractions that look alike do not necessarily represent equal amounts. The wholes must be the same before fractions can represent equal amounts.

Examples:
- One half of a small box of cereal is not the same as one half of a large box of cereal.
- One half of a group of books may not have one half of the weight of the group.

Courseware Connections

Module: Understanding and Adding Fractions
Fractions and Fraction Models

Name	Fraction
Un medio	$\frac{1}{2}$
Un tercio	$\frac{1}{3}$
Un cuarto	$\frac{1}{4}$
Un quinto	$\frac{1}{5}$
Un sexto	$\frac{1}{6}$
Un séptimo	$\frac{1}{7}$
Un octavo	$\frac{1}{8}$
Un noveno	$\frac{1}{9}$
Un décimo	$\frac{1}{10}$

Source: http://www.learn-spanish-online.de; last checked 12/06

Fraction Names in Spanish

Lesson 12 Teach

BUILD THE CONCEPT

Display Visual 23: Fraction Mat. Your goal in this discussion is to help students understand how to name and read a fraction as part of a collection.

- *A fraction is a number that stands for part of something. It is made up of two parts.* Direct attention to the blank fraction on the Visual. *A bar separates the two parts of a fraction. The bottom part is called the denominator. It tells how many equal parts are in the whole. The top part is called the numerator. It tells how many of those parts the fraction stands for.*

- Use half of small self-stick notes to hang up two different-color counters. *I want to write a fraction that stands for the number of white counters.* Use self-stick notes to record the fraction $\frac{1}{2}$. *The 1 stands for the number of white counters. The 2 stands for the number of equal parts, or counters.*

- *What fraction of the counters are gray?* (one half) *How do you know?* (There are two counters. Only one is gray.)

Connect to Vocabulary Make sure that students can distinguish the numerator from the denominator of a fraction.

- Add **denominator, fraction, half**, and **numerator** to the Word Wall.

- **EL** Have students who know the name for one half in their first language share the name. Discuss how it may appear similar to the English word. For example, the Spanish "medio" may make students think of middle, which may lead them to connect to half. Help students to distinguish "half" and "halves" from "have."

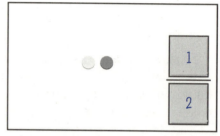

To read a fraction, first read the numerator by saying the number. Then read the denominator. Read the number 2 in the denominator of a fraction as "half".

EXPLORE THE CONCEPT

- Hang two counters of one color and one counter of a second color on the fraction mat. *How do we write the fraction of counters that are gray? Why?* (Put 2 in the numerator because 2 are gray. Put 3 in the denominator because there are 3 in all.)

- *When the denominator of a fraction is 3, we read it as thirds. How do you read the fraction?* (two thirds)

- Repeat the discussion with other fractions such as $\frac{4}{5}$, $\frac{5}{8}$, and $\frac{3}{10}$. Point out that, after half and third, denominators are read by adding "th" to the denominator's number name.

Wrap Up Help students to find some common classroom objects, such as books, with different characteristics. Have them name a fraction of the group. For example, $\frac{3}{8}$ of the books might have a red cover.

Reteach Use Cardstock 5: Coins to relate pennies to dimes. *When there are 10 pennies, the value of one penny is one tenth the value of a dime.* Students should be familiar with this from decimals. Discuss how to write the value as the fraction one tenth, or $\frac{1}{10}$.

There are 8 pets in the pet show. Three of the pets are cats, 4 are dogs, and 1 is a bird. What fraction of the pets are cats? Dogs? Birds? ($\frac{3}{8}$, $\frac{4}{8}$, $\frac{1}{8}$)

APPLY THE CONCEPT
Problem-Solving Strategy: Act It Out

Present the Problem Display Visual 24: Marble Collection. Provide counters for students to use to help them solve the problem. Read the problem set-up and instructions:

- *Gail, Brian, and Red have 24 marbles. Is it possible for all of them to have the fraction of marbles they claim to have? Explain.*
- *Work with a partner. Act out the problem to solve.*

Discuss the Solution After students have had time to solve the problem, help the class discuss their solutions.

- *How did acting out the problem help you to solve the problem?* (Sample answer: We used 24 counters and tried to make $\frac{1}{2}$ of the group, $\frac{1}{4}$, and $\frac{1}{3}$ of the group.)
- *Is it possible for Gail, Brian, and Red to have the fraction of marbles they claim to have? How do you know?* (No. We could not make $\frac{1}{2}$, $\frac{1}{4}$ and $\frac{1}{3}$ of 24 all at the same time.) Discuss how students were able to recognize $\frac{1}{2}$, $\frac{1}{3}$, and $\frac{1}{4}$ of 24.

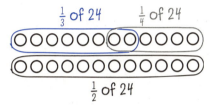

After finding $\frac{1}{2}$ of 24 and $\frac{1}{4}$ of 24, there are not enough marbles left to make $\frac{1}{3}$ of 24.

REFLECT
Vocabulary

- Direct students' attention to the Word Wall. Discuss how to recognize and read fractions. Add **third** and **fourth** to the Word Wall.
- Point out the new terms on the Word Wall. Discuss how to define the terms before asking students to record their definitions in their personal glossaries along with a diagram and/or an example for each.
- Leave the Word Wall up. You will modify it slightly for Concept Builder 13.

Journal Prompt

What is the difference between the numerator and the denominator of a fraction? Use words and numbers to explain. (Answers should convey an understanding that the numerator shows the parts described and the denominator shows the total number of equal parts.)

Assess

There are 10 stickers on the page. Seven of the stickers have stars. The other stickers have moons. What fraction of the stickers have moons? Explain. (Since 3 of the 10 stickers have moons, $\frac{3}{10}$ of the stickers have moons.)

Concept Builder — Lesson 13 Plan

Fractions: Parts of a Whole

TODAY'S CONCEPTS
- Understand fractions as a part of a whole.
- Read fractions.

MATERIALS
- Visual 25: Unit Squares
- Visual 26: 4 by 4 Grids
- Copymaster M5: Grid Paper
- Vocabulary Cards: **denominator**, **fourth**, **fraction**, **half**, **numerator**, **third**

SET UP

Build the Concept
- Display Visual 25: Unit Squares.
- Post a copy of Copymaster M5: Grid Paper.

Apply the Concept
Display Visual 26: 4 by 4 Grids.

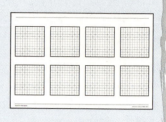

EL WORD WALL

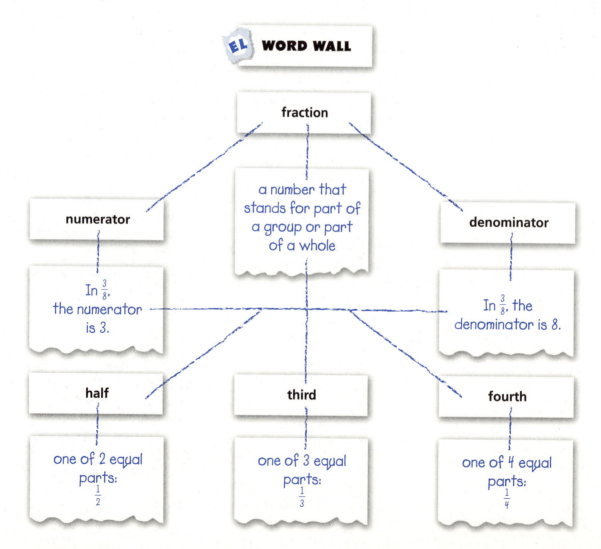

fraction — a number that stands for part of a group or part of a whole

numerator — In $\frac{3}{8}$, the numerator is 3.

denominator — In $\frac{3}{8}$, the denominator is 8.

half — one of 2 equal parts: $\frac{1}{2}$

third — one of 3 equal parts: $\frac{1}{3}$

fourth — one of 4 equal parts: $\frac{1}{4}$

iSucceed MATH

PD PROFESSIONAL DEVELOPMENT

Math Background In this lesson, students name fractions as part of a whole. Fractions as parts of a whole are essentially the same as fractions as parts of a group. The everyday usage exception is that some groups do not have equal-size elements, yet we can talk about a fraction of the items. This means it's OK to talk about half of the students or a third of the books. When you refer to a fraction of a whole, you must refer to equal-size parts.

Drawing Fractions as Parts of a Whole When students use squares or rectangles to draw fractions, they should try to make the parts as equal as they can. At the same time, you should not expect students' drawings to be exact. Copymaster M5: Grid Paper is a good tool.

Circle Model Using the circle model to show fractions as part of a whole is good if the models are provided. Otherwise, the models are probably too difficult to draw. It will probably be much easier for students to draw squares or rectangles to represent the equal parts of a whole.

Error Alert Check that students represent parts of a whole using equal parts. Two parts of a square are not necessarily the same as two equal parts.

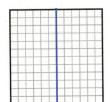 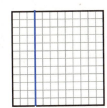

Each square has two parts. Only the square on the left, however, shows two equal parts, or halves.

Courseware Connections

Module: Understanding and Adding Fractions

Fractions and Fraction Models
GET REAL: A Quilting Bee
GET REAL: Clock Fractions

Lesson 13 Teach

BUILD THE CONCEPT

Display Visual 25: Unit Squares. These unit squares are 12 × 12 so that many sets of equal parts can be illustrated. Your goal in this discussion is to help students understand how to name and read a fraction as part of a whole.

- *You know that a fraction can represent a part of a group. A fraction can also represent a part of a whole. The whole must be divided into equal parts to name a fraction.*
- Model one half on a unit square. Discuss how to record and read the fraction. *What fraction of the square is shaded?* (one half)

The square has two equal parts. One of the parts is shaded, so, one half of the square is shaded.

Connect to Vocabulary Post on the Word Wall and discuss: **denominator**, **fourth**, **fraction**, **half**, **numerator**, and, **third**. Point out that the definition of fraction now includes part of a whole as well as part of a group. Help students to see the similarity between the two. Have them identify the numerator and denominator as they name different fractions.

EXPLORE THE CONCEPT

- Discuss different ways to show thirds on unit squares. Contrast the 3 equal parts with 3 parts that are not equal.
- Shade two parts of a unit square divided into thirds. Have students name the fraction for the shaded and unshaded parts. ($\frac{2}{3}$; $\frac{1}{3}$)
- Use the unit square to show other fractions (fourths and sixths). Have students name the shaded and unshaded parts.

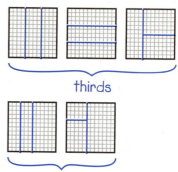

thirds

not thirds

Not all parts are equal. When you use a fraction to name a part of a single thing, the parts must be equal.

Wrap Up Draw these three diagrams on grid paper. *Which of these diagrams shows $\frac{3}{4}$ shaded? Explain how you know.* (All of them have 3 of 4 rows shaded, so all show $\frac{3}{4}$.)

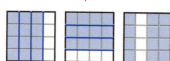

Can you show me some more ways to shade $\frac{3}{4}$?

Reteach Demonstrate different ways to divide a rectangle into equal parts. Continue to stress that the parts must be equal. Have students draw rectangles on Copymaster M5: Grid Paper to show different fractions.

Two ways to show fourths using a rectangle.

Assess

James ate $\frac{2}{8}$ of a pizza. His bothers ate the rest of the pizza. What part of the pizza did his brothers eat? Explain. ($\frac{6}{8}$; There are 8 equal parts; if 2 are gone, then 6 must be left.)

APPLY THE CONCEPT
Problem-Solving Strategy: Draw a Picture

Present the Problem Display Visual 26: 4 by 4 Grids. Distribute copies of Copymaster M5: Grid Paper. Read the problem set-up and instructions:

- *How many different ways can you color the grid to show half of the grid?*
- *Work with a partner. Draw pictures to solve.*

Discuss the Solution After students have had time to solve the problem, help the class discuss their solutions.

- *What are some of the ways you colored the grid to show one half?* (Answers may vary: top and bottom, right and left halves of the grid, or more creative solutions. Each half should have 8 squares. Any combination of 8 colored squares and 8 blank squares corresponds to one half.)
- Challenge students to name the fraction that shows half of the grid. ($\frac{8}{16}$)

REFLECT

Discuss why half of a class is not the same as half of a school. (The wholes are different sizes.) Extend the discussion to include equal parts. *Why do the parts have to be equal to name a fraction as a part of the whole?* (Sample answer: It would not make sense to compare the parts if the parts were different sizes.)

Vocabulary
Direct students' attention to the Word Wall. Discuss how to extend the definition of fraction to include the parts of a whole.

Journal Prompt

How is one half of a square related to one half of a group of two squares? Draw a diagram. (Answers should include some discussion of the difference between a fraction as a part of a whole and as a part of a group. Both fractions name the same number but may not necessarily represent the same amount.)

Assess

Paula and Setsuko used different models to show three fourths. Can both models be correct? Explain. (Yes, as long as both models are divided into 4 equal parts and 3 of the parts are shaded differently than the rest.)

Concept Builder — Lesson 14 Plan

Fractions: The Division Model

TODAY'S CONCEPTS
- Relate fractions and division.
- Interpret and use drawings that represent fractions.

MATERIALS
- Visual 27: Area Model
- Visual 28: Parts of a Group Pattern
- adding machine tape
- counters
- Vocabulary Cards: **denominator**, **dividend**, **division**, **divisor**, **fraction**, **numerator**

SET UP

Build the Concept
Display Visual 27: Area Model.

Explore the Concept
Make and post a 1–26 number line with adding machine tape.

Apply the Concept
Display Visual 28: Parts of a Group Pattern.

EL WORD WALL

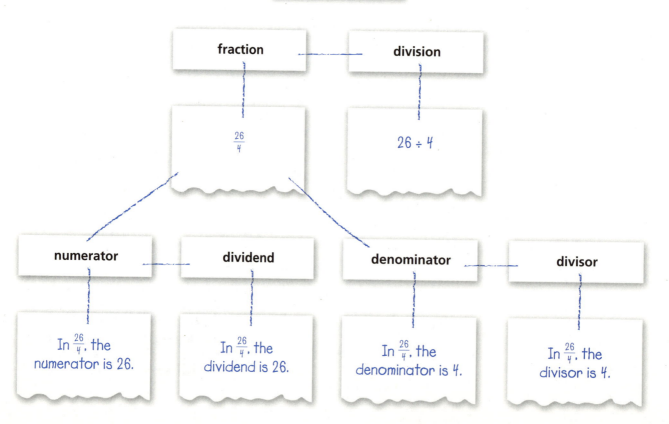

PROFESSIONAL DEVELOPMENT

Math Background The fraction bar means division, so both $\frac{4}{2}$ and $4 \div 2$ mean the same thing. Similarly, $\frac{1}{2} = 1 \div 2$. Just as you can ask how many 2s are in 4 for $4 \div 2$, or $\frac{4}{2}$, so you can ask how many 2s are in 1 for $1 \div 2$, or $\frac{1}{2}$.

Fractions on a Number Line Any fraction can be shown on a number line. A fraction represents equal parts, so equal spaces between whole numbers on a number line can show a fraction.

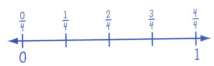

You can show fourths on a number line.

Module: Understanding and Adding Fractions

Fractions on a Number Line

Improper Fractions and Mixed Numbers Although students will consider a fraction in which the numerator is greater than the denominator, the terms *improper fraction* and *mixed number* will not be defined in this lesson. The lesson demonstration should lead students to recognize that $\frac{26}{4} = 6\frac{2}{4}$ without actually having to use any new terms.

Simplest Form Students will consider equivalent fractions in the next lesson. It is important to point out that $\frac{2}{4}$ is not an incorrect way to refer to the fraction. It is traditional to simplify $\frac{2}{4}$ to $\frac{1}{2}$, but doing so is not necessary except in some testing situations.

Writing the Remainder as a Fraction Students will connect fractions to division by considering equal parts, but they will not be dividing in this lesson. It is, however, useful for students to recognize that when there is a remainder in division, an answer such as 6 R2 is not a number. If a numerical answer is needed, students must record the remainder as a number. To write the remainder as a fraction, use the remainder as the numerator and the divisor as the denominator.

Lesson 14 Teach

BUILD THE CONCEPT

Display Visual 27: Area Model. Your goal in this discussion is to help students understand how to connect fractions to division.

- Shade the first diagram to show $\frac{26}{4}$.
- Explain to students that the model shows 6 whole groups of 4 fourths with 2 fourths left over. *This is the same as 6 wholes plus two fourths, or 6 and $\frac{2}{4}$.*
- Connect this to $\frac{26}{4}$ as division by shading the second diagram. Point out that because the fourths are equal groups, you can think of the numerator, 26, as the dividend and the denominator, 4, as the divisor.

Connect to Vocabulary Post on the Word Wall and discuss: **denominator, dividend, division, divisor, fraction,** and **numerator**. Discuss what numerator and denominator mean in terms of division and in terms of fractions. Rather than define the words, however, label the parts to help students see how they match.

Each column in the model represents 4 fourths. There are 26 fourths in the model.

There are 26 shaded squares. You can make 6 groups of 4. There are 2 of the 4 squares in a full column left over.

EXPLORE THE CONCEPT

- Use the adding machine tape to make a number line from 0–26. We can use the number line to show $\frac{26}{4}$.
- *Skip count back by 4 from 26 on the number line. How many full skips of 4 are there?* (6) *How many of the next 4 are left?* (2) Connect $\frac{26}{4}$ to 26 ÷ 4. Point out that you can record the number of skips as $6\frac{2}{4}$.

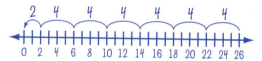

Start skip-counting back by fours from 26. In 26, there are 6 groups of 4, with 2 of the last group of 4 left over.

Wrap Up *Why can you record the number of skips on the number line for $\frac{26}{4}$ as $6\frac{2}{4}$?* (There are 6 whole skips of 4 and 2 left when you try to make another skip of 4.)

Reteach Model the parts of a set using counters to look at groups for $\frac{26}{4}$. You can make 6 groups of 4 with 2 of another group of 4 left over. Point out that 2 of another group of 4 is the same as $\frac{2}{4}$. Connect the amount left over to an alternate way to write the remainder, as $\frac{\text{remainder}}{\text{divisor}}$, or $\frac{2}{4}$.

How many skips of 3 are in $\frac{7}{3}$? Show and explain how that tells you another way to write $\frac{7}{3}$. (There are 2 full skips of 3 with 1 of the next group of 3 left, so $\frac{7}{3} = 2\frac{1}{3}$.)

APPLY THE CONCEPT
Problem-Solving Strategy: Look for a Pattern

Present the Problem Display Visual 28: Parts of a Group Pattern. Provide 24 counters for each pair of students. Read the problem set-up and instructions:

- Use counters to find the number of each group that each fraction represents.
- Work with a partner to solve the problem.

Discuss the Solution After students have had time to solve the problem, help the class discuss their solutions.

- What is $\frac{1}{6}$ of 24? $\frac{1}{8}$ of 24? $\frac{1}{12}$ of 24? (4; 3; 2) Discuss how students found each fraction of the group.
- What pattern did you discover? (You don't need to group counters. You can just divide 24 by the denominator of the fraction.) Discuss how students were able to connect the fraction of the group to division.
- Demonstrate $\frac{2}{3}$ of 24 and $\frac{3}{4}$ of 24 to show that the relationship only works when the numerator is 1.

$\frac{1}{2}$ of 24 = 12 $\frac{1}{6}$ of 24 = 4

$\frac{1}{3}$ of 24 = 8 $\frac{1}{8}$ of 24 = 3

$\frac{1}{4}$ of 24 = 6 $\frac{1}{12}$ of 24 = 2

Look for a pattern that describes the relationship between each fraction and the number of the group it represents. Describe the pattern.

REFLECT

How do you find $\frac{1}{2}$ of any number? $\frac{1}{3}$ of any number? $\frac{1}{4}$ of any number? (Divide the number by 2; divide the number by 3; divide the number by 4)

Vocabulary

Refer students to the Word Wall. Work with them to make another set of examples to illustrate the terms. Encourage them to add new definitions and examples to their personal glossaries.

Journal Prompt

You have 15 quarts of milk and want to distribute it evenly among 4 people. How much will each person get? Explain. ($3\frac{3}{4}$ quarts)

Assess

Write a problem that can be solved by finding a fraction of a group. (Check students' work.)

Concept Builder **Lesson 15** **Plan**

Equivalent Fractions

TODAY'S CONCEPTS
- Find equivalent fractions.
- Recognize equivalent fractions.

MATERIALS
- Visual 29: Stacked Number Lines 1
- Visual 30: Caroline's Claim
- Copymaster M5: Grid Paper
- counters
- small self-stick notes cut in half
- Vocabulary Card: **equivalent fractions**, **fraction**

SET UP
Build the Concept
Display Visual 29: Stacked Number Lines 1.

Apply the Concept
Display Visual 30: Caroline's Claim.

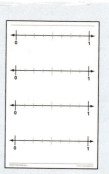

 WORD WALL

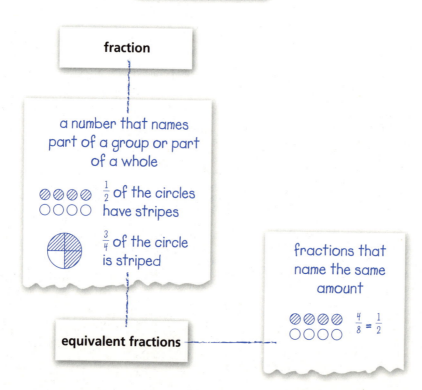

68 iSucceed MATH

PROFESSIONAL DEVELOPMENT

Math Background Equivalent fractions name the same amount. They are used to compare, add, and subtract fractions. Although students will not be adding or subtracting fractions with unlike denominators, they should know how to write equivalent fractions.

Equivalent Fractions To find equivalent fractions, multiply or divide the numerator and the denominator by the same non-zero number. This does not change the value of the fraction because this multiplication has the same overall effect as multiplying by 1.

$$\frac{1}{2} = \frac{1}{2} \times \frac{2}{2} = \frac{2}{4}$$

Since $\frac{2}{2}$ is both of the 2 equal parts of 1 whole, then $\frac{2}{2} = 1$. Any number multiplied by 1 does not change value.

Courseware Connections

Module: Understanding and Adding Fractions

Equivalent Fractions

Alternative Models Students will benefit from using fraction models made from squares or rectangles to identify equivalent fractions. Cardstock C6–7 is a good resource. If you use a ruler model, start simply, with a ruler marked in fourths.

A customary ruler is an excellent model to use to relate halves, fourths, eighths, and sixteenths.

Simplest Form A common application of equivalent fractions is to write a fraction in simplest form. A fraction is in simplest form when its numerator and denominator have no common factor other than 1. Since the value of the fractions is the same, it is not necessary to write a fraction in simplest form for a calculation to be correct.

Example: $\frac{1}{2} = \frac{2}{4}$

Both forms for one half are equivalent and correct.

Lesson 15 Teach

BUILD THE CONCEPT

Display Visual 29: Stacked Number Lines 1. Your goal in this discussion is to help students understand how to identify equivalent fractions.

- *You can show fractions on a number line.* Demonstrate how to show halves and fourths on the first two stacked number lines. Use self-stick notes to label the number lines.
- *Two different fractions can name the same amount. Which two fractions name the same amount? How can you tell?* ($\frac{1}{2}$ and $\frac{2}{4}$; They are in the same positions on the number lines.)
- *Is $\frac{1}{4}$ equivalent to $\frac{1}{2}$? How do you know?* (No; $\frac{1}{4}$ and $\frac{1}{2}$ name different amounts. They are in different positions on the number line.)

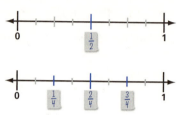

$\frac{1}{2}$ and $\frac{2}{4}$ are equivalent fractions because they name the same amount.

Connect to Vocabulary Emphasize that equivalent fractions have the same value and that they are equal.

- Post **fraction** and **equivalent fraction** on the Word Wall.
- **EL** Some bilingual teachers prefer not to use the word "equal" when compared values are not identical. You may use "equivalent" or "same value" instead. *Equivalent fractions have the same values.* Note that "equivalent" starts the same way as "equal", with "equ-."

EXPLORE THE CONCEPT

- Model and label eighths on the third number line. Discuss how to identify the equivalent fractions.
- Use the fourth number line to show halves, thirds, and sixths. Have students identify equivalent fractions. ($\frac{1}{2}$ and $\frac{3}{6}$, $\frac{1}{3}$ and $\frac{2}{6}$, $\frac{2}{3}$ and $\frac{4}{6}$) *How do number lines help you recognize equivalent fractions?* (They show the position of the fractions. Fractions in the same position are equivalent.)

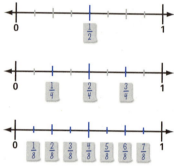

$\frac{1}{2} = \frac{2}{4} = \frac{4}{8}$
$\frac{1}{2}$, $\frac{2}{4}$, and $\frac{4}{8}$ are equivalent fractions.
$\frac{1}{4} = \frac{2}{8}$ So, $\frac{1}{4}$ and $\frac{2}{8}$ are equivalent fractions.
$\frac{3}{4} = \frac{6}{8}$ So, $\frac{3}{4}$ and $\frac{6}{8}$ are equivalent fractions.

Wrap Up List the fractions equivalent to $\frac{1}{2}$ that students have identified: $\frac{1}{2} = \frac{2}{4}$, $\frac{1}{2} = \frac{3}{6}$, $\frac{1}{2} = \frac{4}{8}$. *What relationship do you notice between the numerator and denominator of $\frac{1}{2}$ and the numerator and denominator of the fractions that are equivalent to $\frac{1}{2}$?* (Multiply the numerator and the denominator of $\frac{1}{2}$ by the same number to write the equivalent fraction. Or, the numerator times 2 is the denominator. Or, the numerator is half of the denominator.)

Reteach Have students use Cardstock C6–7: Fraction Models to identify equivalent fractions.

How do you know that $\frac{2}{4} = \frac{3}{6}$? (Both fractions are equal to $\frac{1}{2}$ so they must be equal.)

70 iSucceed MATH: Equivalent Fractions

APPLY THE CONCEPT
Problem-Solving Strategy: Draw a Picture

Present the Problem Display Visual 30: Caroline's Claim. Provide grid paper and counters for students to use. Read the problem set-up and instructions:

- Caroline claims that the two fractions are equivalent. Decide whether her claim is true.
- Work with a partner to solve.

Discuss the Solution After students have had time to solve the problem, help the class discuss their solutions.

- Are the fractions equivalent? (yes) How were you able to show that the fractions are equivalent? (Sample answer: There are 3 groups of 4 counters in 12, so $\frac{4}{12} = \frac{1}{3}$. There are 3 groups of 5 counters in 15, so $\frac{5}{15} = \frac{1}{3}$. Since $\frac{1}{3} = \frac{1}{3}$, then $\frac{4}{12} = \frac{5}{15}$.)
- Discuss all the pictures and methods students used to solve the problem.
- You may wish to make number lines showing thirds and twelfths and thirds and fifteenths to show that both fractions are equivalent to $\frac{1}{3}$.

REFLECT

We noticed that, for $\frac{1}{2} = \frac{2}{4} = \frac{4}{8}$, the numerator times 2 is the denominator. What do you notice about $\frac{4}{12} = \frac{5}{15}$? (The numerator times 3 is the denominator.)

Vocabulary

Direct students' attention to the Word Wall. Discuss how to define the terms before asking students to record definitions and examples in their personal glossaries.

Journal Prompt

Explain with words and pictures to someone who doesn't know about equivalent fractions why $\frac{1}{2} = \frac{7}{14}$. (Answers may include the use of number lines or other fraction models to show that the fractions are equivalent.)

Assess

How many tenths are equivalent to $\frac{3}{5}$? How do you know? ($\frac{6}{10}$; Sample answer: They are in the same position on number lines divided into fifths and tenths.)

Concept Builder — Lesson 16 Plan

Simplest Form

TODAY'S CONCEPTS
- Write fractions in simplest form.
- Recognize equivalent fractions.

MATERIALS
- Visual 31: Fractions and Factors
- Visual 32: Problem Answers
- self-stick notes cut in half
- Vocabulary Cards: **denominator**, **factor**, **greatest common factor (GCF)**, **numerator**, **simplest form**

SET UP
Build the Concept
Display Visual 31: Fractions and Factors.

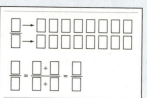

Apply the Concept
Display Visual 32: Problem Answers.

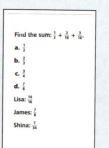

EL WORD WALL

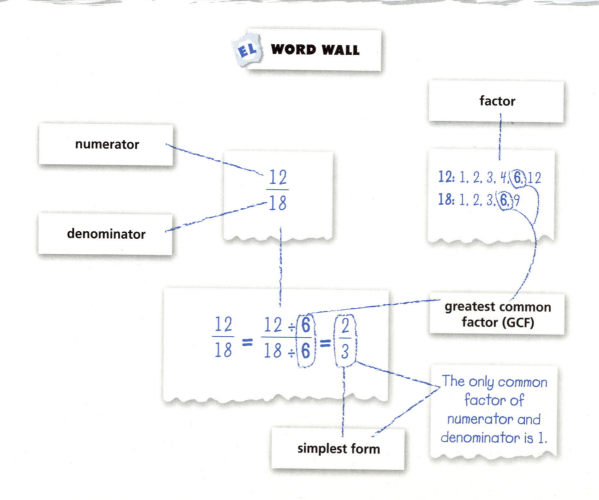

PROFESSIONAL DEVELOPMENT

Math Background Although writing fractional answers in simplest form is not required in this program, it is covered in this lesson. Even if your curriculum does not require simplest form, being able to recognize a fraction in simplest form can be a useful tool for students. A fraction in simplest form may be the correct choice on a multiple choice test and a student who fails to recognize it as the correct choice is at a distinct disadvantage.

Simplest Form Writing a fraction in simplest form is a special case of writing an equivalent fraction. A fraction is in simplest form when its numerator and denominator have no other common factor than one. Simplest form is sometimes referred to as lowest terms or simplest terms.

Greatest Common Factor To write a fraction in simplest form, divide the numerator and the denominator by the greatest common factor of the numerator and the denominator. Or, keep dividing the numerator and the denominator by common factors until the only common factor is one. Each time you divide numerator and denominator by the same number, you are effectively dividing by one.

Example: Write $\frac{25}{30}$ in simplest form.

The GCF of 25 and 30 is 5.

Think: $\frac{25}{30} = \frac{5 \times 5}{6 \times 5} = \frac{5}{6} \times \frac{5}{5} = \frac{5}{6} \times 1$

The simplest form of $\frac{25}{30}$ is $\frac{5}{6}$.

Models Students who have difficulty understanding simplest form may benefit from models showing $\frac{3}{4}$, $\frac{6}{8}$, and $\frac{9}{12}$. Each model represents the same fraction but the model for $\frac{3}{4}$ has the fewest possible pieces.

Courseware Connections

Module: Understanding and Adding Fractions

Simplest Form

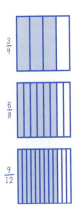

Any way you slice it, the models show the same ratio of filled cells to all cells.

Lesson 16 Teach

BUILD THE CONCEPT

Display Visual 31: Fractions and Factors. Your goal in this discussion is to help students write fractions in simplest form.

- Use halves of small self-stick notes to show the fraction $\frac{4}{8}$ on the Visual. *We are going to find the factors of 4 and 8, the numerator and denominator, to see what they have in common. What are some factors of 4?* (1, 2, 4) *What are some factors of 8?* (1, 2, 4, 8)

- Use self-stick notes to record the factors of each number next to the number. *The factors are listed from least to greatest.*

- *What factors do 4 and 8 have in common?* (1, 2, and 4) *What is the greatest factor they have in common?* (4) *The greatest factor in both sets of factors is called the greatest common factor. The greatest common factor of 4 and 8 is 4.*

- Repeat the process, using $\frac{10}{15}$, $\frac{9}{12}$, and $\frac{14}{18}$. (5; 3; 2)

The greatest common factor of 4 and 8 is 4.

EXPLORE THE CONCEPT

- *A fraction is in simplest form when its numerator is less than its denominator and when the numerator and denominator have no common factor other than one. You can divide the numerator and the denominator of a fraction by the greatest common factor to write the fraction in simplest form.*

- Demonstrate that $\frac{4}{8} = \frac{1}{2}$. *How can we write $\frac{4}{8}$ in simplest form?* (Divide the numerator and denominator by 4.) Since $\frac{1}{2} \times \frac{4}{4} = \frac{4}{8}$ and $\frac{4}{4} = 1$, we know that $\frac{1}{2}$ and $\frac{4}{8}$ are equivalent fractions.

- Repeat for the other fractions. Have volunteers explain how to write the fractions in simplest form. ($\frac{10}{15} = \frac{2}{3}$; $\frac{9}{12} = \frac{3}{4}$; $\frac{14}{18} = \frac{7}{9}$)

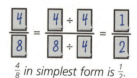
$\frac{4}{8}$ in simplest form is $\frac{1}{2}$.

Connect to Vocabulary Post on the Word Wall and discuss: **denominator**, **factor**, **greatest common factor**, **numerator**, and **simplest form**.

Wrap Up Write the fraction $\frac{24}{40}$. Have students explain how to find the greatest common factor and use it to write the fraction in simplest form. (GCF: 8; $\frac{3}{5}$)

Reteach If students have difficulty finding and using the greatest common factor to write a fraction in simplest form, have them keep dividing by any common factors of the numerator and denominator until 1 is the only remaining common factor.

Example:
$$\frac{24}{40} = \frac{24 \div 2}{40 \div 2}$$
$$= \frac{12}{20} = \frac{12 \div 2}{20 \div 2}$$
$$= \frac{6}{10} = \frac{6 \div 2}{10 \div 2}$$
$$= \frac{3}{5}$$

What is the simplest form of the fraction $\frac{20}{24}$? Explain. ($\frac{5}{6}$; The GCF of the numerator and the denominator is 4. Divide the numerator and the denominator by 4 and the result is $\frac{5}{6}$.)

iSucceed MATH: Simplest Form

APPLY THE CONCEPT

Problem-Solving Skill: Is the Answer Reasonable?

Present the Problem Display Visual 32: Problem Answers. Read the problem set-up and instructions:

- On a test, the answer choices are $\frac{1}{2}$, $\frac{2}{3}$, $\frac{3}{4}$, and $\frac{7}{8}$.
- Lisa, James, and Shina each found a different sum. Whose sum will match the correct answer on the test? What is wrong with the incorrect sum or sums?
- Work with a partner to make a plan to solve the problem. Follow your plan and answer the questions.

Discuss the Solution After students have had time to solve the problem, help the class discuss their solutions.

- *What did you do first?* (Find the correct sum by finding common denominators and adding.)
- *What common denominator did you use?* (The least common denominator is 16, but 32 is also a reasonable denominator.
- *What is true about the four answer choices?* (All are in simplest form.) *How did you decide which choice is correct?* Discuss how students arrived at $\frac{7}{8}$ as the correct choice.
- *Who did the sum correctly?* (Lisa and James)
- *How did you decide what Shina may have done wrong?* (Since her denominator is not a common denominator for halves and sixteenths, students should look for a faulty rule for adding fractions. Shina added the numerators and she added the denominators.)
- *What is wrong with Lisa's answer?* (Although her answer is correct, it is not one of the choices on the test.) *What can she do to select the correct answer?* (Simplify $\frac{14}{16}$ to $\frac{7}{8}$.)

REFLECT

- Discuss the importance of being able to recognize equivalent fractions in simplest form, especially in test situations. *Is it necessarily true that if your answer is not one of the choices on a multiple choice test, your answer is wrong?* (no)
- *What can you do to find the correct answer?* Discuss how the answer choice may be in simplest form, but the result of the computation may not be in simplest form. Encourage students not to immediately assume that their computation is wrong.

Vocabulary

Encourage students to add to the definitions and examples in their personal glossaries.

Journal Prompt

How can you tell that $\frac{25}{40}$ is not in simplest form? What is the fraction in simplest form? Explain. (The GCF of the numerator and the denominator is 5 and not 1, so the fraction cannot be in simplest form; $\frac{5}{8}$.)

Assess

Is $\frac{12}{18}$ equivalent to $\frac{2}{3}$ or to $\frac{3}{4}$? Explain how you know. ($\frac{2}{3}$; The GCF of the numerator and the denominator is 6. Divide the numerator and the denominator by 6 and the result is $\frac{2}{3}$.)

Concept Builder • Lesson 16 • Teach

Concept Builder — Lesson 17 Plan

Relate Fractions to Decimal Numbers

TODAY'S CONCEPTS
- Understand how fractions and decimals are related.
- Recognize equivalent fractions and decimals.

MATERIALS
- Visual 33: Fraction/Decimal Cards
- Visual 34: What Went Wrong?
- Cardstock C8–11: Fraction/Decimal Cards
- Vocabulary Cards: **decimal number**, **equivalent fractions**

SET UP

Build the Concept
Display Visual 33: Fraction/Decimal Cards.

Apply the Concept
Display Visual 34: What Went Wrong?

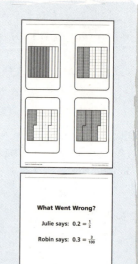

WORD WALL

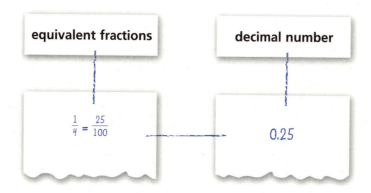

equivalent fractions

$\frac{1}{4} = \frac{25}{100}$

decimal number

0.25

PROFESSIONAL DEVELOPMENT

Math Background Fractions and decimal numbers are rational numbers. All rational numbers can be written in the form $\frac{p}{q}$, where $q \neq 0$. The easiest way to relate equivalent fractions and decimal numbers is to read the numbers. This is why students should be encouraged to read decimals using place value. Doing so makes recognizing the connection between fractions and decimals more apparent.

Write: $0.2 = \frac{2}{10}$

Say: *two tenths equals two tenths*

Write: $0.05 = \frac{5}{100}$

Say: *five hundredths = five hundredths*

Money Models Money continues to be an excellent model to use to represent decimals and to connect to fractions. Students are already familiar with the value of a quarter as $0.25 and with a quarter as $\frac{1}{4}$ of a dollar. You may wish to use Cardstock C5: Coins to model fractions and decimals.

Simplest Form Students need not express fractions in simplest form. It is correct to denote 0.25 as either $\frac{25}{100}$ or $\frac{1}{4}$. Encourage students to continue to refer to number lines or models to recognize equivalent fractions such as $\frac{25}{100}$ and $\frac{1}{4}$.

Recording and Reading Explaining how to write decimal numbers as you are writing them can be very helpful for students. For example, when you write 0.5, point out that you are writing "zero, the decimal point, and 5." Explain that this means there are no ones and the decimal point indicates that you are moving to the tenths place. Then have students read the number as five tenths.

Repeating Decimals and Fractions Be careful to stay away from thirds, sixths, sevenths, and ninths if you make up problems to convert fractions to decimals. Repeating decimals will not be covered in this lesson.

Courseware Connections

Module: Understanding and Adding Fractions

Relating Fractions and Decimals

GET REAL: Buying School Supplies

Lesson 17 Teach

BUILD THE CONCEPT

Display Visual 33: Fraction/Decimal Cards. Your goal in this discussion is to help students relate fractions and decimals.

- *Look at the fraction models. What fraction is shaded on the first card?* ($\frac{7}{10}$) Discuss how to read and write the fraction.
- *You can also use a decimal to represent the number. Why?* (There are 10 equal parts and tenths have 10 equal parts.) Discuss how to read and write the decimal number. (seven tenths; 0.7)
- *Write 0.7 and $\frac{7}{10}$ on the Visual. What do you notice about the way you read the numbers?* (They are read the same way.) Knowing this can help you write a fraction as a decimal number and a decimal number as a fraction.
- Repeat the procedure for hundredths, using the second card, 0.40 and $\frac{40}{100}$.

Connect to Vocabulary Post and discuss: **decimal number** and **equivalent fractions**. Have students provide several examples to connect and illustrate the words.

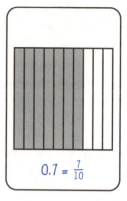

Seven tenths = 0.7 = $\frac{7}{10}$

EXPLORE THE CONCEPT

- Direct students' attention to the third card. *How many fourths does the card show?* (one fourth, or $\frac{1}{4}$) Make sure students see the four equal parts. *The model also shows hundredths. How many hundredths are shaded in the model?* (25 hundredths) If needed, help students see the 2 rows of 10 and the half row of 5. Discuss how to record the fraction and decimal number for the hundredths. ($\frac{25}{100}$; 0.25) Summarize by noting that $\frac{1}{4}$, $\frac{25}{100}$, and 0.25 are equivalent.
- *Suppose you want to write $\frac{1}{4}$ as a decimal number. How will you find an equivalent decimal?* (Find an equivalent fraction with a denominator of 100. Then use the equivalent fraction to write the decimal number.)
- Have a similar discussion for the last card, $\frac{3}{4} = \frac{75}{100} = 0.75$.

Wrap Up Contrast situations in which it is easier to think of a number as a decimal number or as a fraction. For example, you may think of a penny as $0.01 but a quarter as $\frac{1}{4}$ of a dollar.

Reteach Use Cardstock C8–11: Fraction/Decimal Cards as models for equivalent fractions and decimals. Have students use the cards to connect all of the equivalent forms they can. For example, $0.1 = \frac{1}{10} = 0.10 = \frac{10}{100}$.

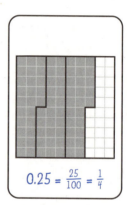

There are many ways to write the same fraction of 100.

How can you write $\frac{1}{5}$ as a decimal number? (First, write an equivalent fraction with a denominator of tenths: $\frac{1}{5} = \frac{2}{10}$. Then write the decimal number: 0.2.)

iSucceed MATH: Relate Fractions to Decimal Numbers

APPLY THE CONCEPT
Problem-Solving Skill: Is the Answer Reasonable?

Present the Problem Display Visual 34: What Went Wrong? Read the problem set-up and instructions:

- *Julie and Robin wrote fractions for the decimal numbers 0.2 and 0.3. Are their answers reasonable? Explain.*
- Ask student pairs to provide explanations for their decisions about the fractions and decimals shown in the problem.

Discuss the Solution After students have had time to solve the problems, help the class discuss their solutions.

- *Is Julie right? Does $0.2 = \frac{1}{2}$? How do you know?* (No; Julie's answer is not reasonable since $\frac{1}{2} = 0.5$ and $0.5 \neq 0.2$.) *What do you think she did wrong?* (Possible answer: Instead of reading the decimal as two tenths and using the decimal name to write the fraction, she used the number in the tenths place as the denominator of the fraction and wrote 1 in the numerator.) Discuss other student insights into Julie's error.
- *Is Robin right? Does $0.3 = \frac{3}{100}$? How do you know?* (No, Robin's answer is not reasonable since $\frac{3}{100} = 0.03$ and $0.3 \neq 0.03$.) *What do you think he did wrong?* (Possible answer: He confused the place just to the right of the decimal point as hundredths when it is tenths.) Discuss other student explanations.

REFLECT

Why is it easier to write a decimal as a fraction than to write a fraction as a decimal? (Using place value to write a decimal as a fraction, you always know that the denominator can be divided evenly by 10. If the fraction does not have a denominator of 10 or 100, you have to find an equivalent fraction before you can write the fraction as a decimal.)

Vocabulary

Encourage students to add to the definitions and examples in their personal glossaries.

Journal Prompt

How are fractions and decimal numbers related? (Answers should mention that decimal place values of tenths and hundredths relate to fractions with denominators of 10 or 100 and that when the denominators are 10 or 100, equivalent fractions and decimal numbers are read the same way.)

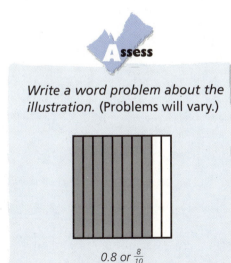

Assess

Write a word problem about the illustration. (Problems will vary.)

0.8 or $\frac{8}{10}$

Concept Builder — Lesson 18 Plan

Compare and Order Fractions

TODAY'S CONCEPTS
- Understand how to use benchmarks to compare fractions.
- Compare and order fractions.
- Understand that it is possible for numbers to be less than zero.

MATERIALS
- Visual 35: Fraction Number Lines
- Visual 36: Camp Clinic Sign-Ups
- Copymaster M2: Number Lines
- Vocabulary Cards: = (is equal to), > (is greater than), < (is less than)

SET UP

Build the Concept
Display Visual 35: Fraction Number Lines.

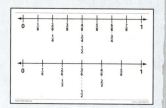

Apply the Concept
Display Visual 36: Camp Clinic Sign-Ups.

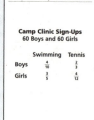

EL WORD WALL

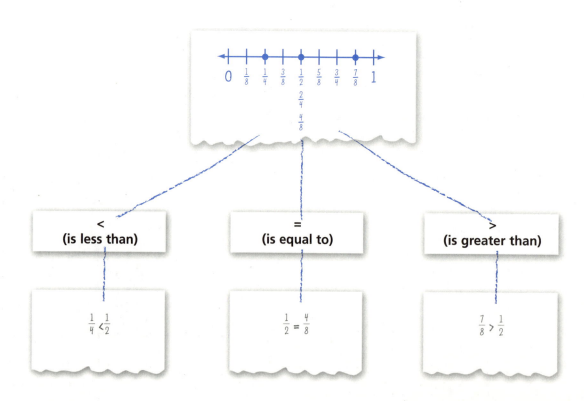

80   iSucceed MATH

PROFESSIONAL DEVELOPMENT

Math Background An important step in comparing and ordering fractions is finding equivalent fractions. In order to locate and compare fractions accurately on a number line, the fractions should have the same denominator. Then, comparing and ordering fractions is as easy as with whole numbers.

Fraction Benchmarks Common benchmarks used to compare fractions are 0, $\frac{1}{2}$, and 1. When the value of the fraction's numerator is much less than the value of its denominator, the fraction is close to 0. When the numerator is about half of the denominator, the fraction is close to $\frac{1}{2}$. When the numerator is close to its denominator, the fraction is close to 1.

Examples: $\frac{1}{8}$ is close to 0

$\frac{6}{10}$ is close to $\frac{1}{2}$

$\frac{11}{12}$ is close to 1

Using Benchmarks to Compare Develop the habit of using benchmarks to compare and order fractions and model it for your students at every opportunity. Although using benchmarks is not always the best method, doing so will often work and can help you work more quickly.

Comparing Fractions and Mixed Numbers Compare the whole numbers before comparing the fractions. Comparing the whole number part may provide enough information to order mixed numbers.

Rational Numbers A number that can be written as a fraction is a rational number. This number type includes negative numbers, which are lightly touched on in this lesson. At this point, expect only that students understand that it is necessary to be able to think of numbers less than 0.

Organize for Learning Use a long piece of adding machine tape to create a generic number line with interval marks and no numbers, using self-stick notes to change the intervals. Students might also make their own number lines and have them available for use. Copymaster M2 is a set of blank number lines that students may use.

Courseware Connections

Module: Understanding and Adding Fractions
- Comparing Fractions
- Ordering Fractions

Lesson 18 Teach

BUILD THE CONCEPT

Display Visual 35: Fraction Number Lines. Your goal in this discussion is to help students understand how to compare and order fractions.

- *How do you use a number line to compare and order numbers?* (A number line shows numbers in order from least to greatest as you read from left to right.)
- *How are the fractions $\frac{4}{8}$, $\frac{2}{4}$, and $\frac{1}{2}$ related? How do you know?* (They are equivalent fractions because they are located at the same place on the number line.)
- *How can you use the number lines to compare $\frac{3}{8}$ and $\frac{3}{4}$?* ($\frac{3}{8}$ is to the left of $\frac{3}{4}$ on the same number line so $\frac{3}{8} < \frac{3}{4}$.) *How can you use the number lines to compare $\frac{3}{8}$ and $\frac{1}{3}$?* ($\frac{3}{8}$ is to the right of $\frac{1}{3}$ and the distance from 0 to 1 is the same, so $\frac{3}{8} > \frac{1}{3}$.)
- *Order $\frac{3}{8}$, $\frac{3}{4}$, and $\frac{1}{3}$ from least to greatest.* ($\frac{1}{3}$, $\frac{3}{8}$, $\frac{3}{4}$)
- *Introduce the benchmarks 0, $\frac{1}{2}$, and 1. Which fractions on the first number line are close to 0? to $\frac{1}{2}$? to 1?* (0: $\frac{1}{8}$, $\frac{1}{4}$; $\frac{1}{2}$: $\frac{3}{8}$, $\frac{5}{8}$; 1: $\frac{3}{4}$, $\frac{7}{8}$)

Connect to Vocabulary Post on the Word Wall: **= (is equal to), > (is greater than),** and **< (is less than)**. Select pairs of fractions from the number lines in the Visual and have students use the vocabulary and symbols to compare the fractions.

EXPLORE THE CONCEPT

- Discuss how to order these numbers: $1\frac{9}{10}$, $2\frac{1}{4}$, and $1\frac{2}{5}$.
- *Which number is the greatest? How do you know?* ($2\frac{1}{4}$, because $2 > 1$.)
- *How can you use benchmarks to compare $1\frac{9}{10}$ and $1\frac{2}{5}$?* (Because 9 is close to 10, $1\frac{9}{10}$ is close to the next whole number, 2. Because $\frac{2}{5}$ is close to $\frac{1}{2}$, $1\frac{2}{5}$ is close to $1\frac{1}{2}$. $1\frac{9}{10} > 1\frac{2}{5}$)
- *What are the numbers from least to greatest?* ($1\frac{2}{5}$, $1\frac{9}{10}$, $2\frac{1}{4}$) Discuss how using benchmarks makes comparing and ordering fractions easier.

Wrap Up Have students suggest a list of five different fractions with denominators from 2 through 5. Discuss how to order the fractions from least to greatest. If time permits, create a second list and order the numbers from greatest to least.

Reteach Have students use Cardstock C6–7: Fraction Models to order fractions by comparing two fractions at a time.

Compare the numerators and denominators of the fractions to their benchmarks. What relationships do you notice? (When the numerator is much less than the denominator, the benchmark is 0. When the numerator is about half of the denominator, the benchmark is $\frac{1}{2}$. When the numerator is a number close to the denominator, the benchmark is 1.)

Which is greater: $\frac{4}{8}$ or $\frac{4}{6}$? How do you know? ($\frac{4}{6}$. Possible explanation: When the numerators are the same, the lower denominator is in the greater fraction.)

82 iSucceed MATH: Compare and Order Fractions

APPLY THE CONCEPT
Problem-Solving Skill: Choose an Estimate or Exact Amount

Present the Problem Display Visual 36: Camp Clinic Sign-Ups. Distribute copies of M2: Number Lines. Read the problem set-up and instructions:

- *Did more boys or girls sign up for the swimming clinic? Did more boys or girls sign up for the tennis clinic?*
- *Choose an estimate or an exact amount to solve. Explain your thinking for each answer.*

Discuss the Solution After students have had time to solve the problem, help the class discuss their solutions.

- *Did more boys or girls sign up for the swimming clinic? Did you use an estimate or an exact amount to solve? Why?* (More girls signed up since $\frac{3}{5} > \frac{4}{10}$. Sample explanation: I used an exact amount since both $\frac{3}{5}$ and $\frac{4}{10}$ are close to $\frac{1}{2}$.)
- *Explain how you found the estimate or the exact amount you used.* (I found an equivalent fraction in tenths for $\frac{3}{5}$: $\frac{3}{5} = \frac{6}{10}$. Then I used a number line to compare the fractions. Since $\frac{6}{10}$ is to the right of $\frac{4}{10}$, it is greater.)
- *Did more boys or girls sign up for the tennis clinic? Did you use an estimate or an exact amount to solve? Why?* (More boys signed up since $\frac{2}{3} > \frac{4}{12}$. Sample explanation: I used an estimate, since it was easy to find benchmarks for the fractions.)
- *Explain how you found the estimate or the exact amount you used.* (Since $\frac{2}{3}$ is closer to 1 and $\frac{4}{12}$ is closer to 0, $\frac{2}{3} > \frac{4}{12}$.)
- *If students used an alternate method for each problem, discuss why and how they used the method to solve.*

REFLECT
What happens if you are at $\frac{1}{2}$ on the number line and want to find the number 1 less? How can you use the number line to find the number? (Possible answer: From $\frac{1}{2}$ to 0 is $\frac{1}{2}$. So if you move another $\frac{1}{2}$ to the left, you will find 1 less than $\frac{1}{2}$. Since you are to the left of zero, you will be at $-\frac{1}{2}$.)

Vocabulary
Encourage students to add new or revised definitions and examples to their personal glossaries.

Journal Prompt

How can benchmarks help you decide how to order $\frac{76}{81}$, $\frac{2}{99}$, and $\frac{50}{93}$? (Possible answer: Using benchmarks, $\frac{2}{99}$ is close to 0, $\frac{50}{93}$ is close to $\frac{1}{2}$, and $\frac{76}{81}$ is close to 1. From least to greatest, the fractions are $\frac{2}{99}$, $\frac{50}{93}$, and $\frac{76}{81}$.)

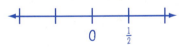

A number line extends in both directions.

Assess

One half is greater than $\frac{1}{3}$. Is $\frac{1}{2}$ of a small pizza greater than $\frac{1}{3}$ of a large pizza? Explain. (You cannot compare the fractions, since the wholes are not the same size.)

Concept Builder **Lesson 19** **Plan**

Model Adding Fractions

TODAY'S CONCEPTS
- Use benchmarks to estimate sums of fractions.
- Understand how to model adding fractions.

MATERIALS
- Visual 37: Number Line Addition 1
- Visual 38: Smoothie Recipe
- Copymaster M2: Number Lines
- Vocabulary Cards: **addend**, **sum**

SET UP
Build the Concept
Display Visual 37: Number Line Addition 1.

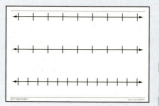

Apply the Concept
- Display Visual 38: Smoothie Recipe.
- Hang a copy of Copymaster M2: Number Lines next to the Visual.

 WORD WALL

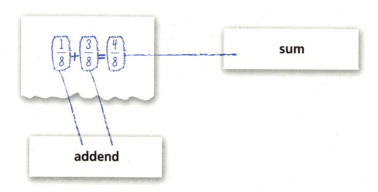

84 iSucceed MATH

PROFESSIONAL DEVELOPMENT

Math Background In this lesson, students will model addition of fractions with like denominators. Students will not be introduced to the algorithm until later. Although they will not model adding fractions with unlike denominators, students will be introduced to the idea in Apply the Concept.

Adding Fractions Adding fractions is just like adding anything with labels. You can add oranges to oranges and ones to ones but you cannot add apples to oranges or tens to ones without somehow making the labels the same. You can add apples to oranges by changing the label to *pieces of fruit*. You can add tens to ones by regrouping. The same is true for fractions. If the denominators are different, you must change something before adding: you find a like denominator for the fractions being added.

Using the Algorithm To use the algorithm to add fractions with like denominators, add the numerators and keep the denominators the same. When the fractions have unlike denominators, rewrite the fractions with like denominators. Then add the fractions.

Add the numerators to get the new numerator. Use the same denominator.

Renaming Fractions If the denominator is greater than the numerator, the value of a fraction is greater than one. In such cases, you may rename the fraction as a mixed number. Students will encounter such a sum in this lesson when they model $\frac{3}{4} + \frac{3}{4}$.

Example: $\frac{3}{4} + \frac{3}{4} = \frac{6}{4} = \frac{4}{4} + \frac{2}{4} = 1\frac{2}{4}$ or $1\frac{1}{2}$

Equivalent Fractions In a multiple-choice testing format, students may not recognize the correct choice if it is in simplest form and the sum is not. Remind students to look for equivalent fractions if they cannot find a sum that matches a choice. It is not necessary, however, to have students record all of their sums in simplest form at this stage.

Courseware Connections

Module: Understanding and Adding Fractions

Adding Fractions Using Models

Adding Fractions with Like Denominators

Adding Fractions with Unlike Denominators

GET REAL: Making a Flag

GET REAL: Sports in School

Lesson 19 Teach

BUILD THE CONCEPT

Display Visual 37: Number Line Addition 1. Your goal in this discussion is to help students understand how to model adding fractions.

- *Trent walks $\frac{2}{8}$ mile to the park. Then he walks $\frac{5}{8}$ mile to the library. How far does he walk in all? What operation can you use to solve this problem?* (Use addition to find the total number of miles.) *What do you need to add to solve the problem?* ($\frac{2}{8} + \frac{5}{8}$)
- *How can you use benchmarks to estimate the sum?* ($\frac{2}{8}$ is about 0, $\frac{5}{8}$ is about $\frac{1}{2}$. The sum should be greater than $0 + \frac{1}{2}$.)
- Label the first number line in eighths from 0–1. Demonstrate how to model the sum. Have students compare the sum to the estimate to check that the sum is reasonable.

Connect to Vocabulary Post on the Word Wall and discuss: **addend** and **sum**. As you work with the class to model fraction sums, have students identify the addends and the sum for each problem.

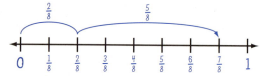

Start at 0 and count two eighths. Then, count five more eighths. Stop at $\frac{7}{8}$.
$\frac{2}{8} + \frac{5}{8} = \frac{7}{8}$

EXPLORE THE CONCEPT

- Repeat the Build the Concept discussion, modeling $\frac{3}{4} + \frac{3}{4}$ ($1\frac{1}{2}$). Label the second number line in fourths from 0–2. Discuss why the sum is greater than one.
- Label the third number line from 0–4 in thirds. Discuss how to model $2\frac{2}{3} + \frac{2}{3}$ ($3\frac{1}{3}$). Be sure to have students first estimate and then model the sum on the number line.
- Use the same number line to model $1\frac{2}{3} + 1\frac{1}{3}$ (3). Discuss why the sum is a whole number.

Wrap Up Check that students recognize how to label a number line to add the fractions. *How will you label a number line to add $1\frac{3}{6} + 1\frac{1}{6}$? Why?* (Label the number line in sixths from 0 through 4. The number line must extend far enough to add the whole numbers.) Have students estimate and find the sum. (Sample estimate: $2\frac{1}{2}$; Sum: $2\frac{4}{6}$)

Reteach Have students model each fraction or mixed number using unit squares. They can color the fraction (or whole number) parts on Copymaster M5: Grid Paper and cut them out. Then they can add the pictures together to find the sum.

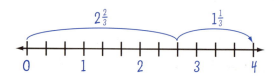

Start at 0 and count $2\frac{2}{3}$. Then, count $1\frac{1}{3}$ more. Stop at 4. $2\frac{2}{3} + 1\frac{1}{3} = 4$

How can you use a number line to model $\frac{2}{5} + \frac{4}{5}$? (Use a number line that shows fifths. Start at 0 and move to $\frac{2}{5}$. Then move another $\frac{4}{5}$. The sum is $1\frac{1}{5}$.)

86 iSucceed MATH: Model Adding Fractions

APPLY THE CONCEPT

Problem-Solving Strategy: Draw a Picture

Present the Problem Display Visual 38: Smoothie Recipe. Distribute copies of Copymaster M2: Number Lines and hang one next to the Visual. Read the problem set-up and instructions:

- *How many cups of berries does Monica use to make a smoothie?*
- *How many cups of fruit? How many cups of ingredients?*
- *Work with a partner. Use a number line to model and solve the problems.*

Discuss the Solution After students have had time to solve the problem, help the class discuss their solutions.

- *What did you add to find the total number of berries?* ($\frac{1}{8} + \frac{1}{4}$) *What is unusual about adding $\frac{1}{8} + \frac{1}{4}$?* (The fractions have different denominators; their wholes are divided into different parts.)

- Discuss how students used number lines. They may have used one number line, labeling eighths and recognizing that $\frac{1}{4}$ is equivalent to $\frac{2}{8}$. Or, they may have drawn two number lines to identify the equivalence.

- *Why do you have to find an equivalent fraction in eighths for $\frac{1}{4}$ to add the fractions?* (Sample answer: The parts must be the same to add, and we know how to model adding fractions with like denominators.) *What is another way to write the problem using an equivalent fraction for $\frac{1}{4}$?* ($\frac{1}{8} + \frac{2}{8}$)

- Follow the same process to find the answers to the other problems. ($\frac{7}{8}$ cup of fruit; $1\frac{5}{8}$ cups of ingredients)

REFLECT

How is adding fractions similar to adding whole numbers? How is it different? Probe for responses like these: The process is essentially the same in that you add like parts. It is different because you cannot use place value the same way. You may have to find an equivalent fraction to add. The denominators of the fractions must be the same before you can add. Then, you just add the numerators. The sum might have a whole number part and a fraction part.

Vocabulary

- Direct students' attention to the Word Wall. Work together to make up several new examples to label with Vocabulary Words.
- Encourage students to add to the definitions and examples in their personal glossaries.

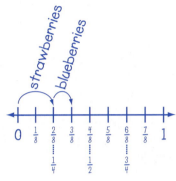

How many cups of berries does Monica use to make a smoothie? ($\frac{3}{8}$ cup)

Journal Prompt

Explain how you know whether the sum of $\frac{5}{6} + \frac{3}{6}$ is greater than or less than one. (Sample answer: Using benchmarks, $\frac{5}{6}$ is close to 1 and $\frac{3}{6}$ is close to $\frac{1}{2}$. The sum will be greater than one because a reasonable estimate of the sum is $1\frac{1}{2}$.)

Assess

Write a word problem that can be solved by adding two fractions with like denominators. Make a model to solve your problem. (Check students' work.)

Concept Builder • Lesson 19 • Teach

Concept Builder — Lesson 20 Plan

Model Subtracting Fractions

TODAY'S CONCEPTS
- Use benchmarks to estimate fraction differences.
- Understand how to model subtracting fractions.

MATERIALS
- Visual 39: Number Line Subtraction 1
- Visual 40: Park Trails
- Copymaster M2: Number Lines
- Vocabulary Cards: **difference**, **missing addend**

SET UP
Build the Concept
Display Visual 39: Number Line Subtraction 1.

Apply the Concept
Display Visual 40: Park Trails.

EL WORD WALL

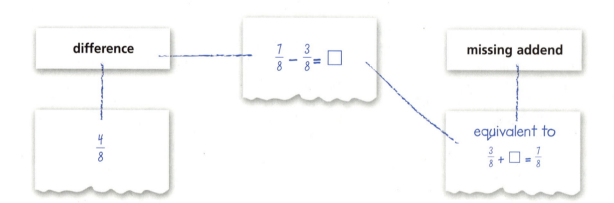

88   iSucceed MATH

PD PROFESSIONAL DEVELOPMENT

Math Background In this lesson, students will model subtracting fractions with like denominators. The lesson closely parallels the previous lesson on modeling adding fractions with like denominators. As a result, you should present and talk about the problems in very similar ways.

Subtracting Fractions As with adding fractions, subtracting fractions is the same as subtracting anything with like labels. To use the algorithm to subtract fractions with like denominators, subtract the numerators and keep the denominators the same. When the fractions have unlike denominators, rename the fractions with like denominators, and then subtract the fractions.

Subtract the numerators to get the new numerator. Use the same denominator.

Courseware Connections

Module: Subtracting Fractions

Subtracting Fractions Using Models

Subtracting Fractions with Like Denominators

Subtracting Fractions with Unlike Denominators

Subtracting Fractions

Missing Addends For some students, it is easier to subtract by thinking of missing addends in an addition sentence. Encourage students to use whichever method they find easier. To make this alternative method accessible to students, write an equivalent sum with a missing addend whenever you write a subtraction problem. This will make it easier for some students to see how to solve the problem.

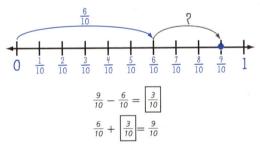

This is a missing-addend model for $\frac{9}{10} - \frac{6}{10} = \square$.

Concept Builder • Lesson 20 • Plan 89

Lesson 20 Teach

BUILD THE CONCEPT

Display Visual 39: Number Line Subtraction 1. Your goal in this discussion is to help students understand how to model subtracting fractions.

- The trail to the lake is $\frac{9}{10}$ mile long. Natalie has walked $\frac{6}{10}$ mile. How much farther is the lake? What operation do you need to use to solve this problem? Why? (Use subtraction to find the difference.)
- What do you need to subtract? ($\frac{9}{10} - \frac{6}{10}$) How can you write the subtraction using addition with a missing addend? ($\frac{6}{10} + \square = \frac{9}{10}$)
- How can you use benchmarks to estimate the difference? ($\frac{6}{10}$ is about $\frac{1}{2}$, $\frac{9}{10}$ is about 1. The difference should be about $\frac{1}{2}$.)
- Label the first number line in tenths from 0–1. Demonstrate how to model the difference as shown. Have students compare the total to the estimate to check that the difference is reasonable.

Connect to Vocabulary Post on the Word Wall: **difference** and **missing addend**. As you work with the class to model fraction differences, have students use the terms as you discuss the problems.

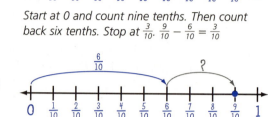

Start at 0 and count nine tenths. Then count back six tenths. Stop at $\frac{3}{10}$. $\frac{9}{10} - \frac{6}{10} = \frac{3}{10}$

$\frac{9}{10} - \frac{6}{10} = \boxed{\frac{3}{10}}$

$\frac{6}{10} + \boxed{\frac{3}{10}} = \frac{9}{10}$

This is a missing-addend model for $\frac{9}{10} - \frac{6}{10} = \square$.

EXPLORE THE CONCEPT

- Label the second number line from 0–3 in fourths. Discuss how to model $1\frac{1}{4} - \frac{3}{4}$ ($\frac{1}{2}$). Be sure to have students first estimate and then model the difference on the number line.
- Use the third number line to model $3\frac{2}{4} - 1\frac{2}{4}$ (2). Discuss why the difference is a whole number.
- Repeat with several other fraction and mixed-number differences.

Wrap Up Post a copy of Copymaster M2: Number Lines. Contrast using the number line to subtract with using the number line to find a missing addend. Model several of the differences using addition to find the missing addend. Connect addition and subtraction as opposite operations that are different ways of looking at the same problem.

Reteach Have students model each fraction or mixed number using unit squares made from Copymaster M5: Grid Paper. They can color the fraction (or whole number) parts. Then have them cross off the number being subtracted to find the difference.

Assess

How can you use a number line to model $\frac{7}{8} - \frac{4}{8}$? (Sample answer: Use a number line that shows eighths. Start at 0 and move to $\frac{7}{8}$. Then count back $\frac{4}{8}$. The difference is $\frac{3}{8}$.)

APPLY THE CONCEPT

Problem-Solving Strategy: Draw a Picture

Present the Problem Display Visual 40: Park Trails. Distribute copies of Copymaster M2: Number Lines. Read the problem set-up and instructions:

- *How much longer is the Waterfall Trail than the High Lake Trail?*
- *Work with a partner. Use a number line to model and solve the problem.*

Discuss the Solution After students have had time to solve the problem, help the class discuss their solutions.

- *What operation did you need to use? Why?* (Subtract to compare.) *What did you subtract?* ($1\frac{7}{8} - 1\frac{1}{2}$) *What is unusual about subtracting $1\frac{7}{8} - 1\frac{1}{2}$?* (Sample answer: The fractions have different denominators. Their wholes are divided into different parts.)
- Discuss how students used the number line to find an equivalent fraction for $\frac{1}{2}$ to subtract. *Why do you need to find an equivalent fraction in eighths for $\frac{1}{2}$ to subtract the fractions?* (Sample answer: The parts must be the same to subtract, and we know how to model subtracting fractions with like denominators.)
- *What is another way to write the problem using an equivalent fraction for $\frac{1}{2}$?* ($1\frac{7}{8} - 1\frac{4}{8}$) *Can you write it using just eighths?* ($\frac{15}{8} - \frac{12}{8}$)

REFLECT

How is subtracting fractions similar to subtracting whole numbers? How is it different? Probe for responses like these: The process is essentially the same. You subtract like parts. The process is different because you cannot use place value the same way. You may have to find an equivalent fraction to subtract. The denominators of the fractions must be the same before you can subtract. Then, you just subtract the numerators. The difference might have a whole number part and a fraction part.

Vocabulary

- Direct students' attention to the Word Wall. Work with them to make up new examples to label with today's vocabulary.
- Encourage students to add to the definitions and examples in their personal glossaries.

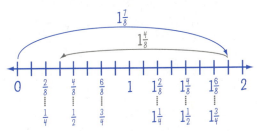

How much longer is the Waterfall Trail than the High Lake Trail? ($\frac{3}{8}$ mile)

Journal Prompt

Explain how you know whether the difference of $1\frac{11}{12} - \frac{2}{12}$ is greater than or less than one. (Using benchmarks, $1\frac{11}{12}$ is close to 2 and $\frac{2}{12}$ is close to 0. The difference will be greater than one because a reasonable estimate of the difference is a little less than 2.)

Assess

Write a word problem that can be solved by subtracting two fractions with like denominators. Make a model to solve your problem. (Check students' work.)

Concept Builder — Lesson 21 Plan

Model Multiplying Fractions

TODAY'S CONCEPT
- Model multiplying fractions.

MATERIALS
- Visual 41: Models for Multiplying Fractions
- Visual 42: Ribbon Lengths
- Copymaster M5: Grid Paper
- Vocabulary Cards: **factor**, **product**

SET UP

Build the Concept
Display a copy of Copymaster M5: Grid Paper.

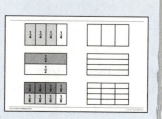

Explore the Concept
Display Visual 41: Models for Multiplying Fractions.

Apply the Concept
Display Visual 42: Ribbon Lengths.

WORD WALL

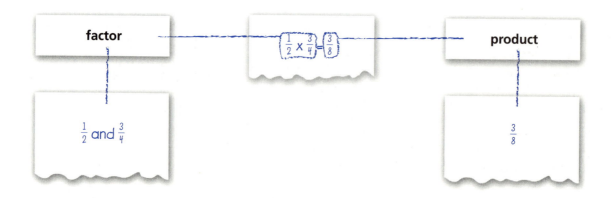

92 iSucceed MATH

PROFESSIONAL DEVELOPMENT

Multiplying with Fractions Stories are a good way to help students think about two factors and the relative size of the product.

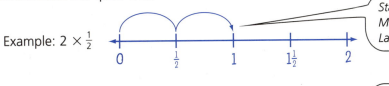

Product   Meaning

$2 \times 4 \rightarrow$ Walk a 4-mile path twice. Product > 4

$\frac{1}{2} \times 4 \rightarrow$ Walk a 4-mile path halfway. Product < 4

$2 \times \frac{1}{4} \rightarrow$ Walk a $\frac{1}{4}$-mile path twice. Product > $\frac{1}{4}$

$\frac{1}{2} \times \frac{1}{4} \rightarrow$ Walk a $\frac{1}{4}$-mile path halfway. Product < $\frac{1}{4}$

$1\frac{1}{2} \times \frac{1}{4} \rightarrow$ Walk a $\frac{1}{4}$-mile path $1\frac{1}{2}$ times. Product > $\frac{1}{4}$

Think about the meaning of multiplication and the meaning of fractions to understand what it means to multiply with fractions.

Courseware Connections

Module: Multiplying Fractions

Multiplying Whole Numbers and Fractions Using Models

Multiplying Whole Numbers and Fractions

Multiplying Fractions Using Models

Multiplying Fractions

Finding Ones

Number Line Models Multiplying a factor by a number between 0 and 1 results in a product less than the first factor. A number line demonstrates this quite well.

Example: $2 \times \frac{1}{2}$

Start at 0. Make 2 jumps of $\frac{1}{2}$ unit each. Land at $\frac{2}{2}$, which is 1.

Example: $\frac{1}{2} \times \frac{3}{4}$

Start at 0. Make $\frac{1}{2}$ of a jump of $\frac{3}{4}$ unit. Land at $\frac{3}{8}$.

Preventing Common Errors Students will not be required to use the algorithm in this lesson, but will be asked to notice the pattern: multiply numerator by numerator to get the numerator of the product, then multiply denominator by denominator to get the denominator of the product. Encourage them to continue to use models until they're comfortable with the algorithm. After students are introduced to the algorithm for multiplying fractions, some may try to apply the basic idea to other operations. If they add fractions by adding the numerators and then the denominators, probe to find out why.

Equivalent Fractions In a multiple-choice testing format, students may not recognize the answer if the answer choice is in simplest form and the product they have found is not. Do not count these products incorrect in everyday work, but help students to look for equivalents if they don't find their products among the choices on multiple-choice tests.

Concept Builder • Lesson 21 • Plan

Lesson 21 Teach

BUILD THE CONCEPT

Display Copymaster M5: Grid Paper. Your goal in this discussion is to help students understand how to use models to multiply fractions.

- *To find the number of things in two groups of two, what do you do?* (Multiply 2 × 2.) *What about one group of two?* (1 × 2)

- *What is 2 × 2?* (4) *1 × 2?* (2) *1 × 1?* (1) *If I multiply one by a number less than one, will my product be greater or less than one?* (less)

- Draw a rectangle and divide it into two equal parts. *How can you use this diagram to find one half of one?* (Color one half of the figure.) *What is one half of one?* (one half) Write $\frac{1}{2} \times 1 = \frac{1}{2}$ on the board.

- Repeat the discussion modeling two thirds of one ($\frac{2}{3} \times 1 = \frac{2}{3}$) and three fourths of one ($\frac{3}{4} \times 1 = \frac{3}{4}$).

- *When you multiply a whole number and a fraction less than one, the product is less than the whole number. Why?* (Because you are finding a part of the whole and a part must be less than the whole.)

Connect to Vocabulary Post and discuss these Vocabulary Cards: **factors** and **product**. As you work with the class to model fraction products, have students identify the factors and the product for each problem.

EXPLORE THE CONCEPT

Display Visual 41: Models for Multiplying Fractions.

- Refer to the models on the left of the Visual. *What fractions do the first two models represent?* ($\frac{3}{4}$ and $\frac{1}{2}$)

- *Each fraction shows a part of a whole. When your factors are both fractions, you find a part of a part. To find $\frac{3}{4}$ of $\frac{1}{2}$, think of laying the model for $\frac{1}{2}$ on the model for $\frac{3}{4}$. The part where the models overlap is the part of the part, or $\frac{3}{4}$ of $\frac{1}{2}$. Label the third model $\frac{3}{4}$ of $\frac{1}{2}$. What is $\frac{3}{4}$ of $\frac{1}{2}$? How do you know?* ($\frac{3}{8}$: When the models are overlapped, they form eighths. Three of the eighths overlap.) Record the product: $\frac{3}{4} \times \frac{1}{2} = \frac{3}{8}$.

Wrap Up Repeat the discussion for the second set of models, showing $\frac{2}{3} \times \frac{3}{4} = \frac{6}{12}$. *How does using models help you understand how to multiply fractions?* (Sample response: Using models shows the part of the part that is the product.)

Reteach Have students use Copymaster M5: Grid Paper to draw models to find fraction products. Have them demonstrate how to find the following products: $\frac{1}{2} \times \frac{1}{4} = \frac{1}{8}$, $\frac{1}{3} \times \frac{1}{2} = \frac{1}{6}$, $\frac{2}{3} \times \frac{1}{2} = \frac{2}{6}$, $\frac{2}{3} \times \frac{1}{4} = \frac{2}{12}$, and $\frac{3}{4} \times \frac{1}{3} = \frac{3}{12}$.

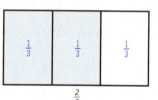

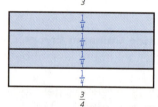

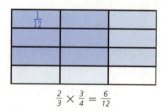

Assess

When you multiply two fractions less than one, how does the product compare to one? Why? (The product is less than one because it represents a part of a part.)

APPLY THE CONCEPT
Problem-Solving Strategy: Combine Strategies
(Write an Equation and Make a Diagram)

Present the Problem Display Visual 42: Ribbon Lengths. Provide students with Copymaster M5: Grid Paper. Read the problem set-up and instructions:

- Haley is designing a costume for the school play. She needs to use two thirds of the cotton ribbon. How long is the piece of cotton ribbon she needs to use?
- Work with a partner. Write an equation and make a diagram to solve the problem.

Discuss the Solution After students have had time to solve the problem, help the class discuss their solutions.

- How did writing an equation help you solve the problem? What equation did you write? (Since she needs part of a part of a yard, the equation is $\frac{2}{3} \times \frac{5}{6} = \square$.)
- Discuss how students make diagrams to model the problem. Encourage volunteers to share their work. How long is the piece of cotton ribbon Haley needs to use? ($\frac{10}{18}$ or $\frac{5}{9}$ of a yard)
- How did combining strategies help you solve the problem? (Each strategy was used to solve a different part of the problem. The diagram provides the solution to the equation.)
- If time permits, find fractions of the other ribbon lengths on the Visual.

REFLECT

What relationship do you notice between the numerators and the denominators of the factors when you multiply fractions? (In the product of two fractions, the product of the numerators is the new numerator. The product of the denominators of the factors is the new denominator.)

Vocabulary

Refer to the Word Wall. Review the Vocabulary terms and encourage students to add new diagrams and examples to their personal glossaries.

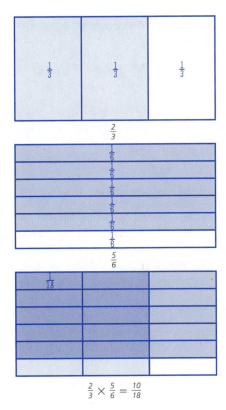

$\frac{2}{3} \times \frac{5}{6} = \frac{10}{18}$

Journal Prompt

Can the product of $\frac{1}{2} \times \frac{3}{4}$ be greater than $\frac{7}{8}$? How do you know without computing? (No. Sample explanation: The greatest factor is $\frac{3}{4}$ and $\frac{3}{4} = \frac{6}{8}$. The product must be less than either factor and $\frac{7}{8} > \frac{6}{8}$.)

Assess

Draw a diagram to show how to multiply $\frac{1}{3}$ by $\frac{5}{8}$. (Check students' work; $\frac{5}{24}$.)

Concept Builder Lesson 22 Plan

Reciprocals

TODAY'S CONCEPTS
- Understand the meaning of reciprocals.
- Find the reciprocal of a number.

MATERIALS
- Visual 43: Reciprocal Patterns
- Visual 44: What Is My Reciprocal?
- Vocabulary Cards: **factor**, **product**, **reciprocals**

SET UP
Build the Concept
Display Visual 43: Reciprocal Patterns.

Apply the Concept
Display Visual 44: What Is My Reciprocal?

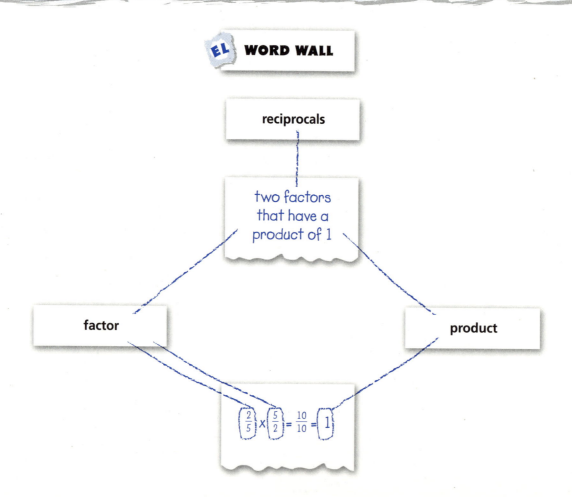

EL WORD WALL

96   iSucceed MATH

PROFESSIONAL DEVELOPMENT

Math Background "Reciprocal" is a term that refers to the multiplicative inverse of a number. When you multiply a number and its multiplicative inverse, the product is one, the identity element of multiplication. The reciprocal of $\frac{a}{b}$ is $\frac{b}{a}$ because $\frac{a}{b} \times \frac{b}{a} = 1$ where $a \neq 0$ and $b \neq 0$. It is important to note that the multiplicative inverse of a number is different from its additive inverse. When you add a number and its additive inverse, the sum is zero, which is the identity element of addition. For any number x ($x \neq 0$), the multiplicative inverse is $\frac{1}{x}$ and the additive inverse is $-x$.

Module: Multiplying Fractions
Reciprocals

Reciprocals Every number except zero has a reciprocal. To write the reciprocal of a number, write the number as a fraction. Then reverse the numerator and the denominator.

Examples of reciprocals:

$\frac{2}{3}$ and $\frac{3}{2}$ because $\frac{2}{3} \times \frac{3}{2} = \frac{6}{6} = 1$

4 and $\frac{1}{4}$ because $4 = \frac{4}{1}$ and $\frac{4}{1} \times \frac{1}{4} = \frac{4}{4} = 1$

$1\frac{1}{4}$ and $\frac{4}{5}$ because $1\frac{1}{4} = \frac{5}{4}$ and $\frac{5}{4} \times \frac{4}{5} = \frac{20}{20} = 1$

Lesson 22 Teach

BUILD THE CONCEPT

Display Visual 43: Reciprocal Patterns. Your goal in this discussion is to help students understand how to write the reciprocal of a number.

- Direct students to look at the left half of the Visual. Discuss why $\frac{1}{2} \times 2 = 1$ and $\frac{1}{3} \times 3 = 1$. *Use the pattern of the first four products to find the last two products.* (1, 1) *What seems to be special about the factors whose product is 1?* (One is a whole number and the other is a fraction with a numerator of 1 and a denominator that's the same as the whole number.)

- When the product of two factors is one, the numbers are reciprocals. One eighth is the reciprocal of eight and eight is the reciprocal of $\frac{1}{8}$. *What is the reciprocal of $\frac{1}{3}$?* (3) *What is the reciprocal of $\frac{1}{2}$?* (2)

Connect to Vocabulary Stress that reciprocals are factors and their product is always one.

- Add the Vocabulary Cards **reciprocal**, **factor**, and **product** to the Word Wall.
- Have students find the reciprocal of several more unit fractions and whole numbers, such as $\frac{1}{9}$, 10, and 4.

EXPLORE THE CONCEPT

- Refer to the right half of the Visual. Discuss the patterns. *How are the numerators and denominators of $\frac{2}{3}$ and $\frac{3}{2}$ related?* (They are reversed.) *How are the numerators and denominators of $\frac{3}{4}$ and $\frac{4}{3}$ related?* (They are reversed.) *What do you notice about the product when the numerator and the denominator of a fraction are reversed?* (The product is one.) *How are $\frac{2}{3}$ and $\frac{3}{2}$ related? Explain.* (They are reciprocals because their product is one.)

- *What do you think the next two products are? Explain.* (Both are one because they follow the same pattern. The numerator and denominator are reversed, so the product should be one.)

Wrap Up Ask students to find the reciprocals of $\frac{5}{9}$ ($\frac{9}{5}$), $\frac{10}{3}$ ($\frac{3}{10}$), and $\frac{7}{8}$ ($\frac{8}{7}$). *If the product of two numbers is a fraction, can the numbers be reciprocals?* (Yes, if the numerator and the denominator of the fraction are the same number, the fraction is equal to one. $\frac{5}{9} \times \frac{9}{5} = \frac{45}{45}$; $\frac{10}{3} \times \frac{3}{10} = \frac{30}{30}$; $\frac{7}{8} \times \frac{8}{7} = \frac{56}{56}$)

Reteach Have students use Copymaster M5: Grid Paper to draw models to find reciprocals of whole numbers. For example, to show that $\frac{1}{5}$ is the reciprocal of 5, shade 5 squares. One fifth of those squares is one, so the reciprocal of 5 must be $\frac{1}{5}$.

Assess

Can a number have more than one reciprocal? Why? (No. Explanations should include noting that equivalent fractions name the same amount. Although the fractions may be represented differently, they represent only one unique amount.)

APPLY THE CONCEPT
Problem-Solving Strategy: Draw a Diagram
Problem-Solving Skill: Check for Reasonableness

Present the Problem Display Visual 44: What Is My Reciprocal? Pass out copies of Copymaster M5: Grid Paper. Read the problem set-up and instructions:

- *Jared and Julia want to find the reciprocal of the number. Jared says the reciprocal is $\frac{8}{9}$ and Julia says the reciprocal is $\frac{8}{11}$. Whose answer is correct?*

- *Work with a partner. Make a diagram if it can help you decide how to solve the problem.*

Discuss the Solution After students have had time to solve the problem, help the class discuss their solutions.

- *Can both students be correct? Explain.* (No, $\frac{8}{9}$ and $\frac{8}{11}$ are not equivalent fractions so they cannot both be correct.)

- *How did making a diagram help you solve the problem?* (Sample answer: Making the diagram helped me see that $1\frac{1}{8}$ is equivalent to $\frac{9}{8}$. Once I recognized that $1\frac{1}{8} = \frac{9}{8}$, I could find the reciprocal of the number. The reciprocal of $\frac{9}{8}$ is $\frac{8}{9}$.)

- Discuss any other methods students might have used to write $1\frac{1}{8}$ as a fraction and how they identified the reciprocal.

REFLECT

Does zero have a reciprocal? Explain. (No, every number multiplied by zero is zero. The product of zero and any other number, including zero, can never be equal to one.)

Vocabulary

- Direct students' attention to the Word Wall. Work with students to make up new examples to show that the product of reciprocals is always one.

- Discuss how to define the terms before asking students to record new definitions and examples in their personal glossaries.

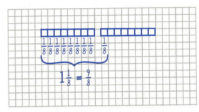

Jared's answer is correct because $1\frac{1}{8} = \frac{9}{8}$. The number to multiply by $\frac{9}{8}$ to get 1 is $\frac{8}{9}$.

Journal Prompt

Explain the reciprocal of a number. What is it and what can you do with it? (Answers should include checking that the product of a number and its reciprocal is one.)

Assess

Write a whole number and find its reciprocal. Then write a fraction and find its reciprocal. (Answers may vary.)

Concept Builder — **Lesson 23 Plan**

Model Dividing Fractions

TODAY'S CONCEPTS
- Model dividing fractions.
- Use the reciprocal to divide fractions.

MATERIALS
- Visual 45: Models for Dividing Fractions
- Visual 46: Patterns in Fraction Division
- Copymaster M5: Grid Paper
- Vocabulary Cards: **dividend**, **divisor**, **quotient**, **reciprocals**

SET UP

Build the Concept
Display a copy of Copymaster M5: Grid Paper.

Explore the Concept
Display Visual 45: Models for Dividing Fractions.

Apply the Concept
Display Visual 46: Patterns in Fraction Division.

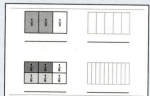

EL WORD WALL

dividend — $3 \div \tfrac{1}{2} = 6$ — quotient

divisor

reciprocals

$3 \div \tfrac{1}{2} = 3 \times \tfrac{2}{1}$

100 iSucceed MATH

PROFESSIONAL DEVELOPMENT

Using Models to Divide Some students may more readily grasp the idea of dividing fractions by using the "goes-into" or "fits into" model. Rephrase division problems by asking, *How many times does the divisor go into the dividend?* This way of thinking about division makes using models to divide fractions much more accessible to students.

Dividing with Fractions Dividing with fractions can involve dividing with whole numbers, fractions, and mixed numbers. Use the table to help make sense of these fraction-division settings.

Division	Meaning
$4 \div 2$	4 divided into equal 2-unit pieces
$4 \div \frac{1}{2}$	4 divided into equal $\frac{1}{2}$-unit pieces
$\frac{1}{2} \div 4$	$\frac{1}{2}$ divided into equal 4-unit pieces
$\frac{1}{2} \div \frac{1}{4}$	$\frac{1}{2}$ divided into equal $\frac{1}{4}$-unit pieces
$1\frac{1}{2} \div \frac{1}{4}$	$1\frac{1}{2}$ divided into equal $\frac{1}{4}$-unit pieces

If the dividend is less than the divisor, as in $\frac{1}{2} \div 4$, then the quotient must be a fraction. Since there are 8 halves in 4, then there is only $\frac{1}{8}$ of 4 in a half.

Preventing Common Errors Although students will not be formally introduced to the algorithm, they will be introduced to the idea of multiplying by the reciprocal in Apply the Concept. Encourage students to continue to use models until they're comfortable using the algorithm. Some students may try to adapt the multiplication algorithm to divide because it is both fast and easy. They may try to divide across the numerators and across the denominators. Ask students who routinely fail to find correct quotients to explain their thinking.

Equivalent Fractions As with other operations involving fractions on a multiple-choice test, students may not recognize the correct choice if it is in simplest form and the quotient they have found is not. Help students to look for equivalent fractions if they cannot find an answer choice that matches their quotient.

Courseware Connections

Module: Dividing Fractions

Dividing Whole Numbers by Fractions

Dividing Fractions by Whole Numbers

Dividing Fractions by Fractions

Lesson 23 Teach

BUILD THE CONCEPT

Post a copy of Copymaster M5: Grid Paper. Your goal in this discussion is to help students understand how to use models to divide fractions.

- Draw one whole on Grid Paper. *To divide fractions, think about what the division means. We can use this picture to find $1 \div \frac{1}{2}$.*
- *The division means we want to find how many halves are in one. Draw the whole as two halves to find the quotient. What is $1 \div \frac{1}{2}$? Why?* (2; There are two halves in 1.)
- *Model $2 \div \frac{1}{3}$.* (6) Discuss how the diagram and using words to rephrase the problem make it easy to divide a whole number by a fraction.
- Use the Grid Paper to create models for other division examples such as $8 \div \frac{1}{2} = 16$, $4 \div \frac{1}{4} = 16$, $3 \div \frac{1}{5} = 15$, and so on.

Connect to Vocabulary Post on the Word Wall and discuss: **quotient**, **dividend**, and **divisor**. As you work with the class to divide fractions, have students use the vocabulary.

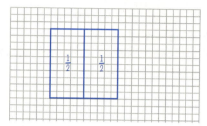

There are two halves in 1, so $1 \div \frac{1}{2} = 2$.

EXPLORE THE CONCEPT

Display Visual 45: Models for Dividing Fractions.

- *Refer to the models on the left side on the Visual. We can use models to divide a fraction by a whole number. To find $\frac{2}{3} \div 2$, first use a model for $\frac{2}{3}$. Label the model. The problem $\frac{2}{3} \div 2$ means, How many twos are in $\frac{2}{3}$? or What is one of 2 equal parts of $\frac{2}{3}$? When you divide $\frac{2}{3}$ of a rectangle into two equal parts, each small rectangle is $\frac{1}{6}$ of the whole. What is $\frac{2}{3} \div 2$? How do you know?* ($\frac{2}{6}$; Each of the two shaded parts is $\frac{1}{6}$.) Record the division: $\frac{2}{3} \div 2 = \frac{2}{6}$.
- *Now find $\frac{3}{5} \div \frac{3}{10}$. Refer to the right side of the Visual. Use a model for each fraction. Think: How many $\frac{3}{10}$s will fit in $\frac{3}{5}$? Show how two sets of $\frac{3}{10}$s are in $\frac{3}{5}$ on the models. What is $\frac{3}{5} \div \frac{3}{10}$? How do you know?* (2; Two $\frac{3}{10}$s will fit in $\frac{3}{5}$.) Record the division under the model: $\frac{3}{5} \div \frac{3}{10} = 2$.

Wrap Up *How does using models help you divide fractions?* (Sample response: It helps me understand ways to think about what it means to divide the fractions.)

Reteach Have students use Copymaster M5: Grid Paper to draw models to divide fractions. Have them copy the models as you draw them to demonstrate how to divide fractions such as: $2 \div \frac{1}{4}$ (8), $\frac{1}{2} \div 4$ ($\frac{1}{8}$), and $\frac{1}{2} \div \frac{1}{4}$ (2).

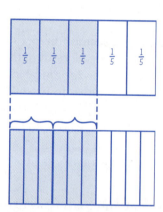

Two groups of $\frac{3}{10}$ will fit into $\frac{3}{5}$, so $\frac{3}{5} \div \frac{3}{10} = 2$.

When you divide a whole number by a fraction, will the quotient be less than or greater than the whole number? Give an example. (Greater. Check students' examples.)

iSucceed MATH: Model Dividing Fractions

APPLY THE CONCEPT
Problem-Solving Strategy: Look for a Pattern

Present the Problem Display Visual 46: Patterns in Fraction Division. Provide students with copies of Copymaster M5: Grid Paper to use if needed. Read the problem set-up and instructions:

- *Look back at the quotients you have already found. Write them, then complete the products shown in the table.*
- *Work with a partner. Compare the quotient and product in each row. Is there a pattern?*

Discuss the Solution After students have had time to solve the problem, help the class discuss their solutions.

- *What did you notice when you compared the quotient and product in each row? Is there a pattern? If so, describe it.* (Yes, the quotient and product in each row are the same.) You may need to help students find equivalents to $\frac{2}{6}$ and $\frac{30}{15}$ to verify their results.
- *How are the problems in each row the same and different?* (They have the same first number, reciprocals for second number, opposite operations, and the same result.)
- *How can a reciprocal help you find a quotient?* (To divide by a fraction, leave the dividend the same. Multiply it by the reciprocal of the divisor.) Discuss how students noticed and interpreted the pattern to solve the problem.
- Try a few more examples to confirm students' rule. ($8 \div \frac{1}{2} = 16$ and $8 \times \frac{2}{1} = 16$; $4 \div \frac{1}{4} = 16$ and $4 \times \frac{4}{1} = 16$; $3 \div \frac{1}{5} = 15$ and $3 \times \frac{5}{1} = 15$)

REFLECT
What can you do if you need to find $\frac{1}{3} \div \frac{1}{2}$ and you forget the rule for dividing by fractions? What is the quotient? (Answers should include making a diagram to find the quotient; $\frac{2}{3}$.)

Vocabulary
- Post **reciprocal** on the Word Wall.
- Discuss all of today's terms before asking students to add new terms and examples to their personal glossaries.

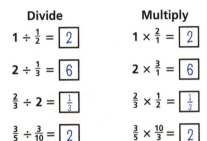

Divide	Multiply
$1 \div \frac{1}{2} = \boxed{2}$	$1 \times \frac{2}{1} = \boxed{2}$
$2 \div \frac{1}{3} = \boxed{6}$	$2 \times \frac{3}{1} = \boxed{6}$
$\frac{2}{3} \div 2 = \boxed{\frac{1}{3}}$	$\frac{2}{3} \times \frac{1}{2} = \boxed{\frac{1}{3}}$
$\frac{3}{5} \div \frac{3}{10} = \boxed{2}$	$\frac{3}{5} \times \frac{10}{3} = \boxed{2}$

To divide, you can multiply by the reciprocal of the divisor.

Journal Prompt
The question for $6 \div 2$ is, How many 2s fit into 6? What is the question for $6 \div \frac{1}{2}$? (How many halves fit into 6?) *How can you find the quotient of $6 \div \frac{1}{2}$?* (Make a model, count by halves to 6, or multiply 6 by the reciprocal of $\frac{1}{2}$: $6 \times 2 = 12$.)

Assess
Multiply by the reciprocal to find the quotient of $\frac{3}{4} \div \frac{1}{2}$. ($\frac{3}{4} \div \frac{1}{2} = \frac{3}{4} \times \frac{2}{1} = \frac{6}{4}$)

Concept Builder — Lesson 24 Plan

Mixed Numbers

TODAY'S CONCEPTS
- Write a mixed number or a whole number as a fraction.
- Write a fraction as a mixed number.
- Relate mixed numbers to decimal numbers.

MATERIALS
- Visual 47: Stacked Number Lines 2
- Visual 48: Mixed Number Sense
- Vocabulary Cards: **fraction**, **mixed number**, **whole number**

SET UP
Build the Concept
Display Visual 47: Stacked Number Lines 2.

Apply the Concept
Display Visual 48: Mixed Number Sense.

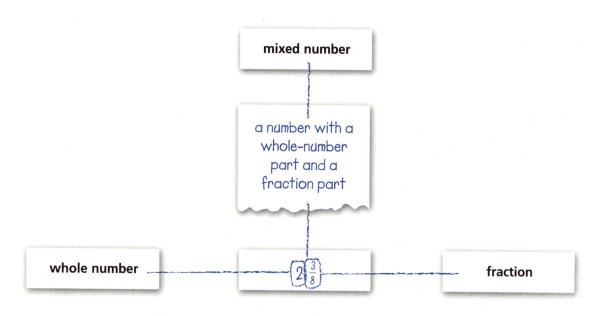

104   iSucceed MATH

PROFESSIONAL DEVELOPMENT

Math Background A fraction with a numerator greater than its denominator has a value greater than one. If the numerator and the denominator are equal, the fraction is equal to one. You can rewrite fractions like these as mixed numbers or as whole numbers. There are at least two ways to write a fraction as a mixed number.

1. Break up the fraction into as many ones as possible. What's left is the fraction part.
$$\frac{12}{5} = \frac{5}{5} + \frac{5}{5} + \frac{2}{5} = 2\frac{2}{5}$$

2. Use the rule. Divide the numerator by the denominator. Use the remainder to write the fraction part of the quotient. To write a mixed number as a fraction, write the whole-number part as a fraction. Then add the fractions. This rule works because of the division meaning of fractions. (See Concept Builder 14.)

Improper Fraction Some math textbooks refer to a fraction with a numerator greater than its denominator as an improper fraction. This term is not used in this program. A fraction with a numerator greater than its denominator is a fraction with a value greater than one. While this form is correct, students may need to rename the fraction as a mixed number in many situations.

Mixed Numbers and Decimal Numbers Mixed numbers are very similar to decimal numbers. In fact, fractions with denominators of 10 and 100 are read exactly the same way as their decimal counterparts. Mixed numbers are generally easier to read than decimal numbers because you read the whole number and then the fraction without having to remember the denominator—it is given. As with decimals, the whole-number part of a mixed number is separated from the fraction part by "and."

Write: $1\frac{3}{4}$

Say: *one and three fourths*

Courseware Connections

Module: Mixed Numbers

Mixed Numbers Defined

Rewriting Fractions and Mixed Numbers

Relating Mixed Numbers and Decimals

Comparing and Ordering Mixed Numbers

GET REAL: A 100-Meter Dash

Lesson 24 Teach

BUILD THE CONCEPT

Display Visual 47: Stacked Number Lines 2. Your goal in this discussion is to help students to read, write, and rename mixed numbers.
Be sure to include all students in the discussion.

- Point to the top number line. Remind students of decimal/fraction equivalents. They know how to read decimal numbers greater than one. Point to $2\frac{3}{10}$ as you read the number on the number line.

- Write $2\frac{3}{10}$ on the board. *This number is a mixed number. It has a whole-number part, 2, and a fraction part, $\frac{3}{10}$.*

- Have students read the numbers as you point to several other mixed numbers on the number line.

- Point to $3\frac{4}{5}$ as you read the number on the second number line. Discuss how to read other mixed numbers on this number line. Have volunteers locate points as you read them.

Connect to Vocabulary Post on the Word Wall and discuss how **whole number** and **fraction** relate to **mixed number**.

 Connect the parts of a mixed number to "mixed," a word that suggests that something is made of different parts.

EXPLORE THE CONCEPT

- Point to 1 on the top number line. *How can we write 1 as a fraction on this number line? How do you know?* ($\frac{10}{10}$; The next tenth after $\frac{9}{10}$ must be $\frac{10}{10}$. It is labeled "1" on the number line) Extend to other numbers greater than 1, such as $1\frac{1}{10}$, $1\frac{7}{10}$, 2, $2\frac{3}{10}$.

- Repeat the discussion for whole numbers and mixed numbers, using the second number line.

- Demonstrate how to rename a mixed number as a fraction. Write $1\frac{5}{10}$ on the board. *What is 1 as a fraction with a denominator of 10?* ($\frac{10}{10}$). *Think of 1 as $\frac{10}{10}$ and add this to $\frac{5}{10}$ to rename $1\frac{5}{10}$ as a fraction.* Write $1\frac{5}{10} = 1 + \frac{5}{10} = \frac{10}{10} + \frac{5}{10} = \frac{15}{10}$.

- *Where is $\frac{22}{5}$ on the second number line? Mark the point. How can we rename this as a mixed number?* (It is $\frac{2}{5}$ past 4 on the number line, so it is $4\frac{2}{5}$.) *Yes, since $\frac{5}{5} + \frac{5}{5} + \frac{5}{5} + \frac{5}{5} + \frac{2}{5} = \frac{22}{5}$ and $\frac{5}{5} = 1$, then $\frac{22}{5} = 4\frac{2}{5}$.*

Wrap Up *How do you know when a fraction can be renamed as a whole number?* (If the numerator is a multiple of the denominator, the fraction is equal to a whole number.)

Reteach Use an inch ruler or Cardstock C6–7: Fraction Models, Cardstock C8–11: Fraction/Decimal Cards or Copymaster M5: Grid Paper to model mixed numbers.

Assess

How can you to write $\frac{7}{3}$ as a mixed number?
($\frac{7}{3} = \frac{3}{3} + \frac{3}{3} + \frac{2}{3} = 2\frac{1}{3}$)

APPLY THE CONCEPT

Problem-Solving Skill: Use Logical Reasoning

Present the Problem Display Visual 48: Mixed Number Sense. Direct students' attention to the list of situations, and read the instructions:

- *Work with a partner. Decide whether the mixed number makes sense in each situation.*
- *If it makes sense, leave it alone. If not, change the situation so that it does make sense.*

Discuss the Solution After students have had time to solve the problem, help them discuss their solutions.

- *Which situations make sense? Explain.* ($1\frac{1}{4}$ miles to the park and $2\frac{3}{4}$ cups milk for a recipe make sense. These are measurements that have fractional parts.)
- *Which situations do not make sense? Explain.* ($1\frac{1}{2}$ buses and $3\frac{2}{3}$ birds do not make sense. You cannot have $\frac{1}{2}$ of a bus or $\frac{2}{3}$ of a live bird. These things are counted in wholes.) Discuss how students changed the situations to make sense. (Possible answers: 2 buses and 4 birds make sense.)

REFLECT ON THE MATH

How can you describe a mixed number to someone who does not know the meaning of the term? (Answers should include an understanding that a mixed number has a fraction part and a whole-number part. When the numerator of a fraction is greater than its denominator, the fraction can be renamed as a mixed number.)

Vocabulary

Direct students' attention to the Word Wall. Discuss how to define each term before asking students to record their definitions in their personal glossaries along with a diagram and/or an example.

Journal Prompt

Explain how to write $2\frac{3}{4}$ as a fraction. ($\frac{11}{4}$; Possible explanation: Use a number line, or write 2 as $\frac{8}{4}$, and add $\frac{8}{4} + \frac{3}{4}$.)

Assess

Write two mixed-number situations that do not make sense and explain what is wrong with them. (Check students' work.)

Concept Builder • Lesson 24 • Teach

Concept Builder 25 Plan

Add Mixed Numbers

TODAY'S CONCEPTS
- Model adding mixed numbers.
- Rename fraction sums.

MATERIALS
- Visual 49: Number-Line Addition 2
- Visual 50: Tio's and Lauren's Sums
- Vocabulary Cards: **addend, common denominators, rename, sum**

SET UP
Build the Concept
Display Visual 49: Number-Line Addition 2.

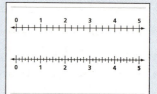

Apply the Concept
Display Visual 50: Tio's and Lauren's Sums.

WORD WALL

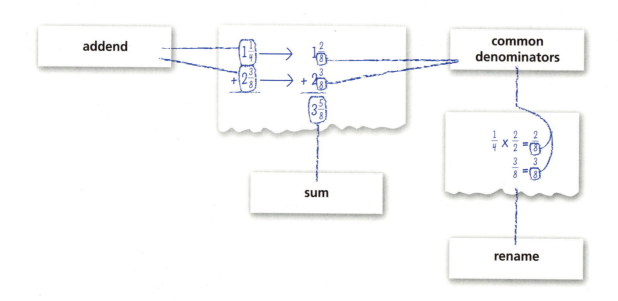

108   iSucceed MATH

PROFESSIONAL DEVELOPMENT

Math Background Adding mixed numbers is the same as adding fractions with the additional step of adding the whole-number parts. If the numerator of the fraction-sum is greater than its denominator, the fraction should be renamed with a whole-number part and a fraction part.

Example:

$$\begin{array}{rcl} 4\frac{1}{2} & \rightarrow & 4 + \frac{2}{4} \\ +\,5\frac{3}{4} & \rightarrow & 5 + \frac{3}{4} \\ \hline 10\frac{1}{4} & & 9 + \frac{5}{4} \\ & & 9 + \frac{4}{4} + \frac{1}{4} \end{array}$$

Courseware Connections

Module: Mixed Numbers

Adding Mixed Numbers with Like Denominators

Adding Mixed Numbers with Unlike Denominators

Adding Mixed Numbers

Adding Fractions

Renaming Fractions Renaming fractions in which the numerator is greater than the denominator is analogous to regrouping in whole numbers. Instead of regrouping ones for tens, regroup based on the denominator.

Common Denominators You may wish to review finding common multiples to help students find a common denominator. Although the least common denominator may make it easier to simplify the sum, sometimes it is faster and more accurate to use the product of the denominators as a common denominator. This works because of the Identity Property of Multiplication: Multiplying any factor by 1 does not change the value of that factor.

Preventing Common Errors Watch for students who rush through the addition and attempt to use the rules for multiplying fractions to add. Remind them that the operations are different and that the same rules do not apply.

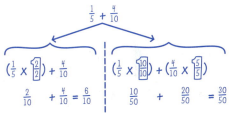

Since $\frac{6}{10} = \frac{30}{50} = \frac{3}{5}$, either method of evaluating the expression is acceptable.

Lesson 25 Teach

BUILD THE CONCEPT

Display Visual 49: Number-Line Addition 2. Your goal in this discussion is to help students understand how to add mixed numbers.

- *I want to add $1\frac{3}{4} + 2\frac{1}{2}$. Why will I use a number line that shows fourths?* (You must be able to count both fourths and halves to add the fractions.) Show $1\frac{3}{4}$ on the number line.
- *To add $2\frac{1}{2}$, first move 2 units to the right of $1\frac{3}{4}$.* Discuss how to count the units on the number line. *I still need to move $\frac{1}{2}$ unit more. How do I move the extra half-unit from $3\frac{3}{4}$?* (Count 2 more fourths because $\frac{1}{2} = \frac{2}{4}$.) Mark and label the movement. *What is the sum?* ($4\frac{1}{4}$)

Connect to Vocabulary Post on the Word Wall and discuss: **addend**, **common denominator**, **sum**, and **rename**. As you work with the class to add mixed numbers, have students use the vocabulary words to discuss the problems.

- Use the second number line on the Visual to model $1\frac{3}{4} + 2\frac{5}{8} = 4\frac{3}{8}$.

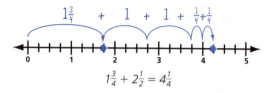

EXPLORE THE CONCEPT

- Demonstrate how to expand the addends to add. Connect to using expanded form to add whole numbers. The ideas are analogous.
- Add the fractions. *Why do we write equivalent fractions?* (You need a common denominator to add the fractions. $\frac{1}{2} \times \frac{2}{2} = \frac{2}{4}$) Then, add the whole numbers.
- The sum is $3\frac{5}{4}$. However, this is not an easy number to understand. Since $\frac{5}{4}$ is greater than 1, you can rename it as a mixed number. *What is $\frac{5}{4}$ as a mixed number? How do you know?* ($\frac{5}{4} = \frac{4}{4} + \frac{1}{4} = 1\frac{1}{4}$) Write $3\frac{5}{4} = 3 + 1 + \frac{1}{4}$ on the board. *What is a different name for the sum?* ($4\frac{1}{4}$)

Wrap Up *How can you use an estimate to check that $4\frac{1}{4}$ is a reasonable sum for $1\frac{3}{4} + 2\frac{1}{2}$?* (The sum is close to $2 + 2\frac{1}{2} = 4\frac{1}{2}$. The sum is reasonable.)

Reteach Have students use Copymaster M5: Grid Paper to make models of the mixed numbers, using unit squares. They can color the fraction parts and cut them out. Then, they can combine the pictures to find the sum. Remind them to make wholes whenever possible.

Assess

Show how to add $3\frac{1}{2}$ to $1\frac{5}{8}$. (Students may use a number line or rename with common denominators to calculate the sum. Either way, the sum is $5\frac{1}{8}$.)

110 iSucceed MATH: Add Mixed Numbers

APPLY THE CONCEPT

Problem-Solving Skill: Check for Reasonableness

Present the Problem Display Visual 50: Tio's and Lauren's Sums. Read the problem set-up and instructions:

- *Tio and Lauren added mixed numbers in two different problems.*
- *Work with a partner. Check each student's sum. Decide whether the sum is reasonable. Explain why or why not. You may use words and pictures to help.*

Discuss the Solution After students have had time to solve the problem, help them discuss their solutions.

- *Is Tio's sum reasonable? How do you know?* (Yes. Sample answer: First, I estimated the sum as $1 + 2 = 3$. The estimate is close to the exact answer. Then, I checked the sum, using 8 as a common denominator. The sum is $2\frac{9}{8}$ or $3\frac{1}{8}$.) Discuss all methods students used to check for reasonableness.
- *Is Lauren's sum reasonable? How do you know?* (No. Sample answer: First, I estimated the sum as $2 + 2 = 4$, which is greater than $2\frac{7}{9}$. The sum did not seem reasonable, so I looked at what she did. I noticed that she added the fractions by adding the numerators and adding the denominators. This is not correct.) You may want to find the exact sum to compare to Lauren's answer as well. ($2\frac{9}{6} = 3\frac{3}{6}$ or $3\frac{1}{2}$)

REFLECT

At which two times might you need to rename when adding mixed numbers? (If there are unlike denominators, rename the fractions with like denominators to add the fractions. If the fraction sum is greater than 1, rename the fraction as a mixed number.)

Vocabulary

Refer to the Word Wall. Discuss the example, then suggest that students add to the definitions and examples in their personal glossaries.

Journal Prompt

How is adding mixed numbers like adding fractions? How is it different? (Sample answer: You follow the same rules for adding fractions that you use to add the fraction parts of the mixed numbers. It is different because you add the whole-number parts and rename any fractions greater than 1 to combine with the whole-number part of the answer.)

Assess

Write two mixed numbers. How would you explain to a friend the key steps needed to add the mixed numbers? (Answers should include adding the fraction parts and the whole-number parts of the mixed numbers, using common denominators and renaming fractional sums that are greater than 1 to combine with the whole-number part of the answer.)

Concept Builder — Lesson 26 Plan

Subtract Mixed Numbers

TODAY'S CONCEPTS
- Model subtracting mixed numbers.
- Rename fractions.

MATERIALS
- Visual 51: Number-Line Subtraction 2
- Visual 52: Regrouping to Subtract Fractions
- Copymater M5: Grid Paper
- Vocabulary Cards: **common denominators, difference, regroup, rename, subtract**

SET UP

Build the Concept
Display Visual 51: Number-Line Subtraction 2.

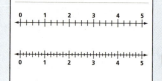

Apply the Concept
Display Visual 52: Regrouping to Subtract Fractions.

EL WORD WALL

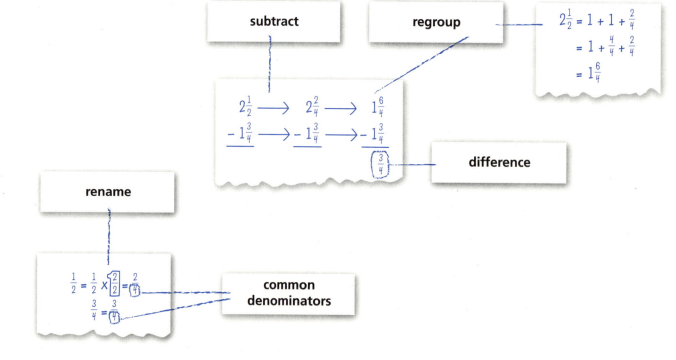

112   iSucceed MATH

PD PROFESSIONAL DEVELOPMENT

Math Background This lesson closely parallels the lesson on adding mixed numbers. Students first subtract on the number line and then use the algorithm to solve the same problem. Be aware that, when students write the fraction in expanded form to subtract, the minus sign is distributed to both the whole-number part and the fraction part of the mixed number to subtract. This is an application of the Distributive Property.

$$2\tfrac{3}{4} - 1\tfrac{1}{2} = 2\tfrac{3}{4} + [(-1)(1 + \tfrac{1}{2})]$$
$$= 2\tfrac{3}{4} + (-1) + (-\tfrac{1}{2})$$
$$= 2 + \tfrac{3}{4} - 1 - \tfrac{1}{2}$$

This is an application of the Distributive Property.

Regrouping to Subtract Fractions Students will be introduced to regrouping to subtract fractions in Apply the Concept. You may choose to introduce the algorithm along with models, depending on the directions students take when solving the problem. To use the algorithm, the denominator of the fraction determines the way to regroup.

Examples:

$$\begin{array}{r} 2\tfrac{1}{3} \\ -1\tfrac{2}{3} \end{array} \rightarrow 1 + \tfrac{3}{3} + \tfrac{1}{3} \rightarrow \begin{array}{r} 1\tfrac{4}{3} \\ -1\tfrac{2}{3} \end{array}$$

$$\begin{array}{r} 3\tfrac{2}{5} \\ -1\tfrac{3}{5} \end{array} \rightarrow 2 + \tfrac{5}{5} + \tfrac{2}{5} \rightarrow \begin{array}{r} 2\tfrac{7}{5} \\ -1\tfrac{3}{5} \end{array}$$

Common Denominators As with addition, any common denominator works for subtracting fractions.

Another Way to Subtract Fractions You can write mixed numbers as fractions in order to compute.

Examples:

$$\begin{array}{r} 2\tfrac{1}{3} \rightarrow \tfrac{3}{3} + \tfrac{3}{3} + \tfrac{1}{3} \rightarrow \tfrac{7}{3} \\ -1\tfrac{2}{3} \rightarrow \quad \tfrac{3}{3} + \tfrac{2}{3} \rightarrow -\tfrac{5}{3} \\ \hline \tfrac{2}{3} \end{array}$$

$$\begin{array}{r} 3\tfrac{2}{5} \rightarrow \tfrac{5}{5} + \tfrac{5}{5} + \tfrac{5}{5} + \tfrac{2}{5} \rightarrow \tfrac{17}{5} \\ -1\tfrac{3}{5} \rightarrow \quad \tfrac{5}{5} + \tfrac{3}{5} \rightarrow -\tfrac{8}{5} \\ \hline \tfrac{9}{5} = 1\tfrac{4}{5} \end{array}$$

Courseware Connections

Module: Subtracting Fractions

Subtracting Mixed Numbers with Like Denominators

Subtracting Mixed Numbers with Unlike Denominators

Subtracting Fractions

Subtracting Fractions and Mixed Numbers from Whole Numbers

Subtracting Mixed Numbers

GET REAL: Small Mammals

GET REAL: World Television Viewing

Lesson 26 Teach

BUILD THE CONCEPT

Display Visual 51: Number-Line Subtraction 2. Your goal in this discussion is to help students understand how to subtract mixed numbers.

- To subtract $2\frac{3}{4} - 1\frac{1}{2}$, I will use a number line that shows fourths. Why? (You must be able to count both fourths and halves to subtract the fractions.) Show $2\frac{3}{4}$ on the number line.
- To subtract $1\frac{1}{2}$, first, move 1 unit to the left of $2\frac{3}{4}$. Show the move. I still need to move another $\frac{1}{2}$ unit to the left. How can I move $\frac{1}{2}$ unit from $1\frac{3}{4}$? (Move 2 more fourths because $\frac{1}{2} = \frac{2}{4}$.) What is the difference? ($1\frac{1}{4}$)

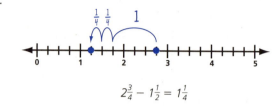

$2\frac{3}{4} - 1\frac{1}{2} = 1\frac{1}{4}$

Connect to Vocabulary Post on the Word Wall and discuss: **common denominator**, **difference**, **rename**, and **subtract**.

- Model $4\frac{3}{4} - 2\frac{5}{8} = 2\frac{1}{8}$, encouraging students to use today's vocabulary.

EXPLORE THE CONCEPT

- Demonstrate how to expand the mixed numbers to subtract. Connect to using expanded form to subtract whole numbers. The ideas are analogous.
- Subtract the fractions. *Why do we write equivalent fractions?* (You need a common denominator to subtract the fractions. $\frac{1}{2} \times \frac{2}{2} = \frac{2}{4}$) Check that students do not confuse the operation of subtraction with writing the mixed number in expanded form. Then subtract the whole numbers. *What is the difference?* ($1\frac{1}{4}$)

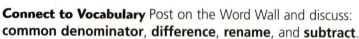

Subtract the fraction parts. Then subtract the whole-number part of the mixed numbers.

Wrap Up How can you use an estimate to check that $1\frac{1}{4}$ is a reasonable difference for $2\frac{3}{4} - 1\frac{1}{2}$? (Possible answer: The difference is close to $3 - 2 = 1$, so it is reasonable.)

Reteach Show students how to write mixed numbers as fractions before subtracting.

Show how to subtract $1\frac{1}{8}$ from $4\frac{3}{4}$. (Students may use a number line or rename with common denominators to calculate the difference. Either way, the difference is $3\frac{5}{8}$.)

iSucceed MATH: Subtract Mixed Numbers

APPLY THE CONCEPT
Problem-Solving Skill: Solve in More Than One Way

Present the Problem Display Visual 52: Regrouping to Subtract Fractions. Have Copymaster M5: Grid Paper available for students to use to make number lines or to make models if they choose. Read the problem set-up and instructions:

- *How can you find the difference of the mixed numbers? Use whatever method you choose to solve.*
- *Work with a partner. Look back and check the difference after you solve the problem.*

Discuss the Solution After students have had time to solve the problem, help the class discuss their solutions.

- What was different about this difference? ($2\frac{1}{2} - 1\frac{3}{4}$ is not an easy difference) Students may use the same tools in different ways to reach the difference. ($2\frac{1}{2} - 1\frac{3}{4} = \frac{3}{4}$) For example, one student might use the number line and count back while another might think of addition and finding a missing addend on the number line.
- Ask students to explain how they looked back and checked the difference.
- If students do not suggest it, then model regrouping to subtract.

$$\frac{1}{2} \times \boxed{\frac{2}{2}} = \frac{2}{4}$$

$$\begin{array}{l} 2\frac{1}{2} \to 2\frac{2}{4} \to 1 + 1 + \frac{2}{4} \to 1 + \boxed{\frac{4}{4}} + \frac{2}{4} \to 1\frac{6}{4} \\ -1\frac{3}{4} \to 1\frac{3}{4} \to 1 + \frac{3}{4} \longrightarrow 1 + \frac{3}{4} \to -1\frac{3}{4} \\ \phantom{-1\frac{3}{4} \to 1\frac{3}{4} \to 1 + \frac{3}{4} \longrightarrow 1 + \frac{3}{4} \to} \frac{3}{4} \end{array}$$

REFLECT

What are two different situations when it is necessary to rename when subtracting mixed numbers? (If there are unlike denominators, rename the fractions with like denominators to subtract the fractions. If you have to regroup to subtract, you will have to rename the fraction before you can subtract from it.)

Vocabulary

Add to the Word Wall **regroup** as it relates to the subtraction of mixed numbers. Discuss and encourage students to add examples to the definitions in their personal glossaries.

Journal Prompt

How is subtracting mixed numbers like subtracting fractions? How is it different? (Follow the same rules for subtracting fractions that you use to subtract the fraction parts of the mixed numbers. It is different because you may have to regroup a whole to a fraction to subtract.)

Assess

Write two mixed numbers. How would you explain to a friend the key steps needed to subtract mixed numbers? (Answers should include subtracting the fraction parts, using common denominators, and checking whether a fraction must be regrouped, regrouping when necessary, and then subtracting the whole-number parts of the mixed numbers.)

Concept Builder — Lesson 27 Plan

Multiply Mixed Numbers

TODAY'S CONCEPTS
- Model multiplying mixed numbers.
- Use an algorithm to multiply mixed numbers.

MATERIALS
- Visual 53: Multiplying Mixed Numbers
- Visual 54: Carnival Booth
- Vocabulary Cards: **factor**, **mixed number**, **product**

SET UP

Build the Concept
Display Visual 53: Multiplying Mixed Numbers.

Apply the Concept
Display Visual 54: Carnival Booth.

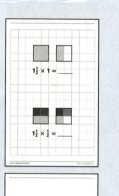

WORD WALL

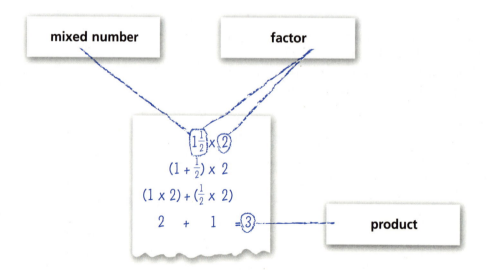

116 iSucceed MATH

PROFESSIONAL DEVELOPMENT

Math Background Students know how to multiply multi-digit whole numbers, decimal numbers, and fractions. Multiplying mixed numbers is essentially the same as multiplying any other rational numbers. When you multiply whole numbers, you multiply every place in a number by every other place. With multi-digit whole numbers, you multiply the ones, then the tens, then the hundreds, and so on. The same rule applies to mixed numbers.

Ways to Multiply Mixed Numbers You can apply the rules for multiplying in three different ways:

1. Use the Distributive Property. Break up one or both factors into whole number and fraction parts, then multiply each part of one factor by each part of the other factor.

   Example:
   $$1\tfrac{2}{3} \times 1\tfrac{1}{2} = 1\tfrac{2}{3} \times (1 + \tfrac{1}{2})$$
   $$= (1\tfrac{2}{3} \times 1) + (1\tfrac{2}{3} \times \tfrac{1}{2})$$
   $$= 1\tfrac{2}{3} + (\tfrac{5}{3} \times \tfrac{1}{2})$$
   $$= 1\tfrac{2}{3} + \tfrac{5}{6}$$
   $$= 1\tfrac{4}{6} + \tfrac{5}{6}$$
   $$= 1\tfrac{9}{6}$$
   $$= 1 + \tfrac{6}{6} + \tfrac{3}{6}$$
   $$= 2\tfrac{1}{2}$$

2. Rewrite each factor in fraction form, then multiply like any other pair of fraction factors.

   Example:
   $$1\tfrac{2}{3} \times 1\tfrac{1}{2} = \tfrac{5}{3} \times \tfrac{3}{2}$$
   $$= \tfrac{15}{6}$$
   $$= \tfrac{6}{6} + \tfrac{6}{6} + \tfrac{3}{6}$$
   $$= 2\tfrac{1}{2}$$

3. Rewrite each factor in decimal form, then multiply like any other pair of decimal factors.

   Example:
   $$1\tfrac{4}{5} \times 1\tfrac{1}{2} = 1.8 \times 1.5$$
   $$= 2.70$$

Organize for Learning The method students use to find a product does not matter as much as finding the product accurately. Some students will prefer to break apart factors, especially when one factor is a whole number. Others will do better by writing both factors as fractions or as decimals. Some decimals (as thirds or sixths) are not as easy to use as others (as halves or fourths).

Distributive Property According to the Distributive Property, when one of the factors of a product is written as a sum, multiplying each addend before adding does not change the product. If you feel that your students need to focus on one technique at a time, consider teaching this lesson over 3 or 4 days.

Courseware Connections

Module: Multiplying Fractions

Multiplying Mixed Numbers and Whole Numbers Using Models

Multiplying Mixed Numbers and Whole Numbers

Multiplying Mixed Numbers and Fractions

Multiplying Mixed Numbers

GET REAL: Designing a Park

GET REAL: Olympic Speed Skating

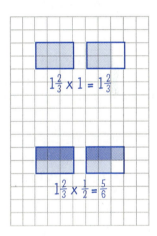

Model $1\tfrac{2}{3} \times 1\tfrac{1}{2} = 1\tfrac{2}{3} \times (1 + \tfrac{1}{2})$.

Lesson 27 Teach

BUILD THE CONCEPT

Display Visual 53: Multiplying Mixed Numbers. Your goal in this discussion is to help students model the multiplication of mixed numbers.

- You can use what you know to multiply mixed numbers.

- Have students help guide you through the steps of multiplying $1\frac{1}{2} \times 1\frac{1}{2}$. What is $1\frac{1}{2}$ written as a fraction? ($\frac{3}{2}$) How can you write $1\frac{1}{2} \times 1\frac{1}{2}$ with factors that are fractions? ($\frac{3}{2} \times \frac{3}{2}$) How do you find the product? (Multiply the numerators. Multiply the denominators.) Record each step as you find the product: $1\frac{1}{2} \times 1\frac{1}{2} = \frac{3}{2} \times \frac{3}{2} = \frac{9}{4}$.

- How can you write the product as a mixed number? (one way: $\frac{9}{4} = \frac{4}{4} + \frac{4}{4} + \frac{1}{4} = 2\frac{1}{4}$)

Connect to Vocabulary Post on the Word Wall and discuss: **factor**, **product**, and **mixed number**. Check that students can differentiate among the terms and apply them correctly in discussion. Have them identify the factors and product in each problem they solve.

EL Remind students that a mixed number is "mixed" because it has a whole number part and a fraction part. In everyday speech, something *mixed* is "made of different things."

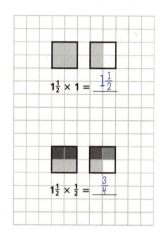

$1\frac{1}{2} \times 1\frac{1}{2} = 1\frac{1}{2} + \frac{3}{4} = 2\frac{1}{4}$

EXPLORE THE CONCEPT

- Explore other ways to find the product of $1\frac{1}{2}$ and $1\frac{1}{2}$. Model breaking up the factors to multiply.

$1\frac{1}{2} \times \boxed{1\frac{1}{2}} = 1\frac{1}{2} \times \boxed{(1 + \frac{1}{2})}$

$= (1\frac{1}{2} \times 1) + (1\frac{1}{2} \times \frac{1}{2})$

$= \quad 1\frac{1}{2} \quad + (1 + \frac{1}{2}) \times \frac{1}{2}$

$= \quad 1\frac{1}{2} \quad + (1 \times \frac{1}{2}) + (\frac{1}{2} \times \frac{1}{2})$

$= \quad 1\frac{1}{2} \quad + \quad \frac{1}{2} \quad + \quad \frac{1}{4}$

$= 2\frac{1}{4}$

- Next, link to multiplying decimals. *What decimal number is equivalent to $1\frac{1}{2}$?* (1.5) Review how to multiply 1.5 × 1.5. (2.25) The numbers $2\frac{1}{4}$ and 2.25 have the same value.

Wrap Up Discuss how to use different ways to find the product $1\frac{3}{4} \times 2 = 3\frac{1}{2}$.

Reteach Use a number line to demonstrate how to multiply $1\frac{1}{2} \times 1\frac{1}{2}$. Divide the number line into quarters. Break $1\frac{1}{2}$ into parts to find the product of $1\frac{1}{2} \times 1$ and $1\frac{1}{2} \times \frac{1}{2}$. Fold the number line in half to show that the product of $1\frac{1}{2} \times \frac{1}{2}$ is $\frac{3}{4}$. Add this part to the length of $1\frac{1}{2} \times 1$, or $1\frac{1}{2}$. The product is $1\frac{1}{2} + \frac{3}{4}$, or $2\frac{1}{4}$.

How can you break apart a mixed number to multiply $2\frac{1}{2} \times 1\frac{1}{2}$? What is the product? (One way: write $2\frac{1}{2} = 2 + \frac{1}{2}$. Next, multiply each part by $1\frac{1}{2}$. Another way: write $1\frac{1}{2} = 1 + \frac{1}{2}$ and multiply each part by $2\frac{1}{2}$. The product is $3\frac{3}{4}$.)

118 iSucceed MATH: Multiply Mixed Numbers

APPLY THE CONCEPT

Problem-Solving Strategy: Use Simpler Numbers

Present the Problem Display Visual 54: Carnival Booth. Read the problem set-up and instructions:

- Students are decorating a booth for the school carnival. They use $2\frac{1}{2}$ yards of ribbon streamers. The streamers cost $1.30 per yard.
- Work with a partner to find how much the ribbon costs.

Discuss the Solution After students have had time to solve the problem, help the class discuss their solutions.

- *How would you solve this problem if the students used 3 yards of ribbon?* Discuss why using simpler numbers makes it easier to come up with a plan for solving the problem. Thinking about using 3 yards of ribbon makes it easier to recognize that you need to multiply to solve the problem.
- Encourage students to estimate the solution. (Sample estimate: $3 \times 1 = 3$, so the answer should be about $3)
- Compare solution methods used to solve the original problem. Some students will use fractions ($2\frac{1}{2} \times 1\frac{3}{10} = 3\frac{1}{4}$); some will use decimals ($2.5 \times 1.3 = 3.25$). Either way, the ribbon costs $3.25.

REFLECT

- Have students explain which factor they changed to a simpler number and then explain why they simplified the factor.
- Have students compare the estimated product to the exact product for reasonableness.

Vocabulary

- Refer students to the Word Wall. Work together to write another example.
- Ask students to check definitions and add examples to their personal glossaries.

Journal Prompt

Compare $1\frac{1}{2} \times 2\frac{1}{2}$ to 1.5×2.5. Explain why both products have the same value. Which method is easier for you to use to multiply? Why? (Answers should refer to writing the equivalent fractions and decimals, verifying each product, and explaining advantages of the preferred method.)

Assess

Solve the carnival booth problem if the students used 4 yards of ribbon. ($5.20)

Concept Builder
Lesson 28 Plan

Divide Mixed Numbers

TODAY'S CONCEPTS
- Understand how to model dividing mixed numbers.
- Divide mixed numbers.

MATERIALS
- Visual 55: Divide with a Number Line
- Visual 56: Unit Fraction Division Patterns
- Vocabulary Cards: **divide, dividend, divisor, quotient, reciprocals**

SET UP
Build the Concept
Display Visual 55: Divide with a Number Line.

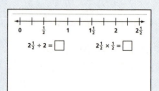

Apply the Concept
Display Visual 56: Unit Fraction Division Patterns.

EL WORD WALL

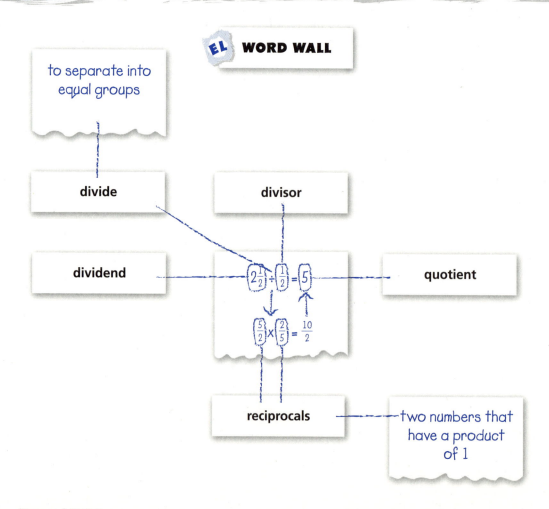

120   iSucceed MATH

PROFESSIONAL DEVELOPMENT

Error Analysis Multiplication and division are inverse operations. Students who are in a hurry, or who are good at memorizing rules without really distinguishing their meanings, may apply a rule such as *multiply by the reciprocal* in the wrong place. Check that students recognize and are able to explain what they are doing in each step of a solution. Turning division and multiplication expressions into questions may help.

Example:
$2\frac{1}{2} \div \frac{1}{2}$ asks, *How many $\frac{1}{2}$s are in $2\frac{1}{2}$?*
$2\frac{1}{2} \times \frac{1}{2}$ asks, *What is $\frac{1}{2}$ of a group of $2\frac{1}{2}$?*

Reciprocals Reciprocals come in pairs. The product of a pair of reciprocals is always 1. The rule for dividing fractions is: Find the reciprocal of the divisor and multiply that by the dividend. The division meaning of fractions shows why this works.

Example:
You know that $4 \div 2 = \frac{4}{2}$
This means that $4 \div \frac{1}{2} = \frac{4}{\frac{1}{2}}$

This complex fraction can be simplified by multiplying numerator and denominator by 2:
$$\frac{4 \times 2}{\frac{1}{2} \times 2}$$

This simplifies to $\frac{4 \times 2}{1}$ or $4 \times \frac{2}{1}$.

Unit Fractions A unit fraction has a numerator of 1. It is easy to divide by a unit fraction because all you have to do is multiply by its whole-number reciprocal. This means that you can use mental math to divide by unit fractions.

Courseware Connections

Module: Dividing Fractions

Dividing Mixed Numbers by Whole Numbers

Dividing Mixed Numbers by Fractions and Mixed Numbers

GET REAL: Planning a Bake Sale

Lesson 28 Teach

BUILD THE CONCEPT

Display Visual 55: Divide with a Number Line. Your goal in this discussion is to help students model the division of mixed numbers.

- Review why dividing by a number is the same as multiplying by the reciprocal of that number. Write $2\frac{1}{2} \div 2$, and have students identify the dividend ($2\frac{1}{2}$) and divisor (2).
- *How can you use this number line to find $2\frac{1}{2} \div 2$?* (Fold the number line into 2 parts.) Fold the number line in half to find the quotient: $1\frac{1}{4}$. *This is the same result as you get from multiplying $2\frac{1}{2}$ by one half. Why?* (In both operations, you are finding half the length of $2\frac{1}{2}$.)

Connect to Vocabulary Post on the Word Wall and discuss: **divide, dividend, divisor, reciprocals,** and **quotient.**

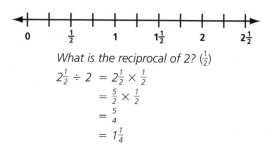

What is the reciprocal of 2? ($\frac{1}{2}$)

$$2\frac{1}{2} \div 2 = 2\frac{1}{2} \times \frac{1}{2}$$
$$= \frac{5}{2} \times \frac{1}{2}$$
$$= \frac{5}{4}$$
$$= 1\frac{1}{4}$$

EXPLORE THE CONCEPT

- Before introducing the algorithm, make sure that students are able to find the reciprocal of a mixed number.
- Write $2\frac{1}{2} \div 1\frac{1}{2}$. *Do you think the quotient will be greater than or less than the quotient of $2\frac{1}{2} \div 2$? Why?* (Greater because you are dividing $2\frac{1}{2}$ into smaller pieces.)
- *You can use what you know about dividing fractions to divide mixed numbers.* As much as possible, have students guide you through the steps of dividing $2\frac{1}{2}$ by $1\frac{1}{2}$.
- *How can you rewrite the division expression using fractions instead of mixed numbers?* ($\frac{5}{2} \div \frac{3}{2}$) *What is the reciprocal of $\frac{3}{2}$?* ($\frac{2}{3}$) *How do you divide fractions?* (Multiply the dividend by the reciprocal of the divisor.) Record each step as you discuss how to find the quotient. ($2\frac{1}{2} \div 1\frac{1}{2} = 1\frac{2}{3}$)

Wrap Up *How is dividing mixed numbers like dividing fractions? How is it different?* (The steps are the same except that you must first rename the mixed numbers as fractions.)

Reteach Draw pictures to model the division of $2\frac{1}{2}$ by 2.

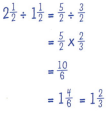

$$2\frac{1}{2} \div 1\frac{1}{2} = \frac{5}{2} \div \frac{3}{2}$$
$$= \frac{5}{2} \times \frac{2}{3}$$
$$= \frac{10}{6}$$
$$= 1\frac{4}{6} = 1\frac{2}{3}$$

To divide, find the reciprocal of the divisor, then multiply.

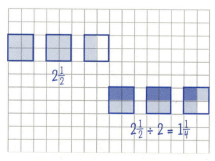

Show $2\frac{1}{2}$. Divide the models into 2 equal parts. Count the fourths: $2\frac{1}{2} \div 2 = \frac{5}{4}$ or $1\frac{1}{4}$.

Assess

How can you use a number line to divide $4\frac{1}{2}$ by $1\frac{1}{2}$? (Sample answer: Count how many times $1\frac{1}{2}$ appears in $4\frac{1}{2}$: 3 times. $4\frac{1}{2} \div 1\frac{1}{2} = 3$)

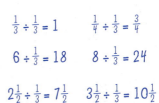

APPLY THE CONCEPT
Problem-Solving Strategy: Look for a Pattern

Present the Problem Display Visual 56: Unit Fraction Division Patterns. Read the problem set-up and instructions:

- *Work with a partner. Complete the division problems to look for a pattern. Describe the pattern in words.*
- *How do you think the pattern might change if you divide the same dividends by $\frac{1}{3}$?*

Discuss the Solution After students have had time to solve the problem, help the class discuss their solutions.

- *What are the missing quotients?* ($\frac{1}{2}$, 16, 7) *Compare each dividend to the quotient. How does the quotient compare to the dividend?* (The quotient is double the dividend.) *Why?* (Dividing by $\frac{1}{2}$ has the same result as multiplying by 2.)
- Discuss how students extended the pattern to dividing by $\frac{1}{3}$ and why. (Dividing by $\frac{1}{3}$ has the same result as multiplying by 3, so the quotient will triple the dividend.)

$\frac{1}{3} \div \frac{1}{3} = 1 \qquad \frac{1}{4} \div \frac{1}{3} = \frac{3}{4}$

$6 \div \frac{1}{3} = 18 \qquad 8 \div \frac{1}{3} = 24$

$2\frac{1}{2} \div \frac{1}{3} = 7\frac{1}{2} \qquad 3\frac{1}{2} \div \frac{1}{3} = 10\frac{1}{2}$

Complete the division to discover what happens to the pattern when you divide by $\frac{1}{3}$.

REFLECT

Explain how to find the reciprocal of a mixed number. Discuss writing the mixed number as a fraction and then interchanging the numerator and denominator to write the reciprocal. Work examples to show steps in the explanation.

Vocabulary

Discuss why the reciprocal of a fraction with 1 in the numerator is always a whole number. Have students add any new information or examples to the definitions in their personal glossaries.

Journal Prompt

Tell how to find the reciprocal of $4\frac{2}{3}$. (Sample answer: Write $4\frac{2}{3}$ as a fraction, $\frac{14}{3}$. Reverse the order of numerator and denominator. The reciprocal is $\frac{3}{14}$.)

Assess

How can you use mental math to divide by a fraction with 1 in the numerator? (Multiply the dividend by the denominator of the unit fraction.)

Skill Builder Lesson 29 Plan

Use a Calculator Appropriately

TODAY'S SKILLS
- Choose a computation method.
- Decide when to use a calculator to compute.

MATERIALS
- Visual 57: Choose a Method
- Visual 58: Calculator Choices
- self-stick notes
- Vocabulary Cards: **calculator, computation method, mental math, paper and pencil**

SET UP
Build the Skill
Display Visual 57: Choose a Method.

Apply the Skill
Display Visual 58: Calculator Choices.

Problem One
Each dinner at the zoo banquet costs $8.35. Service charge is $2.00 each. How much will dinner for 245 patrons cost the zoo?

Problem Two
Souvenir pens come 300 to a box. The zoo orders 80 boxes. How many pens does the zoo order?

Problem Three
There are 228 students. A bus will hold 42 students. How many students are on the last bus?

What is the cost of buying a dozen CDs at $12.95 each if the tax on the total purchase is $0.78?

David's total: $163.20
Olivia's total: $156.18

WORD WALL

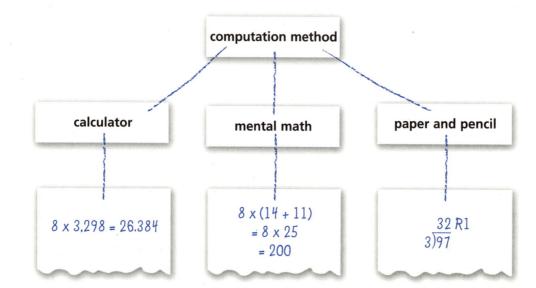

124   iSucceed MATH

PROFESSIONAL DEVELOPMENT

Math Background This lesson focuses on choosing a method of computation for problem solving. If your curriculum includes the use of calculators, use this lesson. If it does not, you may choose not to use the lesson. The lesson does not require the use of calculators; however, if it is possible to have calculators available, students will benefit from the practice. If calculators are not available to students, the actual computation may be skipped after the method is decided upon.

Use of Calculators When a curriculum includes the use of calculators, the calculators are usually used when the computation concept is subsidiary to the math skill. For example, when learning about the area of a circle or the volume of a solid, a calculator may be allowed to simplify the computation process. Keep in mind, however, that calculators are usually not allowed on the computation section of any standardized tests.

Calculator Operations Not all calculators are the same. Some calculators have a constant key, and others do not. Some follow the order of operations; others do not. The best way to find out what a calculator does is to check the directions in the manual.

Check your calculator for order of operations with this expression: $8 + 4 \div 2$. If the display shows 10, the calculator has order of operations. If it shows 6, it does not.

Greater Numbers on a Calculator Display An answer will sometimes be greater (or less) than the calculator display will hold. The calculator may truncate the answer or it may round the answer. It may also use exponents to show very large or very small numbers. Check the calculator instruction book to find out.

Calculator Note Using a calculator often seems to help students validate their answers, even when they can easily compute without the calculator. Encourage students not to rely on calculators just because they are available and seem to make the computation easier.

Courseware Connections

A calculator button in each courseware lesson allows students to use a calculator when appropriate.

Lesson 29 Teach

BUILD THE SKILL

Display Visual 57: Choose a Method. Your goal in this discussion is to help students choose the best computation method for a problem.

- *Sometimes, a calculator is the easiest method to use for computation. Other times, mental math or paper and pencil may be better methods.*
- *Choose a method for Problem 1.* Read the problem and discuss why using a calculator is a good method to use. (The multiplication is difficult.) If calculators are available, have students find the total. ($2,535.75)
- *When using a calculator, you should always estimate the answer since it is possible to make errors when pressing number, operation, or other keys.* Have students estimate to check that the total is reasonable. (Sample estimate: $10 × 200 = $2,000)
- Read Problem 2. *What is a good method for solving this problem? Why?* (mental math; The numbers are easy to multiply. 300 × 80 = 24,000) Point out that, for this problem, mental math is quicker than using a calculator.

Connect to Vocabulary Post on the Word Wall and discuss: **calculator**, **computation method**, **mental math**, and **paper and pencil**.

EXPLORE THE SKILL

- Read Problem 3. *Try to fill the buses. What is a good method to use to solve this problem? Why?* (paper and pencil, so you can easily find the remainder, which tells the number of students on the last bus.) Work out the division on the chalkboard. (5 R18; 18 students are on the last bus.)
- Point out that a calculator will show the remainder as a decimal. In this case, 5.428571429. . . . Elicit that the quotient displayed in this form does not make sense for solving the problem.
- *The calculator could be used to check the answer to Problem 3.* (Multiply the divisor by the quotient. Then add in the remainder. The result on the calculator should be 228.)

Wrap Up Have students suggest problems that are appropriate for each computation method and explain their choices.

Reteach Provide students with a list of examples using different operations. Discuss the best method for evaluating the following expressions: 260 + 140; 379 + 5,968; 2,050 − 643; 430 − 99; 5,600 ÷ 70; and 2,128 ÷ 38.

Assess

Julia has $815 in her bank account. She withdrew $278.50. What method would you use to find the balance in the account? Explain. (Sample answer: Use a calculator since the numbers are not easy to subtract with mental math.)

APPLY THE SKILL

Problem-Solving Skill: Is the Answer Reasonable?

Present the Problem Display Visual 58: Calculator Choices. Read the problem set-up and instructions:

- *CDs cost $12.95 each. What is the total cost of 12 CDs if the total tax is $0.78?*
- *David and Olivia each solved the same problem using a calculator. Who is correct? How do you know?*
- *Work with a partner to decide whose answer is reasonable. Then identify an error the other student may have made.*

Discuss the Solution After students have had time to solve the problem, help the class discuss their solutions.

- *Who is correct? How do you know?* (Olivia is correct. Sample answer: Using paper and pencil to check the answer shows that the correct amount is $156.18.)
- *How did you decide what the other student may have done wrong?* (Sample explanation: The total is not that far off from the actual amount. David may have entered the decimal point in the wrong place when he added the tax to the total cost.)

REFLECT

- *Is a calculator always the best way to perform a calculation when solving a problem? Explain.* (Sample answer: No, use a calculator when the numbers are difficult to compute with. Mental math is easier with some numbers, and paper and pencil is best when you must interpret the remainder to solve a division problem.)
- *When you do use a calculator for a computation, what should you always do after you have the answer? Why?* (You should always look back and use an estimate to make sure that the answer is reasonable. Entering a wrong number or decimal point can be a big mistake.)

Vocabulary

Direct students' attention to the Word Wall. Discuss, then ask students to add definitions and examples to their personal glossaries.

Journal Prompt

Describe situations in which each of the following is the best method to use to solve a problem: calculator, mental math, and paper and pencil. (Answers should include using a calculator when the numbers are difficult to compute, mental math for easier numbers such as tens, and paper and pencil for some division problems.)

Assess

Jake adds 596.08 + 78.39 on a calculator. The calculator display reads 1379.98. Does the answer make sense? Explain. (No, an estimate of the total is about 600. He probably pressed the decimal point key in the wrong place.)

UNIT 3

Positive and Negative Numbers

Lessons

30 Integers (Grade 5)* 130

31 Add Integers (Grade 5) 134

32 Subtract Integers (Grade 5) 138

33 Multiply Integers (Grade 6) 142

34 Divide Integers (Grade 6) 146

35 Rational Numbers (Grade 7) 150

36 Compare and Order Rational Numbers (Grade 7) 154

37 Add and Subtract Rational Numbers (Grade 7) 158

38 Multiply and Divide Rational Numbers (Grade 7) 162

*Indicates grade level at which topic is typically introduced; your curriculum may differ.

MATERIALS

- Volume II Unit 3 Lesson Visuals 59–76
- Copymasters M2: Number Lines
- adding machine tape
- small self-stick notes
- yarn and pushpins
- counters

VOCABULARY CARDS

addend, decimal number, difference, divide, factor, fraction, integers, mixed number, negative number, opposites, positive number, product, quotient, rational number, subtraction, sum, whole number, zero

Introduction

This unit applies the place-value and number skills concepts from units 1 and 2 to numbers less than one. It also covers rational numbers: numbers, including decimal numbers, fractions, and negative numbers and showing how to work in mixed-format settings.

One very important theme of this unit is that patterns established with positive numbers apply as well to negative numbers.

128   iSucceed MATH

Common Errors

Example: Find the difference between 75 and −49.

Error: The student writes 26.

Intervention: This student does not have a mental image of 'difference' as 'distance between on the number line in a particular direction.' Start simple and work your way up to the original problem:

- To find 7 − 4, find 4 on the number line. Find 7 on the same number line. To get from 4 to 7, you must move right (in the positive direction). Count the number of units between 4 and 7. There are 3 units in the positive direction between 4 and 7, so 7 − 4 = 3.

- To find 7 − (−4), find −4 on the number line. Find 7 on the same number line. To get from −4 to 7, you must move right (in the positive direction). Count the number of units between −4 and 7. There are 11 units in the positive direction between −4 and 7, so 7 − (−4) = 11.

- To find 75 − 49, think about 49 and 75 on a number line. The distance between these numbers is 26 units, the direction is positive, so 75 − 49 = 26.

- To find 75 − (−49), find −49 and 75 on the number line. The distance between these numbers must be greater than 26 units. From −49 to 0 is 49 units, then from 0 to 75 is another 75 units. The difference between 75 and −49 is the same as the sum of 75 and 49!

Rational numbers are numbers that can be written in fraction form. Whole numbers, integers, fractions, and decimal numbers are all rational. Equivalence is a key concept for comparing or computing with rational numbers.

Example: Order these numbers from least to greatest: 6, 2.5, −7, $4\frac{1}{3}$.

Error: The student writes $4\frac{1}{3}$, 6, −7, 2.5.

Intervention: This student ignored indicators that some of these numbers are not positive whole numbers. Help the student to first decide whether fractions or decimal numbers are easier to work with. Since $\frac{1}{3}$ is a repeating decimal number, fractions may be a good choice in this case. Now the list reads: 6, $2\frac{1}{2}$, −7, $4\frac{1}{3}$. Next, ask the student to identify any numbers that are less than zero. The only number in that category is −7, so it is the least number in the list. Last, ask the student to use the whole-number parts of the remaining numbers to order them: −7, $2\frac{1}{2}$, $4\frac{1}{3}$, 6.

Concept Builder — Lesson 30 Plan

Integers

TODAY'S CONCEPTS
- Identify and represent integers on a number line.
- Understand integers and their opposites.

MATERIALS
- Visual 59: Thermometer and Vertical Number Line
- Visual 60: Positive or Negative?
- Vocabulary Cards: **integers, negative number, opposites, positive number, zero**

SET UP
Build the Concept
Display Visual 59: Thermometer and Vertical Number Line.

Apply the Concept
Display Visual 60: Positive or Negative?

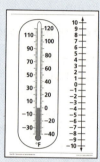

EL WORD WALL

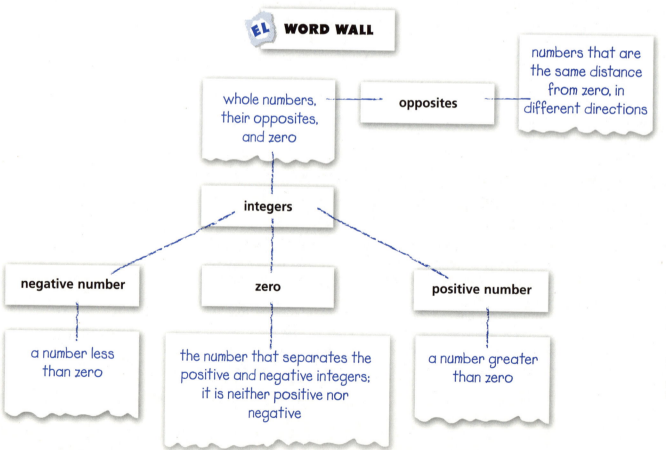

- **integers**: whole numbers, their opposites, and zero
- **opposites**: numbers that are the same distance from zero, in different directions
- **negative number**: a number less than zero
- **zero**: the number that separates the positive and negative integers; it is neither positive nor negative
- **positive number**: a number greater than zero

PROFESSIONAL DEVELOPMENT

Math Background Whole numbers are the counting numbers 1, 2, 3, and so on. Integers are all of the whole numbers, their opposites, and zero. The set of integers does not include fractions or decimals. They are included with integers in the set of rational numbers. The negative numbers are denoted with a negative sign that precedes the number. The positive numbers may be written with a plus symbol, but it is not necessary. The easiest way to think of the sign (+ or −) on any number is as a direction sign. The positive numbers lie to the right of (or above) zero. The negative numbers lie to the left of (or below) zero.

Zero and Opposites Zero separates the positive and negative numbers. Zero is neither positive nor negative, and it is its own opposite. Opposites lie the same distance from zero in opposite directions.

Absolute Value In later grades, students will apply the term absolute value to their understanding of rational numbers and their opposites. The distance of a number from zero on the number line is called the absolute value of the number. Because it is a distance, the absolute value is always positive. Two vertical lines denote the absolute value.

Write: $|-3| = 3$; $|3| = 3$

Say: *The absolute value of negative three is three; the absolute value of three is three.*

Courseware Connections

Module: Positive and Negative Numbers

Graphing Integers

Relating Integers and Word Expressions

Comparing and Ordering Integers

Number Opposites

GET REAL: Daily Temperatures

Lesson 30 Teach

BUILD THE CONCEPT

Display Visual 59: Thermometer and Vertical Number Line. Your goal in this discussion is to help students understand how to identify and represent integers and their opposites.

- *Sometimes, we need numbers that are less than zero. How does the thermometer show temperatures below zero?* (The numbers below zero have minus signs.) *Why do we need the minus signs?* (to distinguish them from positive numbers) Read several positive and negative temperatures. Locate each temperature as you read it.

- *The thermometer is a vertical number line. You begin counting down from zero the same way you count up from zero. The positive numbers on this thermometer are like the counting numbers. They are called positive integers. Can you think of a positive number that is not a positive integer?* (any positive decimal number or fraction, like $1\frac{1}{2}$, 2.7, or $\frac{7}{9}$)

- *The negative numbers you see are called negative integers. The negative and positive integers, plus zero, are all of the integers.*

Connect to Vocabulary Help students to talk about and use integers in sentences.

- Add **integers**, **positive number**, **negative number**, and **zero** to the Word Wall.

EXPLORE THE CONCEPT

- This number line shows integers. *You must write the minus sign when you write a negative integer. You do not need to write a plus sign with a positive integer.*

- Have students locate 1 and −1 on the number line. *Both 1 and −1 are 1 unit away from zero on the number line. They are called opposites. Opposites have different signs but are the same distance from zero. Can someone give me another set of opposite integers from this number line?*

- Add **opposites** to the Word Wall.

- **EL** Point out that "opposite" has a common definition that is similar to its definition in mathematics. Consider example pairs such as hot and cold, wet and dry, and so on.

Wrap Up Have students find the opposites of several integers, such as 4 (−4), 8 (−8), −3 (3), and −7 (7). Show that the numbers are opposites by folding the number line at zero. An integer and its opposite are the same distance from zero.

Reteach Use the adding machine tape from your kit or Copymaster M2 to make an integers number line. You can show the same number line in vertical and horizontal forms by changing its orientation. Have students locate points, read points you select, and find opposite pairs using the number line.

Assess

On a horizontal number line, where do the negative integers lie? The positive integers? Use words and pictures to show your answer. (The negative integers lie to the left of zero, and the positive integers lie to the right of zero.)

132   iSucceed MATH: Integers

APPLY THE CONCEPT

Problem-Solving Skill: Use Logical Reasoning

Present the Problem Display Visual 60: Positive or Negative? Direct students' attention to the list of situations.

- *Read each situation. Would a positive integer or a negative integer best describe the situation?*
- *Work with a partner to explain your answers.*

Discuss the Solution After students have had time to solve the problem, help them discuss their solutions.

- *Which situations can you describe by using a positive integer? Why?* (receiving a gift of money, because the amount of money you have increases; very hot temperature, because hot temperatures are above zero; hiking to the top of a mountain, because you are going higher than sea level, which generally corresponds to zero)
- *Which situations can you describe by using a negative integer? Why?* (owing money, because the amount of money that is yours is less than zero if you must borrow the money; temperature in Antarctica in winter; depth of a submarine, because the submarine is below sea level, which corresponds to zero)

REFLECT

Encourage students to suggest other contrasting situations that can be described by positive or negative integers.

Vocabulary

Direct students' attention to the Word Wall. Discuss how to define the terms before asking students to record their definitions in their personal glossaries along with diagrams and/or examples.

Journal Prompt

Define what it means for numbers to be opposites. Include an example. (Answers should include an understanding that opposites are located the same distance but in different directions from 0 on the number line.)

Assess

What are two examples of positive integers? Negative integers? Opposites? (Sample answers: 1 and 2; −1 and −2; 1 and −1, 2 and −2)

Concept Builder **Lesson 31 Plan**

Add Integers

TODAY'S CONCEPT
- Model adding integers on a number line.

MATERIALS
- Visual 61: Integer Number Line 1
- Visual 62: Badwater Basin
- Copymaster M2: Number Lines
- yarn and push pins
- small self-stick notes
- Vocabulary Cards: **addend**, **integers**, **sum**

SET UP
Build the Concept
- Display Visual 61: Integer Number Line 1.
- Cut pieces of yarn 3 and 5 units long, as measured on Visual 61.

Apply the Concept
Display Visual 62: Badwater Basin.

Lowest Point in North America
Badwater Basin
Death Valley National Park
Elevation: −282 feet

EL WORD WALL

addend

sum

integers

134 iSucceed MATH

PROFESSIONAL DEVELOPMENT

Math Background In this lesson, students will not be introduced to a formal algorithm for adding integers. They will work with adding integers only on a number line. For this reason, have multiple copies of Copymaster M2: Number Lines available for students to use.

Using Counters To model adding integers with counters, use two colors. One color stands for positive; the other color stands for negative. Use the colors to model each addend. When the counters match up, one negative and one positive, they form a zero pair. The remaining counters will be one color. Count them, and use their sign, to find the sum. See *Math at Hand* 201–204.

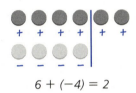

$6 + (-4) = 2$

Adding Integers The following rules explain how to add integers without a number line or counters.

- When the signs are the same, add the numbers. The sign of the sum is the same sign as the sign of the addends.
- If the signs are different, subtract absolute values of the addends (greatest − least). The sign of the sum is the sign of the addend with the greater absolute value.

Integer Word Problems Take special care with how you phrase word problems if you make them up for students. If you want to model a computation situation, be sure that the language you use does not imply a positive answer when what you want is a negative answer. For example: *The home team lost 2 yards and then lost 2 more yards; how many yards did the team lose?* This problem does not model $-2 + (-2) = -4$. The question calls for a positive answer. If the team loses a negative number of yards, you have created a double negative.

Courseware Connections

Module: Positive and Negative Numbers

Adding Positive and Negative Integers

Adding Negative Integers to Negative Integers

Lesson 31 Teach

BUILD THE CONCEPT

Display Visual 61: Integer Number Line 1. Your goal is to help students to model adding integers.

- Distribute copies of Copymaster M2: Number Lines. Have students work on their number lines as you model the sums.
- *One way to think about adding is with a number line. Use the number line to add 3 + 5. Tell me what to do.* Use yarn to show starting at 0 and ending at 3. Label the 3 with a self-stick note.
- Use your second piece of yarn to show starting at 3 and moving 5 units right to end at 8. Label the action (+ 5) and the sum (8).
- *Why did we move to the right on the number line to find the sum?* At this point, students may believe that you always move to the right to add. Express skepticism, but move on.

Connect to Vocabulary Post on the Word Wall and discuss: **addend**, **integers**, and **sum**.

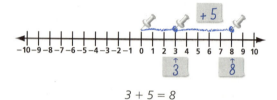

$3 + 5 = 8$

EXPLORE THE CONCEPT

- *Now use the number line to add −3 + (−5). What will I do first?* Demonstrate moving 3 units to the left of 0 to show the first addend.
- *If I were adding 5, which way would I go from here?* (right) *Which way do you think I should go to add −5?* (left: move 5 units of −1 each) *I end at −8. What is −3 + (−5)?* (−8) *Why did we move to the left on the number line to find the sum?* (Negative 5 is the opposite of 5, so you go in the opposite direction to add.)
- Use the same technique to demonstrate how to add 3 + (−5) *Why do we move to the left?* (The negative sign tells you to move left to add.) *What is 3 + (−5)?* (−2)
- Repeat to find the sum of −3 + 5. (2)

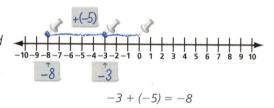

$-3 + (-5) = -8$

Wrap Up Discuss how the four sums are similar and how they are different. Have students use their number lines to find another set of integer sums. (2 + 4 = 6; −2 + (−4) = −6; 2 + (−4) = −2; −2 + 4 = 2)

Reteach Model integer addition with counters. Explain which color represents positive integers and which represents negative integers. Make sure students understand how zero-sum pairs are formed.

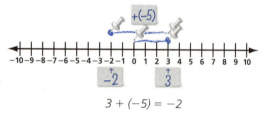

$3 + (-5) = -2$

A zero sum pair has one positive and one negative counter.

Use −8, −2, 2, and 8 to model four integer-addition examples on number lines. (8 + 2 = 10; 8 + (−2) = 6; −8 + (−2) = −10; −8 + 2 = −6)

APPLY THE CONCEPT
Problem-Solving Strategy: Write an Equation

Present the Problem Display Visual 62: Badwater Basin. Provide students with Copymaster M2: Number Lines, or counters. Read the problem set-up and instructions:

- *The Lang family visited Death Valley National Park. The family hiked in Badwater Basin the first day. The next day, the family hiked to an elevation 100 feet higher than in Badwater Basin.*
- *Work with a partner to find their elevation at the end of the hike.*

Discuss the Solution After students have had time to solve the problem, help them discuss their solutions.

- *Explain how you can use a number line to represent the problem situation.* (One way: Use intervals of 100 to label a number line from -300 to 100. Put a point between -300 and -200 to show -282. Draw an arrow to the right to show adding 100. The arrow ends at -182.) Discuss different ways to use number lines to represent the problem.
- *What equation represents the problem? Explain.* ($-282 + 100 = -182$; 100 feet higher means the new elevation is 100 feet greater than the starting elevation. The solution from the number line is -182.)
- *What was their elevation at the end of their hike?* (-182 ft)

REFLECT
How is adding integers like adding whole numbers? How is it different? (Adding positive integers is the same as adding whole numbers. Adding negative integers is different. The negative sign means move in the opposite direction to add.)

Vocabulary
Review the use of today's vocabulary by referring to the Word Wall. Ask students to add examples to the definitions and diagrams in their personal glossaries.

Journal Prompt

What is the sum of an integer and its opposite? How do you know? (Zero. Sample explanation: To find the sum, move the direction and number of units indicated by the first integer. To add the opposite, move the same number of units in the opposite direction. You return to zero. For example, $-1 + 1 = 0$.)

Assess

Write a story that goes with $-4 + 2$. Then find the sum. (Check students' work; -2.)

Concept Builder — Lesson 32 Plan

Subtract Integers

TODAY'S CONCEPT
- Model subtracting integers on a number line.

MATERIALS
- Visual 63: Integer Number Line 2
- Visual 64: Temperature Report
- Copymaster M2: Number Lines
- yarn and pushpins
- Vocabulary Cards: **difference**, **integers**, **opposites**, **subtraction**

SET UP
Build the Concept
- Display Visual 63: Integer Number Line 2.
- Cut pieces of yarn 7 units and 3 units long as measured on the Visual. Knot the ends.

Apply the Concept
Display Visual 64: Temperature Report.

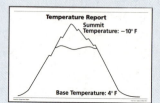

WORD WALL

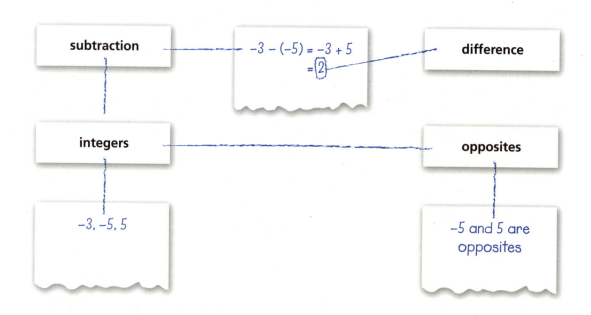

subtraction — $-3 - (-5) = -3 + 5 = 2$ — difference

integers — opposites

$-3, -5, 5$

-5 and 5 are opposites

138   iSucceed MATH

PROFESSIONAL DEVELOPMENT

Math Background The easiest way to understand integer subtraction is to think of subtracting as adding the opposite. Because addition and subtraction are inverse operations, subtracting a number has the same result as adding its opposite. This idea cannot be introduced with whole-number addition and subtraction because you need the opposites of the whole numbers, which are the negative integers.

Examples:
$$6 - 4 \rightarrow 6 + (-4) = 2$$
$$-6 - 4 \rightarrow -6 + (-4) = -10$$
$$-6 - (-4) \rightarrow -6 + 4 = -2$$
$$6 - (-4) \rightarrow 6 + 4 = 10$$

Courseware Connections

Module: Positive and Negative Numbers
- Subtracting Positive Integers
- Subtracting Negative Integers
- GET REAL: Temperatures Around the World

EL Notation In this program, when an operation sign is followed immediately by a negative number, we place the negative number in parentheses. This technique should help students to distinguish between the two uses of + and −.

Using Counters If you decide to use counters to model integer subtraction, continue to have students subtract by adding the opposite. They can rewrite the subtraction as addition and then use counters the same way they did for adding integers.

Example:
$-6 - (-4) = -6 + 4$

Use 6 negative counters. | Use 4 positive counters. | There are 4 zero pairs.

1. Show counters for the first addend.
2. Add counters for the second addend.
3. Look for zero pairs of counters. The remaining counters give the sum. $-6 - (-4) = 2$

Integer Word Problems Continue to be very careful about phrasing word problems if you make them up for students.

Lesson 32 Teach

BUILD THE CONCEPT

Display Visual 63: Integer Number Line 2. Your goal in this discussion is to help students understand how to model subtracting integers.

- *How are addition and subtraction related?* (They are opposite operations.)
- Begin by subtracting positive numbers. Write $7 - 3$ on the board. *How do we show this on the number line?* Use self-stick notes and yarn to model the subtraction. *Who can show me an addition problem with the same digits and the same result?* ($7 + (-3)$) *Yes; you can add opposites to subtract.*
- Distribute copies of Copymaster M2: Number Lines. Have students work on their own number lines as you model on the Visual.
- *Let's find $-7 - 3$. What is the opposite of 3?* (-3) *How can we rewrite the subtraction as addition?* $-7 + (-3)$ Review how to find this sum on the number line. (-10)

$7 - 3 = 7 + (-3) = 4$

Connect to Vocabulary Post on the Word Wall and discuss: **subtraction**, **integers**, **opposites**, and **difference**.

EXPLORE THE CONCEPT

- Now demonstrate how to subtract negative numbers. Emphasize that you still add the opposite to subtract.
- Use the yarn on the number line to demonstrate $7 - (-3)$. *If subtracting a positive number is the opposite of adding, then subtracting a negative number must be the opposite of subtracting. What's that?* (adding) Write $7 - (-3) = 7 + 3 = 10$
- Finally, consider $-7 - (-3)$. *What is the opposite of -3?* (3) *How can we rewrite the subtraction as adding the opposite?* ($-7 + 3$) Review how to find this sum on the number line. (-4)

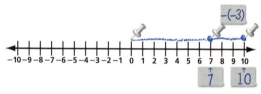

$7 - (-3) = 7 + 3 = 10$

Wrap Up Provide students with additional examples, such as $1 - (-4) = 5$, $-2 - (-1) = -1$, and $-8 - 1 = -9$. Make sure students change the subtraction to adding the opposite. Then, they can find the sums by using their number lines.

Reteach Have students use counters to model integer addition after they rewrite the subtraction as adding the opposite.

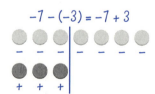

There are 3 zero-sum pairs. Four negative counters are left. $-7 - (-3) = -4$

Compare finding the difference of $-5 - 4$ to finding the difference of $-5 - (-4)$. ($-5 - 4 = -5 + (-4) = -9$ while $-5 - (-4) = -5 + 4 = -1$)

140   iSucceed MATH: Subtract Integers

APPLY THE CONCEPT

Problem-Solving Strategies: Solve in More Than One Way, (Write an Equation, Draw a Diagram)

Present the Problem Display Visual 64: Temperature Report. Provide students with Copymaster M2: Integer Number Lines. Read the problem set-up and instructions:

- *Weather stations at the base and at the summit of the mountain reported the temperatures at 6 A.M.*
- *Work with a partner to find the difference in the temperature from the base to the summit.*
- *Write an equation. If you need to, use a number line to help you solve the problem.*

Discuss the Solution After students have had time to solve the problem, help the class discuss their solutions.

- *What was your first step in solving the problem?* (Sample answer: Difference means subtraction, so I wrote a subtraction expression to show the temperature difference from the base to the summit: $4 - (-10)$.) *How did you find the value of your expression?* (Sample answer: I rewrote the subtraction by adding the opposite: $4 - (-10) = 4 + 10$. Since $4 + 10 = 14$, the difference in the temperature was 14°F.)
- Discuss other methods students may have used to solve the problem. For example, some students may plot points for both temperatures on the number line and count the number of units between to find the difference.

REFLECT

What is the difference of an integer and its opposite? How do you know? (Twice the integer, because you are adding the number to itself when you add the opposite of the opposite.)

Vocabulary

Encourage students to add diagrams and examples to their personal glossaries.

Journal Prompt

Do the rules for subtracting integers work for whole-number subtraction? (Yes, the same rules work as long as you can write the opposite.)

Assess

Write a story that goes with $-2 - (-3)$. Then, find the difference. (Check students' work; 1.)

Concept Builder — Lesson 33 Plan

Multiply Integers

TODAY'S CONCEPTS
- Use number lines to model multiplying integers.
- Understand patterns of integer multiplication.
- Multiply integers, using an algorithm.

MATERIALS
- Visual 65: Multiply Integers on Number Lines
- Visual 66: Integer Puzzles
- Vocabulary Cards: **factor**, **integers**, **product**

SET UP
Build the Concept
Display Visual 65: Multiply Integers on Number Lines.

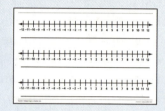

Apply the Concept
Display Visual 66: Integer Puzzles.

EL WORD WALL

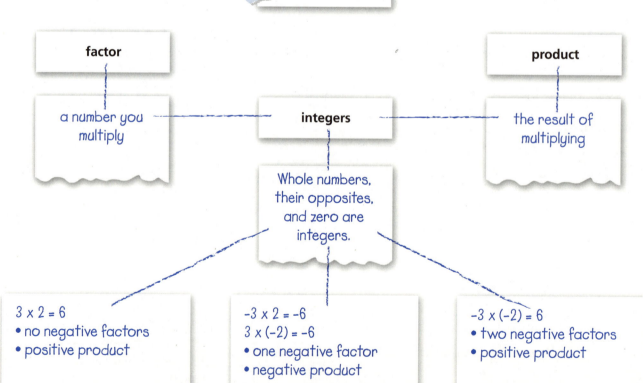

PROFESSIONAL DEVELOPMENT

Math Background When you add integers, if the signs on the addends are the same, then the sum has that sign. (6 + 2 = 8, and −6 + (−2) = −8). Addends with different signs can have either positive or negative sums. (6 + (−2) = 4, but −6 + 2 = −4). For multiplication, you can always tell the sign of the product before multiplying. In both multiplication and division, negatives always come in pairs. Both operations involve three numbers. If any one of them is negative, then one more of them must also be negative.

Examples:

2 positive factors → positive product

2 negative factors → positive product

1 positive and 1 negative factor → negative product

Mnemonic Encourage students to use a mnemonic to remember the sign of a product along the lines of: *I like <u>like</u>, so I'm positive. I don't like <u>unlike</u>, so I'm negative.* Challenge students to invent their own mnemonics.

Beyond the Number Line The number line works well to model integer multiplication, as long as at least one of the two factors is positive: −4 × 3 can be modeled as three groups of −4. However, this model breaks down when both factors are negative. To conceptualize the multiplication of two negatives, it is best to forego the number line and rely on the pattern started with the number line: two negative factors have a positive product because they are both alike.

Courseware Connections

Module: Positive and Negative Numbers

Multiplying Integers

Lesson 33 Teach

BUILD THE CONCEPT

Display Visual 65: Multiplying Integers on Number Lines. Your goal in this discussion is to help students understand how to multiply integers.

- You are paid $3 per hour for 4 hours of chores. Use an integer to describe the change in the amount of money you have. Model 4×3 on first number line. Write $4 \times 3 = 12$.

- Each day for 4 days, you take $3 from your box of coins. Use an integer to describe the change in the amount of money in the box. Model $4 \times (-3)$ on the second number line. Write $4 \times (-3) = -12$.

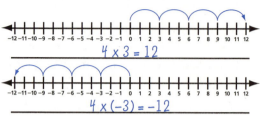

It is easy to model multiplying by a positive number on a number line.

Connect to Vocabulary Post on the Word Wall and discuss: **factor**, **integers**, and **product**.

EXPLORE THE CONCEPT

- Copy the table shown. *What product do I find when I multiply a positive by a positive?* (positive) *A positive by a negative?* (negative)

- Discuss what happens when you multiply a negative by a negative. Point out that multiplying by a negative gives the opposite product as multiplying by a positive.

  Example:
  Since $4 \times 2 = 8$, then $4 \times (-2) = -8$, or the opposite of 8. It stands to reason that $-4 \times (-2) = 8$, or the opposite of -8.

- Together with students, fill in the table.

Multiply	+	−
+	+	−
−	−	+

Record the signs of products of integers here.

Wrap Up *Write rules for multiplying integers of the same and different signs.* (Rules should convey that like signs result in positive products; unlike signs result in negative products.)

Reteach Use the idea that multiplying by a positive number keeps the same sign that you began with, and multiplying by a negative number gives a sign different from what you began with. Use examples such as -4×3 has a negative product, the <u>same</u> sign that you began with; $4 \times (-3)$ has a negative product, <u>different</u> from the sign that you began with. It follows that $-4 \times (-3)$ has a positive product, <u>different</u> from the sign that you began with.

Which product is greater, $8 \times (-7)$ or $-6 \times (-5)$? Explain why you can tell it is greater without multiplying. (The first product is negative, so it is less than the second product, which is positive because it is the result of multiplying two negative factors.)

APPLY THE CONCEPT

Problem-Solving Strategy: Solve Multi-Step Problems

Problem-Solving Skill: Use Logical Reasoning

Present the Problem Display Visual 66: Integer Puzzles. Read each puzzle aloud. Have students work with partners.

- Puzzle 1: A *is an unknown integer (not zero). The product of* $5 \times A$ *is less than* A. *Is* A *a positive or a negative integer?*
- Puzzle 2: B *is an unknown integer (not zero). The product of* $-5 \times B$ *is greater than* B. *Is* B *a positive or a negative integer?*

Discuss the Solution After they have had time to solve the problem, have students discuss their solutions.

- *How did you decide whether* A *was positive or negative?* (Sample answer: I first tried positive numbers for A. The product of $5 \times A$ was always greater than A for positive values of A. Then I tried negative values for A. The product of $5 \times A$ was now less than A, so I knew my answer made sense. I tried other negative values; all seemed to work, so I concluded that my answer was correct.)
- *How did you decide whether* B *was positive or negative?* (Sample answer: I first tried positive numbers for B. The product of $-5 \times B$ was always less than B for positive values of B. Then I tried negative values for B. The product of $-5 \times B$ was now greater than B, so I knew my answer made sense. After testing other negative values, I concluded that my answer was correct.)
- *What are the answers?* (A is negative; B is negative.)

REFLECT

Work with students to write their own integer puzzles.

Vocabulary

- Direct students' attention to the Word Wall. Discuss how the Word Wall shows all four types of integer multiplication and the products that result from each.
- Remind students that the term "integer" refers to the set of numbers that includes all positives and negatives (and zero) but no fractional or decimal numbers. Differentiate integer from whole number by pointing out that the whole numbers do not include any negative numbers.
- Ask students to add new definitions and/or examples to their personal glossaries.

Journal Prompt

Discuss whether the following statement is true: A number multiplied by itself is always positive. (Answers should recognize that the statement is true because if the number is positive, then a positive multiplied by itself is positive. If the number is negative, then a negative multiplied by itself also results in a positive. Either way, the square of a number is positive.)

Assess

What is the product of: $-4 \times (-4) \times (-4)$?

(-64)

Concept Builder — Lesson 34 Plan

Divide Integers

TODAY'S CONCEPTS
- Use number lines to model dividing integers.
- Understand patterns of integer division.
- Divide integers using an algorithm.

MATERIALS
- Visual 67: Division Clouds
- Visual 68: Division Riddles
- small self-stick notes cut in half
- Vocabulary Cards: **integers**, **quotient**

SET UP

Build the Concept
Display Visual 67: Division Clouds.

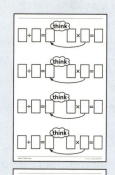

Apply the Concept
Display Visual 68: Division Riddles.

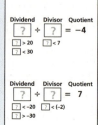

EL WORD WALL

integers — Whole numbers, their opposites, and zero are integers.

quotient — the result of division
dividend ÷ divisor = quotient

- 6 ÷ 2 = 3
  - positive dividend
  - positive divisor
  - positive quotient

- 6 ÷ (−2) = −3
  - positive dividend
  - negative divisor
  - negative quotient

- −6 ÷ (−2) = 3
  - negative dividend
  - negative divisor
  - positive quotient

- −6 ÷ 2 = −3
  - negative dividend
  - positive divisor
  - negative quotient

PROFESSIONAL DEVELOPMENT

Math Background Just as like and unlike signs respectively yield positive and negative products in multiplication, the same pattern holds true in division for quotients.

Inverse Operation Multiplication and division are inverse operations.

Example:
$$-24 \div 6 = -4$$
$$-24 \div (-4) = 6$$
inverses of $-4 \times 6 = -24$

It may be useful to make a habit of restating division as multiplication to show how the distribution of positive and negative numbers among factors and product relates to the distribution of positive and negative numbers among quotient, divisor, and dividend.

Division and Number Lines Number lines are useful for modeling division problems as long as the divisor is not negative. The number line works well for modeling an equation such as $-18 \div 3$ because dividing -18 into 3 equal-sized groups makes sense. However, using a number line for dividing by a negative number is problematic because, for example, it does not make sense to divide 18 into "negative-three" groups. To conceptualize the division of two negatives, it is best to forego the number line and rely strictly on patterns: *like signs result in a positive quotient, unlike signs result in a negative quotient.*

Courseware Connections

Module: Positive and Negative Numbers
Dividing Integers

Lesson 34 Teach

BUILD THE CONCEPT

Display Visual 67: Division Clouds. Your goal in this discussion is to help students understand how to divide integers.

- *Division of integers works much like multiplication of integers. Think about fact families to see how that works.*
- *Think: 5 times what number equals 15?* (3) Use self-stick notes to fill in the first diagram.
- *To divide −15 by 5, think: 5 times what number equals −15?* Point out that the missing number must be negative, because the quotient is negative. Model the example.
- Continue, with $-15 \div (-5) = 3$ and $15 \div (-5) = -3$.
- Repeat with other multiplication and division facts if needed. Leave the last set of facts on the Visual for reference while you complete Explore the Concept.

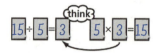

Fifteen divided by 5 equals 3 because 5 times 3 equals 15.

Connect to Vocabulary Post on the Word Wall and discuss: **integers** and **quotient**.

EXPLORE THE CONCEPT

- Copy the table shown onto the board. Leave out all numbers in parentheses. *What is the quotient in the first row?* (4)
- Work through the second example. *Sixteen divided by what number is −4? It's clear that the missing number must be 4 or −4, since 4 times 4 is 16. Which is it?* (It must be positive 4, since dividing a negative by a positive gives a negative.)
- Complete the table with the students. Include additional examples, if necessary.

Dividend ÷ Divisor = Quotient

Dividend	Divisor	Quotient
12	3	(4)
−16	(4)	−4
(−35)	−5	7
−28	−7	(4)
36	(−4)	−9
(−48)	−6	8

Find the missing numbers.

Wrap Up Write rules for dividing integers with the same and different signs. (Wording will vary but should reflect the idea that like signs result in positive quotients; unlike signs result in negative quotients or the idea that negatives always come in pairs for multiplication and division.)

Reteach Make a number line from the adding machine tape in your kit or Copymaster M2. Give examples of division of (a) positive dividend and divisor, and (b) negative dividend and positive divisor. *If you divide −14 into 7 equal groups, what is in each group?* Students should be able to see that each group is −2. Have students work through a variety of other examples.

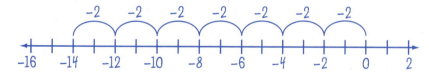

Number line showing $-14 \div \square = 7$.

Assess

Which quotient is greater, $725 \div (-5)$ or $-25 \div (-5)$? Explain how you know it is greater before dividing. (The first quotient is negative so it is much less than the second quotient, which is positive.)

148 iSucceed MATH: Divide Integers

APPLY THE CONCEPT

Problem-Solving Strategy: Guess, Check, and Revise

Problem-Solving Skill: More Than One Answer

Present the Problem Display Visual 68: Division Riddles. Read the problem set-up and instructions:

- Riddle 1: *A division problem has a quotient of −4. Its dividend is greater than 20 and less than 30. Its divisor is less than 7. What is the division problem?*
- Riddle 2: *A division problem has a quotient of 7. Its dividend is greater than −30 and less than −20. Its divisor is less than −2. What is the division problem?*
- *Work with a partner. Assume that all numbers are integers.*

Discuss the Solutions After they have had time to solve the riddles, have the students discuss their solutions.

- *Since 20 is less than our dividend and our dividend is less than 30,* describe how the dividend is related to 20 and 30. (It is between 20 and 30.)
- *To solve riddle 1 what step did you take first? Second? How did you solve the riddle?* (Sample explanation: First I tried different numbers between 20 and 30. I tried dividing them by numbers less than 7. When I found two numbers that had a quotient of −4, I had an answer. $24 \div (-6) = -4$)
- *To solve riddle 1 what step did you take first? Second? How did you solve the riddle?* (Sample explanation: First I tried different numbers between −20 and −30. I tried dividing them by numbers less than −2. When I found two numbers that had a quotient of 7, I had an answer. $-28 \div (-4) = 7$)
- Work with students to find other answers to the riddles. (Riddle 1: $28 \div (-7) = -4$; Riddle 2: $-21 \div (-3) = 7$)

REFLECT

Discuss how the way you decide on the sign of a sum or difference varies from the way to decide on the sign of a product or quotient. Encourage students to think of the number line for every addition and subtraction example. If they then think about inverse operations for multiplication and division, they won't accidentally apply rules for one kind of computation to the other.

Vocabulary

- Direct students' attention to the Word Wall.
- Discuss the four types of integer division and the quotients that result from each.
- Point out that the word "divide" has many meanings in English. Divide can mean "to cut," "to split," "to separate," or "to share." Have students discuss how these synonyms are similar to and different from the mathematical definition of divide.

Journal Prompt

Discuss similarities and differences between multiplying and dividing integers. (Similarities include that they both use signs the same way: like signs give a positive result and unlike signs give a negative result. Differences include terminology (product, quotient, divisor, remainder, etc.).)

Assess

An integer is divided by −7. The quotient is 6. What is the integer? (−42)

Concept Builder Lesson 35 Plan

Rational Numbers

TODAY'S CONCEPT
- Use a number line to represent fractions, mixed numbers, and decimal numbers.

MATERIALS
- Visual 69: Rational Numbers and Opposites
- Visual 70: Number Patterns
- Vocabulary Cards: **decimal number, fraction, integers, mixed number, rational number**

SET UP
Build the Concept
Display Visual 69: Rational Numbers and Opposites.

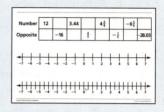

Apply the Concept
Display Visual 70: Number Patterns.

WORD WALL

Leave this Word Wall posted for Concept Builder 36.

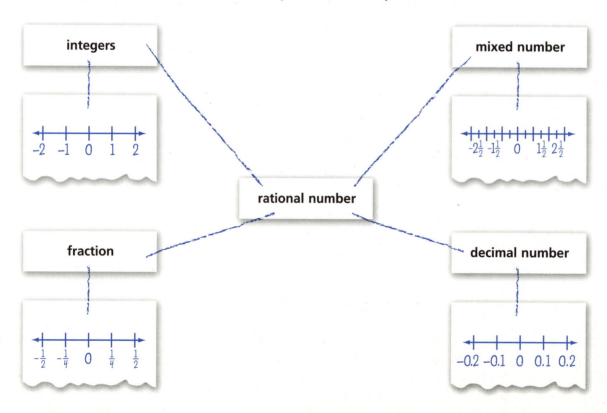

150   iSucceed MATH

PROFESSIONAL DEVELOPMENT

Rational Numbers The Real Numbers include all numbers that can be written as a ratio and all numbers that cannot. If you can write a number as a ratio (in fraction form), then it is a rational number.

Examples of rational numbers:

Whole numbers: 1, 2, 3, . . .

Integers: . . . −1, −2, −3, 0, 1, 2, 3, . . .

Decimal numbers, fractions, and mixed numbers, which name integers and most numbers between integers: $-2\frac{1}{2}$, -1, $\frac{4}{5}$, 75.24

Unless your curriculum requires you to do so, you may not wish to introduce the term "rational number" at this time.

Equivalent Forms Any number that can be expressed as a fraction can be written in decimal form; however, not all decimal numbers can be written in fraction form. These are the irrational numbers.

Examples:

rational number: $-2.4 = 2\frac{4}{10} = 2\frac{2}{5}$

irrational number: 3.121121112 . . . has no fraction equivalent, it is a non-terminating, non-repeating decimal

Approximation This lesson requires students to use number sense when locating fractions, decimal numbers, and mixed numbers on the number line. In the most basic sense, the location of a mixed number like $-4\frac{2}{3}$ is just between -4 and -5. However, most students should be capable of finding a more precise location, recognizing that $-4\frac{2}{3}$ should be closer to -5 than to -4, somewhat past the halfway point between the two.

Courseware Connections

Module: Decimals

Comparing and Ordering Decimals Through Hundredths

Comparing and Ordering Decimals Through Thousandths

Module: Understanding and Adding Fractions

Fractions on a Number Line

Comparing Fractions

Ordering Fractions

Module: Mixed Numbers

Comparing and Ordering Mixed Numbers

Lesson 35 Teach

BUILD THE CONCEPT

Display Visual 69: Rational Numbers and Opposites. Your goal in this discussion is to help students understand positive and negative fractions, mixed numbers, and decimal numbers.

- Refer to the Visual. Have students locate some integers, like 1, 3, −1, and −3 on the first number line.

- Refer to the second number line. *We can also locate fractions, mixed numbers, and decimals on the number line. Where are $\frac{3}{4}$ and $1\frac{1}{2}$?* Help students find and label the approximate location of each number.

- *Where are $2\frac{1}{2}$ and $-2\frac{1}{2}$? What about the decimal numbers 0.7 and −0.7?* Help students find and label the approximate location of each number.

Connect to Vocabulary Post on the Word Wall and discuss: **integers**, **fraction**, **mixed number**, and **decimal number**.

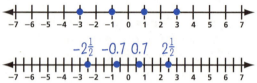

If you can write a number as a fraction or a decimal number, you can find it on the number line.

EXPLORE THE CONCEPT

- *Does anyone remember what we learned about opposites?* (Opposites are the same distance from zero, but on either side of it.) *Do you see any opposites marked on the first number line?* (1, −1 and 3 −3)

- *Opposites do not need to be integers. Find some opposites among the numbers we labeled on the second number line.* ($2\frac{1}{2}, -2\frac{1}{2}$; 0.7, −0.7)

- *What is the opposite of 4.1?* (−4.1) *Of $-\frac{3}{5}$?* ($\frac{3}{5}$) Have students locate and label these numbers and their opposites on the second number line.

- Point out that the term "opposite" can mean "directly across from" or "on the other side" in every-day usage. Compare this to the mathematical usage.

- Have students complete the table on the Visual. If they need help, draw a −30 through 30 number line on the board.

Connect to Vocabulary Add **rational number** to the Word Wall to tie together the rest of today's vocabulary.

Wrap Up *Write a rule for finding the opposite of a number.* (Rules should include the idea that the opposite has the opposite sign but the same numeral.)

Reteach Draw on the board or use a real thermometer to provide visual reinforcement of the idea that positive numbers are on one side of zero and negative numbers are on the other.

Number	12	16	3.44	$-\frac{4}{5}$	$4\frac{3}{8}$	$\frac{1}{5}$	$-6\frac{5}{6}$	28.03
Opposite	−12	−16	−3.44	$\frac{4}{5}$	$-4\frac{3}{8}$	$-\frac{1}{5}$	$6\frac{5}{6}$	−28.03

Complete the table.

Assess

Name a mixed number that you might find between 4 and 5 on a number line. Then, find its opposite. Name a decimal number that you might find between 0 and −1. Then, find its opposite. (Check students' work.)

APPLY THE CONCEPT

Problem-Solving Strategy: Look for a Pattern

Present the Problem Display Visual 70: Number Patterns. Read the problem set-up and instructions:

- *Work with a partner and decide how to fill in the blanks for Pattern A and Pattern B.*
- *Decide what will be the next number in each pattern.*

Discuss the Solutions After students have had time to solve the problems, help the class discuss their solutions.

- *Describe the patterns you found for Pattern A and Pattern B.* Pattern A alternates positive and negative numbers; if all the numbers were positive, they would increase by 0.2 from one to the next. Pattern B changes by -0.25 or $-\frac{1}{4}$ from one to the next, alternating between decimal numbers and mixed numbers.
- *What are the missing numbers in Pattern A?* (1.0, 1.4, -1.6)
- *What are the missing numbers in Pattern B?* ($-1\frac{3}{4}$, -2.5)
- Extend the discussion by asking students to find the tenth number in each pattern. (A: -2; B: -3.0)

REFLECT

Give an example of each of the different kinds of numbers we found on the number lines today, then find the opposites. (Answers should include whole numbers, fractions, mixed numbers, and decimal numbers.)

Vocabulary

- Refer to the Word Wall. Discuss the terms and as many different examples and ways to define as you have time for. Have students record their definitions in their personal glossaries along with a diagram and/or an example for each.
- Leave the Word Wall posted for Concept Builder 36.

Journal Prompt

How do fractions and mixed numbers compare to integers on the number line? (Answers should refer to how fractions and mixed numbers fall between integers on the number line.)

Assess

Make up your own number pattern with positive and negative numbers. Tell how you can find the missing numbers in your pattern. (Check students' work.)

Concept Builder — Lesson 36 Plan

Compare and Order Rational Numbers

TODAY'S CONCEPTS
- Use number lines to compare rational numbers, including positive and negative numbers, fractions, mixed numbers, and decimal numbers.
- Order a list of positive and negative fractions, mixed numbers, and decimal numbers.

MATERIALS
- Visual 71: Rational Number Lines
- Visual 72: Skating Scores
- Vocabulary Cards: **decimal number**, **fraction**, **integers**, **mixed number**, **rational number**

SET UP

Build the Concept
Display Visual 71: Rational Number Lines.

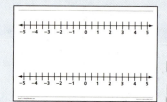

Apply the Concept
Display Visual 72: Skating Scores.

EL WORD WALL

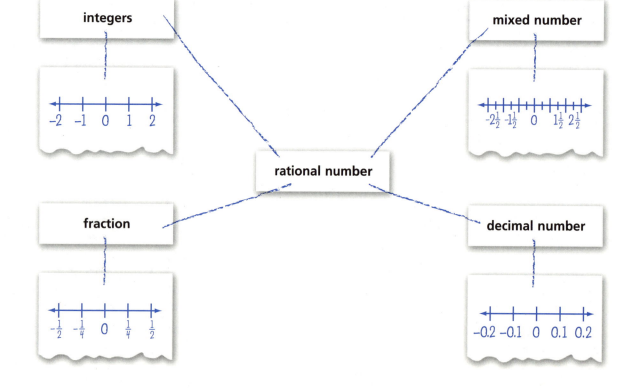

154 iSucceed MATH

PROFESSIONAL DEVELOPMENT

Place Value Students must have a strong grasp of place value in order to compare and order decimal numbers. It might be beneficial to go over the different place values (tens, ones, tenths, hundredths, thousandths, etc.). It might also help students to understand that comparing decimal numbers involves several of the same steps they follow when adding decimal numbers.

1. Align on decimal points.

   7.03
   7.3

2. Tack on zeros.

   7.03
   7.30 → greater

To compare decimal numbers, line up the decimal points and then tack on zeros as needed.

Denominators To compare fractions and mixed numbers, students may need to find common denominators. They may use lists of multiples to find common denominators, or they may find the product of unlike denominators. In many cases, benchmarks of $0, \frac{1}{2}$, and 1, or $0, \frac{1}{4}, \frac{1}{2}, \frac{3}{4}$, and 1 provide enough information to compare fractions with fractions or fractions with decimal numbers.

Examples: Compare $\frac{3}{8}$ to $\frac{5}{6}$.

- Use lists of multiples to find a common denominator.

  8, 16, $\boxed{24}$, 30 → $\frac{3 \times 3}{8 \times 3} = \frac{9}{24}$

  6, 12, 18, $\boxed{24}$, 30 → $\frac{5 \times 4}{6 \times 4} = \frac{20}{24}$

  $\frac{9}{24} < \frac{20}{24}$, so $\frac{3}{8} < \frac{5}{6}$

- Multiply denominators to find a common denominator.

  $6 \times 8 = 48$

  $\frac{3 \times 6}{8 \times 6} = \frac{18}{48}$ and $\frac{5 \times 8}{6 \times 8} = \frac{40}{48}$

  $\frac{18}{48} < \frac{40}{48}$, so $\frac{3}{8} < \frac{5}{6}$

- Use benchmarks.

  $\frac{3}{8} < \frac{1}{2}$ and $\frac{5}{6} > \frac{1}{2}$, so $\frac{3}{8} < \frac{5}{6}$

Courseware Connections

Module: Decimals
- Comparing and Ordering Decimals Through Hundredths
- Comparing and Ordering Decimals Through Thousandths

Module: Understanding and Adding Fractions
- Fractions on a Number Line
- Comparing Fractions
- Ordering Fractions

Module: Mixed Numbers
- Comparing and Ordering Mixed Numbers

Module: Positive and Negative Numbers
- Graphing Integers
- Comparing and Ordering Integers

Lesson 36 Teach

BUILD THE CONCEPT

Display Visual 71: Rational Number Lines. Your goal in this discussion is to help students compare and order positive and negative fractions, mixed numbers, and decimal numbers.

- *Do you remember how a number line can help you compare and order whole numbers?* (A number line shows numbers in order from least to greatest as you read from left to right.)

- Write on the board: 2, −2.5, $3\frac{1}{2}$, $-2\frac{3}{4}$, 2.1, −3.1. *Find each of these numbers on the first number line.* Encourage students to use estimation and number sense to place numbers on the number line. Mark and label each number.

- Use the second number line to mark and label −2.5 and $-2\frac{3}{4}$. Compare −2.5 to $-2\frac{3}{4}$. ($-2.5 > -2\frac{3}{4}$ and $-2\frac{3}{4} < -2.5$) Then, use the same number line to mark and label 2.5 and $2\frac{3}{4}$. Compare 2.5 to $2\frac{3}{4}$. ($2.5 < 2\frac{3}{4}$ and $2\frac{3}{4} > 2.5$)

- Have students list the numbers in order from least to greatest. ($-3.1, -2\frac{3}{4}, -2.5, -2, 2, 2.1, 3\frac{1}{2}$) Then, ask them to order them greatest to least.

Connect to Vocabulary Refer to the Word Wall and review **integers, fraction, mixed number, decimal number,** and **rational number**.

As you go left on the number line, the values are less.

EXPLORE THE CONCEPT

- Write 1.65 and $1\frac{3}{5}$ on the board. *Can you easily place these on the number line or with benchmarks?* (not on these number lines; both numbers are near $1\frac{1}{2}$) *To compare a decimal number and a mixed number that are close in value, you can write them both as either decimal numbers or fractions.* ($1.65 = 1\frac{65}{100}$ and $1\frac{3}{5} = 1\frac{60}{100} = 1.60$)

- *Which number is greater, $-1\frac{3}{5}$ or −1.65?* ($-1\frac{3}{5}$).

- Repeat with other number pairs as time allows.

Wrap Up *How does zero compare to any positive number?* (It is less.) *How does zero compare to any negative number?* (It is greater.) *How do you know?* (On a number line, left is less.)

Reteach Use the adding machine tape in your kit to make two same-length number lines to compare numbers such as 3.7 and $3\frac{1}{2}$. Divide the first number line into 10 sections between 3.0 and 4.0 and color in 7 of them to represent 3.7. Divide the second number line into two sections between 3 and 4 and color in one of them to represent $3\frac{1}{2}$. The students should be able to see clearly that 3.7 is greater. Give them copies of Copymaster M2: Number Lines to keep handy if they continue to need the number line.

How can you decide which number is greater, 4.8 or $4\frac{3}{5}$? (Sample answer: Write $4\frac{3}{5}$ as 4.6, align the decimal numbers and compare; 4.8 is greater.)

156   iSucceed MATH: Compare and Order Rational Numbers

APPLY THE CONCEPT

Problem-Solving Skill: Solve Multi-Step Problems

Present the Problem Display Visual 72: Skating Scores. Read the problem set-up and instructions:

- The chart shows the scores from six different continents for the Continental Skating Championships.
- Work with a partner. Throw out the high and low scores, and decide which team won the championship.

Discuss the Solutions After they have had time to solve the problem, help the students discuss their solutions.

- *What did you do to solve the problem?* (Sample answer: Change all of the scores to decimal numbers; compare scores and throw out the high and low scores; add the remaining scores for each team; compare the sums.)
- *How did you decide who won the competition?* (Sample answer: Compare the two sums. Red Team: 17.50 total points, Green Team: 17.25 points. Since 17.50 > 17.25, then the Red Team won.)

REFLECT

Why do you sometimes write numbers in different forms when comparing or computing? (Converting is helpful when a mixed number is close in value to a decimal number, such as 5.44 and $5\frac{9}{20}$.)

Vocabulary

Direct students' attention to the Word Wall. Encourage them to add any new information or examples to the definitions in their personal glossaries.

Journal Prompt

For comparing numbers, which is usually easier—writing decimal numbers as fractions or writing fractions as decimal numbers? Explain. (Most students will think that it's easier to write fractions as decimals for comparison because they don't need to go through a step of finding common denominators. Be sure that students understand that they should use the method that is most comfortable to them or that is most easily used with the numbers with which they are working.)

Assess

Order these numbers from least to greatest: 7.5, $-1\frac{1}{3}$, $-3\frac{3}{8}$, 0.14, -0.15, $-2\frac{3}{8}$. Explain your work. ($-3\frac{3}{8}$, $-2\frac{3}{8}$, $-1\frac{1}{3}$, -0.15, 0.14, 7.5; write mixed numbers as decimal numbers or decimal numbers as mixed numbers.)

Concept Builder **Lesson 37 Plan**

Add and Subtract Rational Numbers

TODAY'S CONCEPT
- Model adding and subtracting rational numbers on a number line.

MATERIALS
- Visual 73: Adding and Subtracting Rational Numbers
- Visual 74: Pond Depth
- Copymaster M2: Number Lines
- yarn and push pins
- small self-stick notes
- Vocabulary Cards: **difference**, **opposites**, **sum**

SET UP
Build the Concept
- Display Visual 73: Adding and Subtracting Rational Numbers.
- Cut two pieces of yarn $2\frac{3}{4}$ and $1\frac{1}{2}$ units long as measured on Visual 73. Knot the ends.

Apply the Concept
Display Visual 74: Pond Depth.

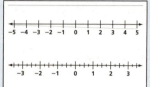

EL WORD WALL

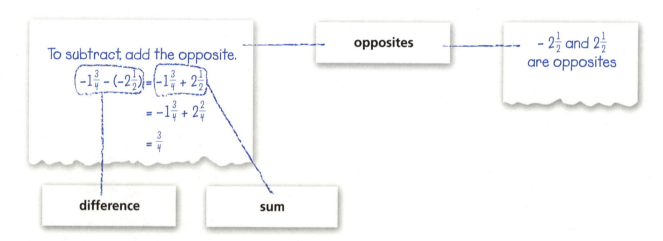

158 iSucceed MATH

PROFESSIONAL DEVELOPMENT

Math Background In this lesson, students will not be introduced to a formal algorithm for adding and subtracting rational numbers. A rational number is any number, positive or negative, that can be written in fraction form. Integers are rational numbers; so are fractions and decimal numbers.

Prepare for Learning Adding and subtracting rational numbers is usually more difficult for students than multiplying and dividing rational numbers. Consider working with students to make a class number-line poster that reviews how to add and subtract two numbers with the same sign (both positive and negative) and with mixed signs.

Adding Rational Numbers The following rules explain how to add rational numbers without a number line.

$(+) + (+) = (+)$

$(-) + (-) = (-)$

$(+6) + (-3) = +3$

$(-6) + (+3) = -3$

Courseware Connections

Module: Positive and Negative Numbers

Adding Positive and Negative Integers

Adding Negative Integers to Negative Integers

Subtracting Positive Integers

Subtracting Negative Integers

- When the signs are the same, add the numbers. The sign of the sum is the same sign as the sign of the addends.
- If the signs are different, pretend that the numbers are positive and subtract greater − lesser. The sign of the sum is the sign of the addend that would be farthest from zero on the number line.
- If the numbers are in different forms (like $1\frac{3}{4}$ and 2.5), find equivalents in the same form.

Subtracting Rational Numbers The easiest way to understand subtraction with signed numbers is to think of subtracting as adding the opposite. Because addition and subtraction are inverse operations, subtracting a number has the same result as adding its opposite.

EL Notation In this program, when an operation sign is followed immediately by a negative number, we place the negative number in parentheses. This technique should help students to distinguish between the two uses of + and −.

Word Problems with Rational Numbers Take special care with how you phrase word problems if you make them up for students. If you want to model a computation situation, be sure that the language you use does not imply a positive answer when what you want is a negative answer.

Example: *The home team lost $2\frac{1}{2}$ yards and then lost 2 more yards; how many yards did the team lose?*

This problem does not model $-2\frac{1}{2} + (-2) = -4\frac{1}{2}$. The question calls for a positive answer. If the team loses a negative number of yards, you have created a double negative.

Lesson 37 Teach

BUILD THE CONCEPT

Display Visual 73: Adding and Subtracting Rational Numbers. Your goal in this discussion is to help students to model adding and subtracting rational numbers.

- Distribute copies of Copymaster M2: Number Lines. Have students work on their number lines as you model the sums.

- Use the first number line to review how to add two integers on a number line. *Start at 0, then move to the first addend. If the second addend is positive, move to the right; if the second addend is negative, move to the left. What is the sum of 1 and −3?* (−2)

- *How should we add* $-2\frac{3}{4} + 1\frac{1}{2}$? Use yarn to show starting at 0 and ending at $-2\frac{3}{4}$ on the second number line. Label $-2\frac{3}{4}$ with a self-stick note. *How do you think I should show adding* $1\frac{1}{2}$? (Move right $1\frac{1}{2}$ units.) Use your second piece of yarn to show starting at $-2\frac{3}{4}$ and moving $1\frac{1}{2}$ units to the right to end at $-1\frac{1}{4}$. *What is* $-2\frac{3}{4} + 1\frac{1}{2}$? ($-1\frac{1}{4}$)

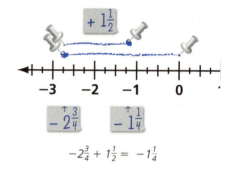

$-2\frac{3}{4} + 1\frac{1}{2} = -1\frac{1}{4}$

EXPLORE THE CONCEPT

- *How are addition and subtraction related?* (They are opposite operations.) *Subtract* $-2 - 1$ *on the first number line. What is the opposite of 1?* (−1) *How can we rewrite the subtraction as adding the opposite?* ($-2 + (-1)$) Have students find the sum on their number lines. (−3)

- Now demonstrate how to subtract rational numbers. Emphasize that you still add the opposite to subtract. Use the yarn on the second number line to demonstrate $-\frac{1}{2} - 1\frac{3}{4}$. ($-\frac{1}{2} + (-1\frac{3}{4}) = -2\frac{1}{4}$)

Connect to Vocabulary Post today's vocabulary on the Word Wall and model several examples for: **difference**, **opposites**, and **sum**.

Wrap Up Work through these additional examples:
$2\frac{3}{4} - 1\frac{1}{2} = 1\frac{1}{4}$
$1\frac{1}{2} - 2\frac{3}{4} = -1\frac{1}{4}$
$-1\frac{1}{2} - (-2\frac{3}{4}) = 1\frac{1}{4}$.

Reteach Go back and review how to add and subtract whole numbers. When students demonstrate mastery, move on to adding and subtracting mixed numbers, then integers. Define subtraction in terms of adding the opposite and have students use number lines to model integer sums and differences. When they can accurately compute integer sums and differences, review how to add and subtract rational numbers in the same form. Gradually introduce sums and differences of rational numbers in different forms.

Why is a number line a useful tool to use to find the sums of rational numbers? (It lets you show the direction and number of units you need to move for each addend.)

160   iSucceed MATH: Add and Subtract Rational Numbers

APPLY THE CONCEPT

Problem-Solving Skill: Make a Plan

Problem-Solving Strategy: Write an Equation

Present the Problem Display Visual 74: Pond Depth. Provide students with copies of Copymaster M2: Number Lines. Read the problem set-up and instructions:

- *Students helping to clean a pond in the city park measured the depth of the pond at its eastern and western ends. Which end is deeper? How much deeper?*
- *Work with a partner to make a plan and write an equation to solve the problem. If you need to, use a number line to help you solve the problem.*

Discuss the Solution After students have had time to solve the problem, help them discuss their solutions.

- *What kind of plan did you make to solve the problem?* Discuss how making a plan helped students understand how to solve the problem. Elicit that the numbers must be written in like form to solve the equation. Students can write both numbers in fraction form ($-4.6 = -4\frac{6}{10}$ or $-4\frac{3}{5}$) or both in decimal form ($-4\frac{2}{5} = -4.4$).
- *Which end is deeper? How do you know?* (western end; $-4.6 < -4.4$)
- *How did you find how much deeper the western end is than the eastern end?* (To find the difference between the depths, write an equation: $-4.6 - (-4.4) = x$ or $-4\frac{3}{5} - (-4\frac{2}{5}) = x$.) *What is the difference?* (-0.2 m)
- *How much deeper is the western end of the pond?* (0.2 m deeper) Discuss why you would not answer with a negative number. ("Deeper" implies a positive number.)

REFLECT

Explain how to interpret the signs of rational numbers to add or subtract rational numbers. (Answers should include rewriting subtraction as addition. Move right to add positive numbers, and move left for negative numbers. The sign of the sum depends upon where you end up on the number line.)

Vocabulary

Refer to the Word Wall. Discuss today's terms. Ask students to add new definitions and examples to their personal glossaries.

Journal Prompt

Do the rules for subtracting integers work for subtracting positive and negative fractions, decimals, and mixed numbers? Show examples. Work with students to provide examples that show that the rules work in all cases.

Assess

What is the sum of a number and its opposite? What is the difference of a number and its opposite? Give an example. (The sum is zero, and the difference is twice the number. Check students' examples.)

Concept Builder — Lesson 38 Plan

Multiply and Divide Rational Numbers

TODAY'S CONCEPTS
- Use number lines to model multiplying and dividing rational numbers.
- Understand patterns of rational-number multiplication and division.

MATERIALS
- Visual 75: Multiplying and Dividing Rational Numbers
- Visual 76: Dive Depth
- Vocabulary Cards: **product**, **quotient**, **rational number**

SET UP

Build the Concept
Display Visual 75: Multiplying and Dividing Rational Numbers.

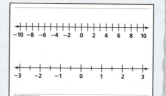

Apply the Concept
Display Visual 76: Dive Depth.

Scuba Class Dives
first dive: 3.4 meters
second dive: $2\frac{1}{2}$ times as deep

EL WORD WALL

rational number

$\frac{2}{3}, -\frac{2}{3}, 4, -4, \frac{8}{3}, -\frac{8}{3}$

same signs
$\frac{2}{3} \times 4 = \frac{2}{3} \times \frac{4}{1} = \frac{8}{3}$
$-\frac{2}{3} \times (-4) = -\frac{2}{3} \times \left(\frac{-4}{1}\right) = \frac{8}{3}$

same signs
$\frac{8}{3} \div 4 = \frac{8}{3} \times \frac{1}{4} = \frac{8}{12} = \frac{2}{3}$
$-\frac{8}{3} \div (-4) = -\frac{8}{3} \times \left(-\frac{1}{4}\right) = \frac{8}{12} = \frac{2}{3}$

product

quotient

different signs
$-\frac{2}{3} \times 4 = -\frac{2}{3} \times \frac{4}{1} = -\frac{8}{3}$
$\frac{2}{3} \times (-4) = \frac{2}{3} \times \left(-\frac{4}{1}\right) = -\frac{8}{3}$

different signs
$-\frac{8}{3} \div 4 = -\frac{8}{3} \times \frac{1}{4} = -\frac{8}{12} = -\frac{2}{3}$
$\frac{8}{3} \div (-4) = \frac{8}{3} \times \left(-\frac{1}{4}\right) = -\frac{8}{12} = -\frac{2}{3}$

PROFESSIONAL DEVELOPMENT

Math Background When you add integers, if the signs on the addends are the same, then the sum has that sign. (3 + 4 = 7, and −3 + (−4) = −7) Addends with different signs can have either positive or negative sums. (3 + (−4) = −1, but −3 + 4 = 1) For multiplication and division, you can always tell the sign on the result before computing. In both multiplication and division, negatives always come in pairs.

Examples:

(+) × (+) = +   (+) ÷ (+) = +
(−) × (−) = +   (−) ÷ (−) = +
(+) × (−) = −   (+) ÷ (−) = −
(−) × (+) = −   (−) ÷ (+) = −

Courseware Connections

Module: Positive and Negative Numbers
  Multiplying Integers
  Dividing Integers

Using the Algorithm Multiply and divide rational numbers using the same algorithms used for positive whole numbers, decimal numbers, fractions, and mixed numbers. The only differences may involve changing one number to the same form as the other one and keeping track of the sign on the product or quotient.

Mnemonic Encourage students to use a mnemonic to remember the sign of a product or quotient along the lines of: *I like like, so I'm positive. I don't like unlike, so I'm negative.* Challenge students to invent their own mnemonics.

Inverse Operation Multiplication and division are inverse operations. It may be useful to make a habit of restating division as multiplication to show how the distribution of positive and negative numbers among factors and product relates to the distribution of positive and negative numbers among quotient, divisor, and dividend.

Beyond the Number Line The number line works well to model multiplication as long as at least one of the two factors is positive. However, this model breaks down when both factors are negative. The same is true for division of negative numbers. To conceptualize the multiplication and division of two negatives, it is best to forego the number line and rely strictly on patterns: *like signs result in a positive product or quotient; unlike signs result in a negative product or quotient.*

Lesson 38 Teach

BUILD THE CONCEPT

Display Visual 75: Multiplying and Dividing Rational Numbers. Your goal in this discussion is to help students model multiplying and dividing rational numbers.

- On the first number line, review how to model $4 \times (-2)$ by making 4 groups of (-2). *What is the product?* (-8)
- Now use the number line to multiply $3 \times (-\frac{1}{2})$. *Where shall we start?* (0) *What is each jump?* $(-\frac{1}{2})$ *How many jumps?* (3) *What is $3 \times (-\frac{1}{2})$?* $(-1\frac{1}{2})$
- *How does the product of $3 \times (-\frac{1}{2})$ compare to the product of $3 \times \frac{1}{2}$?* (The products are opposites.) Connect the rules for choosing the signs of integer products to choosing the signs of rational number products.

Connect to Vocabulary Post on the Word Wall: **rational number**, **product**, and **quotient**. Use these terms as they relate to the examples you have already worked.

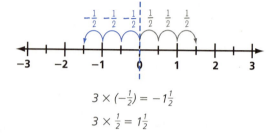

$4 \times (-2) = -8$

$3 \times (-\frac{1}{2}) = -1\frac{1}{2}$

$3 \times \frac{1}{2} = 1\frac{1}{2}$

EXPLORE THE CONCEPT

- You can think about fact families to divide rational numbers. To find $1.8 \div 3$, think: 3 times what number equals 1.8? (0.6) Model the example on the board:
  $1.8 \div 3 = 0.6 \rightarrow 3 \times 0.6 = 1.8$.
- To divide -1.8 by 3, think 3 times what number equals -1.8? (-0.6) Point out that the missing number must be negative, because the quotient is negative. Model the example.
- Continue with $-1.8 \div (-3) = 0.6$, and $1.8 \div (-3) = -0.6$.
- Repeat with other multiplication and division examples as time allows.

Wrap Up Work with students to write rules for multiplying and dividing rational numbers of the same and different signs. (Rules should state that like signs result in positive products and quotients; unlike signs result in negative products and quotients.) You may wish to summarize the rules in a table.

Reteach Review how to multiply and divide whole numbers. When students demonstrate mastery, move on to multiplying and dividing integers. When they can accurately compute integer products and quotients, review how to multiply and divide with decimals and fractions. Gradually introduce products and quotients of rational numbers.

$(+) \times (+) = +$ $(+) \div (+) = +$
$(-) \times (-) = +$ $(-) \div (-) = +$
$(+) \times (-) = -$ $(+) \div (-) = -$
$(-) \times (+) = -$ $(-) \div (+) = -$

Like signs result in positive products and quotients. Unlike signs result in negative products and quotients.

Which quotient is greater, $3.2 \div (-4)$ or $-1.2 \div (-4)$? Explain how you know it is greater before dividing. (The first quotient is negative so it is less than the second quotient, which is positive.)

APPLY THE CONCEPT

Problem-Solving Skill: Make a Plan

Problem-Solving Strategy: Write an Equation

Present the Problem Display Visual 76: Dive Depth. Read the problem set-up and instructions:

- *Jessica went diving with her scuba class. The class had two dives. The second dive was $2\frac{1}{2}$ times as deep as the first dive. How deep was the second dive?*
- *Work with a partner to make a plan, and write an equation to solve the problem.*

Discuss the Solution After students have had time to solve the problem, help them discuss their solutions.

- *What kind of plan did you make to solve the problem?* Discuss how making a plan helped students understand how to solve the problem. Elicit that the numbers must be written in like form to solve the equation. Students can write both numbers in fraction form ($3.4 = 3\frac{4}{10}$ or $3\frac{2}{5}$) or in decimal form ($2\frac{1}{2} = 2.5$).
- *What equation represents the problem? Explain.* (The equation $3.4 \times 2\frac{1}{2} = d$ represents the depth, d, of the second dive. $3.4 \times 2.5 = d$ or $3\frac{4}{10} \times 2\frac{1}{2} = d$) Discuss how students solved the equations in both forms.
- *What was the depth of the second dive?* (8.5 meters or $8\frac{1}{2}$ meters)

REFLECT

Discuss how the way you decide on the sign of a sum or difference varies from the way you decide of the sign of a product or quotient. Encourage students to think of the number line for every addition and subtraction example. If they then think about inverse operations for multiplication and division, they will not accidentally apply rules for one kind of computation to the other.

Vocabulary

Refer to the Word Wall. Work with students to write new examples. Ask them to add new examples to their personal glossaries.

Journal Prompt

Discuss the patterns of the signs when multiplying and dividing rational numbers. (Multiplying or dividing with like signs yields positive products and quotients; multiplying or dividing with unlike signs yields negative products and quotients.

Assess

Compare the product of $(-\frac{1}{2}) \times (-\frac{1}{2}) \times (-\frac{1}{2})$ to the product of $\frac{1}{2} \times (-\frac{1}{2}) \times \frac{1}{2}$. (They are the same: $-\frac{1}{8}$.)

Active Practice

Lessons

Active Practice 1 Fill In 1 Whole (Grade 3)* **168**

Active Practice 2 Order Decimal Numbers (Grade 4) **170**

Active Practice 3 Draw to Add Decimals (Grade 4) **172**

Active Practice 4 Draw to Multiply Decimals (Grade 5) **174**

Active Practice 5 Order Fractions (Grade 5) **176**

Active Practice 6 Giant Inch (Grade 5) **178**

Active Practice 7 Draw to Add Fractions (Grade 4) **180**

Active Practice 8 Integers (Grade 5) **182**

*Indicates grade level at which topic is typically introduced; your curriculum may differ.

MATERIALS

- Volume II Active Practice Cards 1–8
- Volume II Active Practice Recording Sheets 1–8, pages 184–191
- number cubes: 1, 2, 2, 10, 10, 10; 0–5; +/−, 1–6**
- Volume II Cardstock: Fraction/Decimal Cards, Digit Cards
- coins

**See page 2 for instructions on preparing number cubes.

Introduction

The Active Practice for Volume II provides games in which pairs of students generate their own practice exercises. Each of these Active Practice lessons is designed to be taught before any students are assigned to the Active Practice. The Lesson Support file for each Courseware lesson lists Active Practice games that are appropriate for a student who has successfully completed that lesson.

While students play, circulate and observe the interactions of partners as they make decisions and explain their moves. Remind students to complete their Recording Sheets as they play. The Model and Reflect questions in each lesson here provide examples of ways that you can encourage students to think mathematically. The Assess and Reteach tables in each lesson point out specific skills students should be using, and suggest ways to tell whether they are successfully using these skills and how to correct any problems.

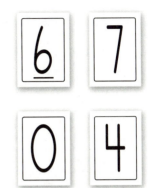

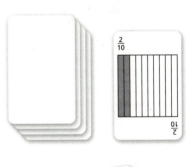

Active Practice 1

Fill In 1 Whole

MATERIALS PER PAIR
- One number cube (1, 2, 2, 10, 10, 10)
- Two Fill In 1 Whole Recording Sheets
- Two pencils

TO PLAY

1. Take turns. Before each turn, tell how many tenths and hundredths are already filled on your recording sheet. **(I have 3 tenths and 7 hundredths filled. I have thirty-seven hundredths filled.)**
2. Roll the number cube. Fill in that many hundredths. Label the last square and write the addition number sentence on your recording sheet. **(0.37 + 0.10 = 0.47)**
3. You win when you have filled 1 whole.

Variations

a. Cross off hundredths starting in the bottom right corner. Tell how many tenths and hundredths you have not yet crossed off. Write the subtraction number sentence. (1 − 0.1 = 0.9) Be the first to cross off 1 whole.

b. On each turn, write the addition number sentence using fractions instead of decimals. ($\frac{37}{100} + \frac{10}{100} = \frac{47}{100}$)

Reinforces Concept- and Skill-Builder Lessons 1, 4–6, 13, 17, 19–20.
Reinforces Courseware Modules Decimals, Adding and Subtracting Decimals, and Understanding and Adding Fractions.

CONCEPTS

- Add tenths and hundredths.
- Write equations to represent operations.

Variations	Additional Concepts
a. Cross off hundredths starting in the bottom right corner. Tell how many tenths and hundredths you have not yet crossed off. Write the subtraction number sentence (1 − 0.1 = 0.9) Be the first to cross off 1 whole.	Subtract fractions.
b. After each turn, write the equation using fractions instead of decimals. ($\frac{37}{100} + \frac{10}{100} = \frac{47}{100}$)	Write equations with decimal equivalents.

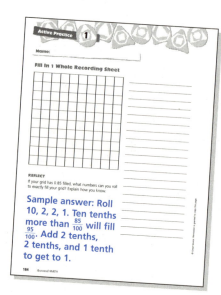

Active Practice 1 Recording Sheet

168   iSucceed MATH: Fill in 1 Whole

MODEL AND REFLECT

As students play, encourage them to think carefully and stretch mathematically by asking questions such as:

- *Who has more tenths filled? Who has more hundredths filled? How many more? How can you tell?*
- *How many more hundredths do you need to fill the whole?*
- *How many more turns do you think you will need to finish?*

Assess and Reteach

Have the student review as needed, lessons in these courseware modules: *Decimals; Adding and Subtracting Decimals; Understanding and Adding Fractions.*

Skills To Check	Indicators	Reteaching
Does the student connect a visual model to a fraction in tenths and hundredths?	The student can correctly tell how many tenths and hundredths are filled.	Use a blank Fill In 1 Whole Recording Sheet. Shade or cover various amounts and have students write the corresponding number.
Can the student add decimal numbers?	The student writes the correct equation.	Use only the first column of the grid. Fill a number of spaces and have the student say how many hundredths are filled. Repeat several times, then progress to filling one column and part of the second, and so on.
Variaton b: Can the student use mental math to add?	Student can say what the new sum will be without counting individual squares.	Have students practice adding whole numbers.

Active Practice 2

Order Decimal Numbers

MATERIALS PER PAIR
- Two sets of Fraction/Decimal Cards, decimal tenths cards only (18 cards) **(Cardstock C9–11)**
- Two Order Decimal Numbers Recording Sheets
- Two pencils

Round 1

| 0 | 0.2 | | | | | 1 |

TO PLAY
1. Shuffle the Fraction/Decimal Cards and place them face down.
2. Take turns. Draw a card. Read the number and tell how you will choose where to write it. **(I drew 2 tenths. I will put it in the second spot because there is only one choice less than 2 tenths.)** Write the number in an empty space on your recording sheet. If there is no empty space that works for your number, you lose your turn.
3. If you are the first to fill in your recording sheet with numbers in order from least to greatest, you win. Play 2 rounds.

Variations
a. Use only the hundredths decimal cards (20 cards). **(Cardstock C8–9)**
b. Use only the tenths and hundredths decimal cards (38 cards). **(Cardstock C8–11)**

Reinforces Concept- and Skill-Builder Lessons 1, 3.
Reinforces Courseware Module: Decimals.

CONCEPTS
- Read and write decimal numbers to tenths.
- Compare and order decimal numbers to tenths.
- Use mathematical reasoning.

Variations	Additional Concepts
a. Use only the hundredths decimal cards (20 cards).	• Read and write decimal numbers in hundredths. • Compare and order decimal numbers to hundredths.
b. Use only the tenths and hundredths decimal cards (38 cards).	• Read and write decimal numbers (tenths and hundredths). • Compare and order decimal numbers (tenths and hundredths).

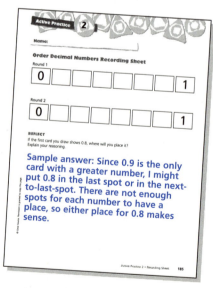

Active Practice 2 Recording Sheet

170   iSucceed MATH: Order Decimal Numbers

MODEL AND REFLECT

As you play a model game, encourage students to think mathematically by asking questions such as:

- *How does the diagram on the card help you name the number?*
- *How do you decide where to place each number?*

Assess and Reteach

Have the student review, as needed, lessons in this courseware module: *Decimals*.

Skills To Check	Indicators	Reteaching
Can the student read and write decimal numbers?	The student correctly names the number on each card and correctly writes the number on the recording sheet.	• Use Copymaster M5: Grid Paper. Have the student shade and label 1 tenth of a 10 × 10 square with words (one tenth) and numbers (0.1). Repeat for 2 tenths, and so forth.
Can the student compare and order decimal numbers?	The student orders the decimal numbers correctly and places them appropriately to save space for numbers that are greater and less.	• Have the student use the shaded diagrams on Cardstock C8–11: Fraction/Decimal Cards to place all of the decimal cards in order from least to greatest • Ask the student to describe how the diagrams on the cards represent the relative size of the numbers.

Active Practice 2

Active Practice 3

Draw To Add Decimals

MATERIALS PER PAIR
- Two sets of Digit Cards without 1s or 2s (16 cards) **(Cardstock C12)**
- Two Draw To Add Decimals Recording Sheets
- Two pencils

TO PLAY
1. Take one 0 card each. Shuffle the other cards and place them face down. Both players draw three cards.
2. Use your three digits and your 0 to make two decimal numbers.
3. Use your numbers to write an addition problem on your recording sheet. Find the sum.
4. You win the round if you have the least sum. Tell how much less. **(I have 64 hundredths and you have 78 hundredths. My sum is 14 hundredths less.)** Play 6 rounds.

Variations
a. Draw five cards. Choose four. Make two decimal numbers with the least sum.
b. Draw five cards. Choose four. Make two decimal numbers with the least difference.

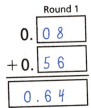

Round 1

Reinforces Concept- and Skill-Builder Lessons 3–6.
Reinforces Courseware Module: Adding and Subtracting Decimals.

CONCEPTS
- Use decimal place value to create small numbers.
- Use mathematical reasoning.
- Add simple decimal numbers.
- Compare decimal numbers.

Variations	Additional Concepts
a. Draw five cards. Choose four. Make two decimal numbers with the least sum.	Use place value to create small decimal numbers.
b. Draw five cards. Choose four. Make two decimal numbers with the least difference.	Subtract decimal numbers.

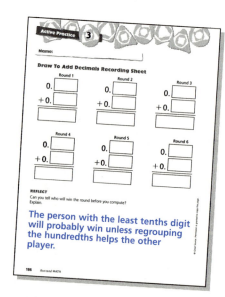

Active Practice 3 Recording Sheet

172 iSucceed MATH: Draw To Add Decimals

MODEL AND REFLECT

As you play a model game, encourage students to think mathematically by asking questions such as:

- *How do you decide where to place each digit?*
- *What is the least decimal number you can make with these digits?*
- *What is the least sum you can make? What digits will you need?*

Assess and Reteach

Have the student review, as needed, this courseware module: *Adding and Subtracting Decimals.*

Skills To Check	Indicators	Reteaching
Does the student understand decimal place value?	The student creates the least decimal numbers possible, and the student knows who has won each round.	Have the student play *Fill In 1 Whole* (Active Practice 1) to review models for tenths and hundredths.
Can the student add and subtract decimal numbers?	The student consistently finds the correct sum or difference.	Have the student play *Fill In 1 Whole* (Active Practice 1) to review adding or subtracting tenths and hundredths.

Active Practice 4

Draw To Multiply Decimals

MATERIALS PER PAIR
- Two sets of Digit Cards (20 cards) **(Cardstock C12)**
- Two Draw To Multiply Decimals Recording Sheets
- Two pencils

TO PLAY
1. Take one 0 card each. Shuffle the other cards. Both players draw three cards.
2. Make a two-digit whole number and a decimal number with tenths. Use them to write a multiplication problem on your recording sheet. Find the product.
3. You win if your product is less. Tell how you know your product is reasonable. **(I know 0.4 is a little less than half. Half of 67 is about 33. I got 26.8, so my product is reasonable.)** Play 6 rounds.

Variations
a. Draw four cards each. Use them with your 0 to make a decimal number less than 1 and a whole number. Try to get the least product.
b. Draw four cards each. Use them with your 0 to make a decimal number less than 1 and a whole number. Try to get the least quotient.

Round 1

$$\begin{array}{r} 67 \\ \times\, 0.4 \\ \hline 26.8 \end{array}$$

Reinforces Concept- and Skill-Builder Lessons 3, 7–11.
Reinforces Courseware Modules Multiplying Decimals; and Dividing Decimals.

CONCEPTS
- Use decimal place value to create small numbers.
- Use mathematical reasoning.
- Verify reasonableness of answers.
- Multiply one-digit decimal numbers by whole numbers.
- Compare decimal numbers.

Variations	Additional Concepts
a. Draw four cards each. Use them with your 0 to make a decimal number less than 1 and a whole number. Try to get the least product.	Multiply multi-digit decimal numbers by whole numbers.
b. Draw four cards each. Use them with your 0 to make a decimal number less than 1 and a whole number. Try to get the least quotient.	Divide decimal numbers by whole numbers.

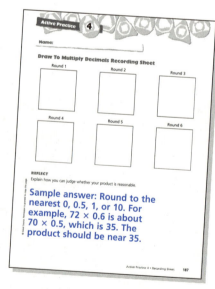

Active Practice 4 Recording Sheet

174 iSucceed MATH: Draw To Multiply Decimals

MODEL AND REFLECT

As you play a model game, encourage students to think mathematically by asking questions such as:

- *How do you decide where to place each digit?*
- *What is the least decimal number you can make with these digits?*
- *What is the least product you can make? What digits will you need?*

Assess and Reteach

Have the student review, as needed, these courseware modules: *Multiplying Decimals; Dividing Decimals.*

Skills To Check	Indicators	Reteaching
Does the student understand decimal place value?	The student knows who has won each round.	Have the student play *Fill In 1 Whole* (Active Practice 1) to review models for tenths and hundredths.
Can the student multiply and divide decimal numbers?	The student consistently finds the correct product or quotient.	Use Cardstock C1–3: Place-Value Models or C4–5: Paper Money and Coins. Have the student model multiplication as repeated addition of tenths or hundredths, or model division as breaking tenths and hundredths into equal groups.

Active Practice 4

Active Practice 5

Order Fractions

MATERIALS PER PAIR
- Two sets Fraction/Decimal Cards, fraction tenths cards only (18 cards) **(Cardstock C9–11)**
- Two Order Fractions Recording Sheets
- Two pencils

Round 1

| | $\frac{2}{10}$ | | | $\frac{6}{10}$ | | |

TO PLAY
1. Shuffle the cards and place them face down.
2. Take turns. Draw a card. Read the number and tell how you will choose where to write it. **(I drew 2 tenths. I will put it in the second spot because there is only one choice less than 2 tenths.)** Write the number in an empty space on your recording sheet. If there is no empty space that works for your number, you lose your turn.
3. If you are the first to fill in your recording sheet with numbers in order from least to greatest, you win. Play 2 rounds.

Variations
a. Use all of the fraction tenths and fraction hundredths from one set of Fraction/Decimal Cards (20 cards). **(Cardstock C8–9)**
b. Use one complete set of Fraction/Decimal cards (40 cards). **(Cardstock C8–11)**

Reinforces Concept- and Skill-Builder Lessons 1, 3, 13, 18, 36.
Reinforces Courseware Modules Understanding and Adding Fractions; and Decimals.

CONCEPTS
- Read and write fractions.
- Compare and order fractions with like denominators
- Use mathematical reasoning.

Variations	Additional Concepts
a. Use all of the fraction tenths and hundredths from one set of Fraction/Decimal Cards (20 cards).	Compare and order fractions with unlike denominators
b. Use one complete set of Fraction/Decimal cards (40 cards).	Compare and order decimal numbers and fractions (tenths and hundredths).

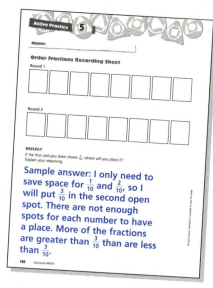

Active Practice 5 Recording Sheet

iSucceed MATH: Order Decimal Numbers

MODEL AND REFLECT

As you play a model game, encourage students to think mathematically by asking questions such as:

- *How can the diagram on the card help you compare the fractions?*
- *How do you decide where to place each number?*

ssess and Reteach

Have the student review as needed, lessons in these courseware modules: *Understanding and Adding Fractions; Decimals.*

Skills To Check	Indicators	Reteaching
Can the student read and write fractions?	The student correctly names the number on each card and correctly writes the number on the recording sheet.	• Use Copymaster M5: Grid Paper. Have the student shade and label 1 tenth of a rectangle with words (one tenth) and numbers ($\frac{1}{10}$). Repeat for 2 tenths, and so forth.
Can the student compare and order fractions (and decimal numbers)?	The student orders the numbers correctly and places them appropriately to save space for numbers that are greater and less.	• Use the shaded diagrams in Cardstock C8–11: Fraction/Decimal Cards. Have the student place all of the fraction cards or all of the decimal cards in order from least to greatest. • Ask the student to describe how the shaded diagrams on the cards can help them to compare the fractions or decimal numbers.

Active Practice 5

Active Practice 6

Giant Inch

MATERIALS PER PAIR
- One coin
- Two Giant Inch Recording Sheets
- Two pencils

$\frac{2}{8} = \frac{1}{4}$

TO PLAY

1. Take turns. Flip the coin. If it lands heads up, shade 2 eighths of the Giant Inch. For tails, shade 1 eighth.
2. Tell how many eighths you have shaded altogether. **(I have 2 eighths shaded.)** Write the fraction. ($\frac{2}{8}$)
3. If you can write the fraction another way with a smaller denominator, write that fraction, too. If you do, you may take another turn. ($\frac{2}{8} = \frac{1}{4}$)
4. If you fill your Giant Inch first, you win the round. Play 3 rounds.

Variations

a. Start with one whole inch. Flip the coin and cross out one or two eighths on each turn. Tell how much you have left.

b. On each turn, write the starting amount, how much you added, and the sum. ($\frac{2}{8} + \frac{1}{8} = \frac{3}{8}$)

Reinforces Concept- and Skill-Builder Lessons 13, 15, 19–20.
Reinforces Courseware Modules Understanding and Adding Fractions; and Subtracting Fractions.

CONCEPTS

- Represent fractions with models.
- Write fractions.
- Add fractions.
- Recognize equivalent fractions.

Variations	Additional Concepts
a. Start with one whole inch. Flip the coin and cross out one or two eighths on each turn. Tell how much you have left.	Subtract fractions.
b. On each turn, write the starting amount, how much you added, and the sum. ($\frac{2}{8} + \frac{1}{8} = \frac{3}{8}$)	Write fraction-addition equations.

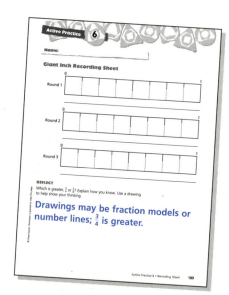

Active Practice 6 Recording Sheet

178 iSucceed MATH: Giant Inch

MODEL AND REFLECT

As students play, encourage them to think carefully and stretch mathematically by asking questions such as:

- *How many more eighths do you need to have one half shaded?*
- *Who has more shaded? How much more? How can you tell?*
- *Do you have more or less than $\frac{3}{4}$ shaded now? How do you know?*

Assess and Reteach

Have the student review, as needed, lessons in these courseware modules: *Understanding and Adding Fractions; Subtracting Fractions.*

Skills To Check	Indicators	Reteaching
Does the student connect a visual model to a fraction?	The student correctly names the amount shaded on each turn.	Fold a sheet of paper and open to model halves. Fold another twice and open to model fourths, and fold another three times to model eighths. Have the student name the fractional parts.
Can the student write fractions to match models?	The student records the correct fraction on each turn.	Help the student understand that the denominator tells how many equal parts are in a whole, and the numerator is the number of shaded parts.
Can the student recognize equivalent fractions?	The student writes $\frac{2}{8} = \frac{1}{4}$, $\frac{4}{8} = \frac{1}{2}$, $\frac{6}{8} = \frac{3}{4}$.	Use Cardstock C6–7: Fraction Models to help students add and find equivalent fractions.

Active Practice 6

Active Practice 7

Draw To Add Fractions

MATERIALS PER PAIR
- Two sets of Digit Cards without zeros (18 cards) **(Cardstock C12)**
- Two Draw To Add Fractions Recording Sheets
- Two pencils

TO PLAY
1. Sort out from the Digit Cards the 2s, 4s, and 8s. These are your denominators. The other cards will be your numerators. Shuffle both stacks and place them face down.
2. Both players draw two denominators and two numerators.
3. Make 2 fractions with your cards. Find the sum on your recording sheet.
4. If your sum is less, you win the round. Explain how you know your sum is less. (My $\frac{7}{8}$ is less than your $\frac{9}{8}$. I know that because $\frac{7}{8}$ is less than one whole and $\frac{9}{8}$ is greater than one whole.) Play 6 rounds.

Round 1

$$\frac{2}{4} + \frac{3}{8} = \frac{7}{8}$$

Variations
a. Find the difference instead of the sum. The least difference wins.
b. Place the 1–9 Digit Cards in a stack. Draw 4 cards and create 2 fractions. The greatest possible sum wins.

Reinforces Concept- and Skill-Builder Lessons 15, 19–20.
Reinforces Courseware Modules Understanding and Adding Fractions; and Subtracting Fractions.

CONCEPTS
- Add simple fractions.
- Compare fractions.
- Find equivalent fractions.
- Use mathematical reasoning.

Variations	Additional Concepts
a. Find the difference instead of the sum. The least difference wins.	Subtract simple fractions.
b. Place the 1–9 Digit Cards in a stack. Draw 4 cards and create 2 fractions. The greatest possible sum wins.	Add fractions with more challenging denominators.

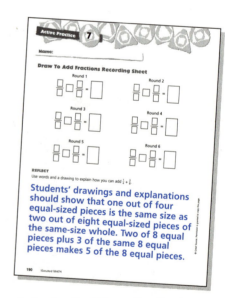

Active Practice 7 Recording Sheet

180 iSucceed MATH: Draw To Add Fractions

MODEL AND REFLECT

As you play a model game, encourage students to think mathematically by asking questions such as:

- *For which denominator is each equal part of the whole greater? Why?*
- *How can you show that $\frac{2}{4}$ has the same value as $\frac{1}{2}$?*
- *What is the least fraction you can make with these digits? The greatest?*

Assess and Reteach

Have the student review, as needed, these courseware modules: *Understanding and Adding Fractions; Subtracting Fractions.*

Skills To Check	Indicators	Reteaching
Does the student understand the relative size of eighths, fourths, and halves?	The student consistently places the greater numerator with the greater denominator when aiming for the least sum.	• Use Copymaster M5: Grid Paper. Draw eighths (2 rows of 4 boxes). Choose a Digit Card. Have the student shade that many eighths, and tell whether the shaded part is greater or less than $\frac{1}{4}$ and than $\frac{1}{2}$. • Have the student play *Giant Inch* (Active Practice 6) to review fractions of a whole.
Does the student know how to convert among halves, fourths, and eighths?	The student correctly adds fractions with different denominators.	• Use Copymaster M5: Grid Paper. Draw eighths (2 rows of 4 boxes). Shade $\frac{1}{4}$, $\frac{1}{2}$, or $\frac{3}{4}$ and have the student tell the fraction shaded and the number of eighths shaded
Does the student understand that only the numerators are added (or subtracted)?	The student consistently finds the correct sum (or difference).	• Have the student play *Giant Inch* (Active Practice 6) to review adding very simple fractions.
Can the student compare unlike fractions?	The student correctly identifies who won the round.	• Use Copymaster M5: Grid Paper. Have the student sketch and shade rectangles divided into eighths to model each sum.

Active Practice 7

Active Practice 8

Integers

MATERIALS PER PAIR
- One 0–5 number cube and a +/− cube
- Two Integers Recording Sheets
- Two pencils

TO PLAY
1. Take turns. Roll the cubes. Name your number and tell how you know where to write it. **(I rolled −1. I will write it just to the left of the 0 because it is one less than 0.)**
2. If there is no empty space that works for your number, you lose your turn.
3. If you are the first to fill in your recording sheet with numbers in order from least to greatest, left to right, you win. Play 2 rounds.

Variations
a. Use three number cubes (1–6, 0–5, and +/−). Make two integers. Add them. After two rounds, the greatest sum wins.
b. Use three number cubes (1–6, 0–5, and +/−). Make two integers. Multiply them. After two rounds, the least product wins.

Reinforces Concept- and Skill-Builder Lesson 30, 36.
Reinforces Courseware Module Positive and Negative Integers.

CONCEPTS
- Compare and order integers −5 through 5.
- Use mathematical reasoning.

Variations	Additional Concepts
a. Use three number cubes (1–6, 0–5, and +/−). Make two integers. Add them. After two rounds, the greatest sum wins.	Add integers.
b. Use three number cubes (1–6, 0–5, and +/−). Make two integers. Multiply them. After two rounds, the least product wins.	Multiply integers.

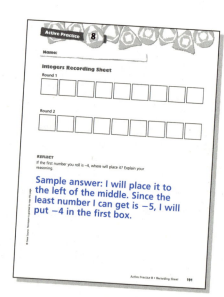

Active Practice 8 Recording Sheet

MODEL AND REFLECT

As you play a model game, encourage students to think mathematically by asking questions such as:

- *What is the greatest number you can make with this cube? What is the least?*
- *How do you decide where to place each number?*
- *Which number is neither positive nor negative?*

Assess and Reteach

Have the student review as needed, lessons in this courseware module: *Positive and Negative Integers.*

Skills To Check	Indicators	Reteaching
Does the student understand that negative and positive integers are on opposite sides of zero on the number line?	The student writes integers a reasonable distance from 0 and on the correct side of 0.	• Use Copymaster M2: Number Lines. Label a number line from −10 through 10. Label 0. Have the student label 1, then −1, 2, then −2, and so forth. • Ask the student to count the number of units from 0 for each negative integer.
Can the student order integers?	The student writes numbers in order from least to greatest.	• Use Copymaster M2: Number Lines. Label a number line from −10 through 10. Ask the student questions such as: *What number is one unit farther from 0 than −3?* (−4) *What number is one unit closer to 0?* (−2)
Variation a: Can the student add integers?	The student does not struggle to find the sum of a positive and a negative integer.	• Use Copymaster M2: Number Lines. Work through finding the first addend, then letting the second addend tell you in which direction and how many units to move to find the sum. • Allow the student to use the number lines to play the game.
Variation b: Can the student multiply integers?	The student does not struggle to find the product of a positive and a negative integer.	• Use Copymaster M2: Number Lines. Work through starting at 0, then using the negative factor to tell you the size of each jump to the left. Use the positive factor to tell you the number of jumps. • Allow the student to use the number lines to play the game.

Active Practice 8

Active Practice 1

Name:

Fill In 1 Whole Recording Sheet

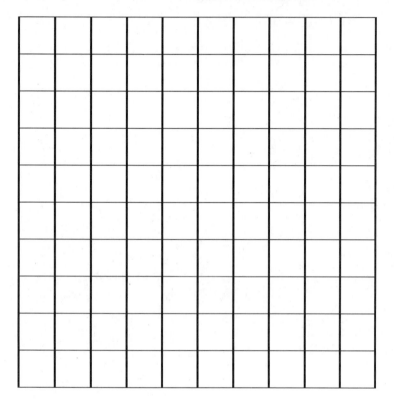

REFLECT

If your grid has 0.85 filled, what numbers can you roll to exactly fill your grid? Explain how you know.

Active Practice 2

Name: _____

Order Decimal Numbers Recording Sheet

Round 1

0							1

Round 2

0							1

REFLECT

If the first card you draw shows 0.8, where will you place it? Explain your reasoning.

Active Practice 3

Name:

Draw To Add Decimals Recording Sheet

Round 1

0.⬜
+ 0.⬜
———

Round 2

0.⬜
+ 0.⬜
———

Round 3

0.⬜
+ 0.⬜
———

Round 4

0.⬜
+ 0.⬜
———

Round 5

0.⬜
+ 0.⬜
———

Round 6

0.⬜
+ 0.⬜
———

REFLECT

Can you tell who will win the round before you compute? Explain.

Active Practice 4

Name:

Draw To Multiply Decimals Recording Sheet

Round 1

Round 2

Round 3

Round 4

Round 5

Round 6

REFLECT

Explain how you can judge whether your product is reasonable.

Active Practice 5

Name:

Order Fractions Recording Sheet

Round 1

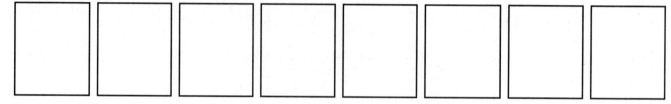

Round 2

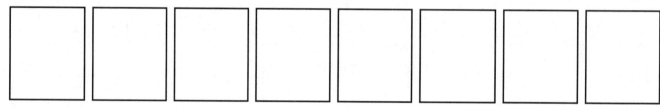

REFLECT

If the first card you draw shows $\frac{3}{10}$, where will you place it? Explain your reasoning.

188   iSucceed MATH

Active Practice 6

Name:

Giant Inch Recording Sheet

Round 1

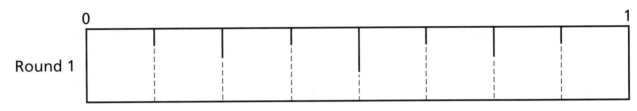

Round 2

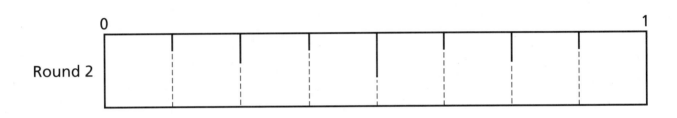

Round 3

REFLECT

Which is greater, $\frac{3}{4}$ or $\frac{3}{8}$? Explain how you know. Use a drawing to help show your thinking.

Active Practice 7

Name:

Draw To Add Fractions Recording Sheet

Round 1

$$\frac{\square}{\square} \square \frac{\square}{\square} = \square$$

Round 2

$$\frac{\square}{\square} \square \frac{\square}{\square} = \square$$

Round 3

$$\frac{\square}{\square} \square \frac{\square}{\square} = \square$$

Round 4

$$\frac{\square}{\square} \square \frac{\square}{\square} = \square$$

Round 5

$$\frac{\square}{\square} \square \frac{\square}{\square} = \square$$

Round 6

$$\frac{\square}{\square} \square \frac{\square}{\square} = \square$$

REFLECT

Use words and a drawing to explain how you can add $\frac{1}{4} + \frac{3}{8}$.

Active Practice 8

Name:

Integers Recording Sheet

Round 1

☐ ☐ ☐ ☐ ☐ ☐ ☐ ☐ ☐

Round 2

☐ ☐ ☐ ☐ ☐ ☐ ☐ ☐ ☐

REFLECT

If the first number you roll is –4, where will place it? Explain your reasoning.

Place-Value Charts

Name:

Number Lines

Name:

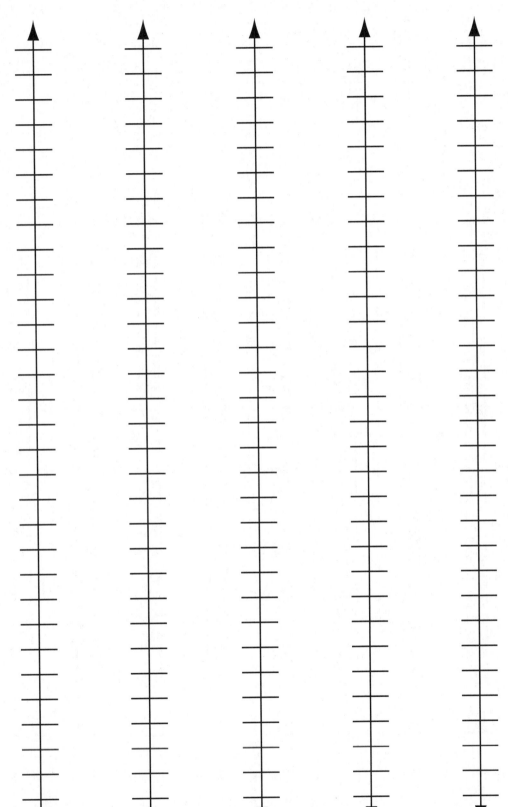

Place-Value Models

Name:

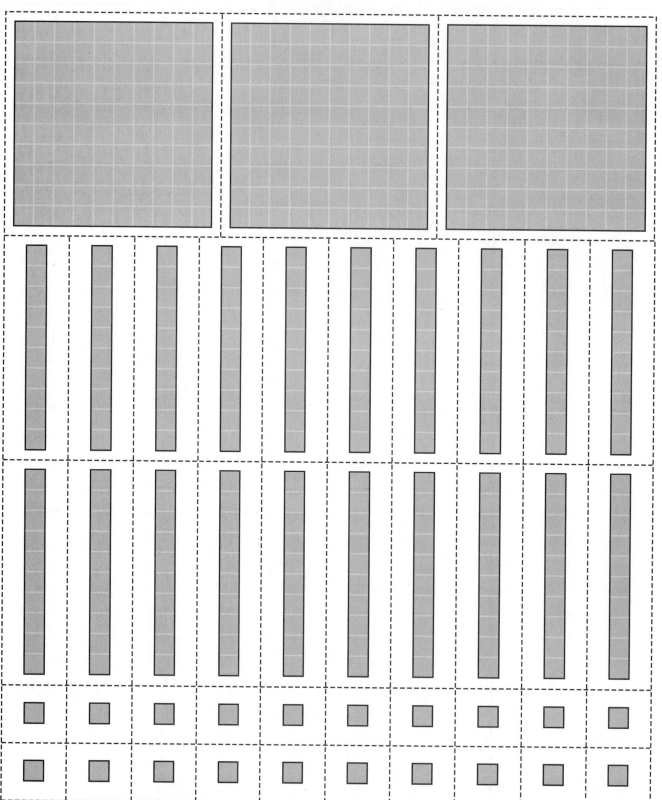

Place-Value Addition and Subtraction

Name:

M4 • Place-Value Addition and Subtraction

Grid Paper

Name:

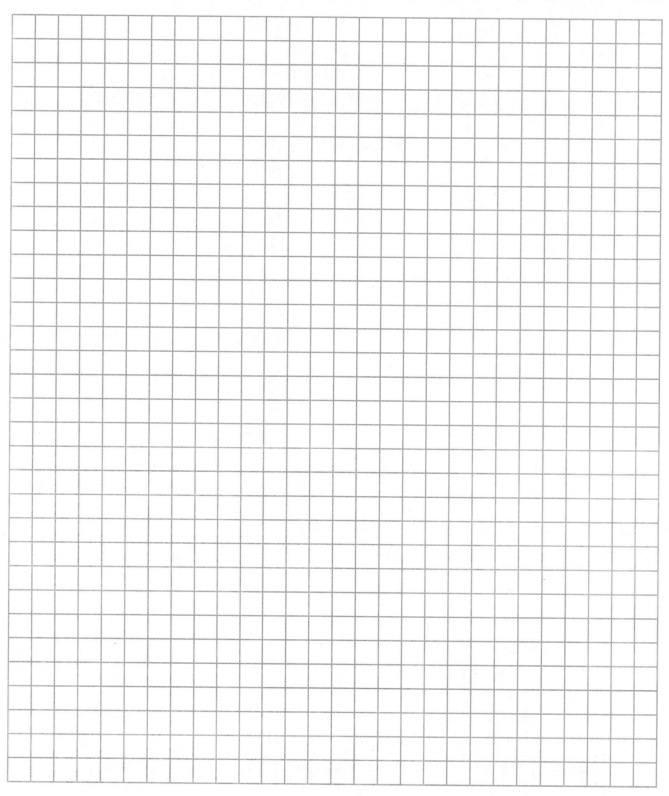

Hundred Charts

Name:

1	2	3	4	5	6	7	8	9	10
11	12	13	14	15	16	17	18	19	20
21	22	23	24	25	26	27	28	29	30
31	32	33	34	35	36	37	38	39	40
41	42	43	44	45	46	47	48	49	50
51	52	53	54	55	56	57	58	59	60
61	62	63	64	65	66	67	68	69	70
71	72	73	74	75	76	77	78	79	80
81	82	83	84	85	86	87	88	89	90
91	92	93	94	95	96	97	98	99	100

1	2	3	4	5	6	7	8	9	10
11	12	13	14	15	16	17	18	19	20
21	22	23	24	25	26	27	28	29	30
31	32	33	34	35	36	37	38	39	40
41	42	43	44	45	46	47	48	49	50
51	52	53	54	55	56	57	58	59	60
61	62	63	64	65	66	67	68	69	70
71	72	73	74	75	76	77	78	79	80
81	82	83	84	85	86	87	88	89	90
91	92	93	94	95	96	97	98	99	100

1	2	3	4	5	6	7	8	9	10
11	12	13	14	15	16	17	18	19	20
21	22	23	24	25	26	27	28	29	30
31	32	33	34	35	36	37	38	39	40
41	42	43	44	45	46	47	48	49	50
51	52	53	54	55	56	57	58	59	60
61	62	63	64	65	66	67	68	69	70
71	72	73	74	75	76	77	78	79	80
81	82	83	84	85	86	87	88	89	90
91	92	93	94	95	96	97	98	99	100

iSucceed MATH © Great Source. Permission is granted to copy this page.

Index

A

Absolute value, 131

Active practice model lesson, 168–183

Active practice recording sheet, 184–191

Addition
   addend, 22, 84, 86, 108, 110, 134
   algorithm, 24, 85
   checking, 30–33
   decimal numbers, 22–25, 168–169, 172–173
   fractions, 84–87, 178–179, 180–181
   integers, 134–137
   mixed numbers, 108–111
   rational numbers, 158–161
   regrouping, 24
   sum, 22, 84, 86, 108, 110, 134, 158, 160
   using a number line, 86, 87, 136, 160
   using models, 24, 84–87, 135
   using place value, 24

Approximation, 151

C

Calculator, 124–128

Choose a computation method, 126

Common denominators, 108, 112–114, 155

Compare
   decimals, 18–21, 170–171, 172–173, 174–175
   fractions, 80–83, 176–177, 180–181
   integers, 182–183
   mixed numbers, 81
   rational numbers, 154–157
   using a number line, 21, 82, 156
   using benchmarks, 81, 82
   symbols (<, =, >), 18, 80, 82

Copymasters
   grid paper M5, 196
   hundred charts M6, 197
   number lines M2, 193
   place-value addition and subtraction M4, 195
   place-value charts M1, 192
   place-value models M3, 194

Counting numbers, 131

D

Decimal numbers
   addition, 22–25, 168–169, 172–173
   and fractions, 15, 23, 76–79, 117, 118, 152, 156
   and mixed numbers, 152
   and money, 12, 14–17, 77
   compare, 18–21, 170–171, 172–173, 174–175, 176–177
   decimal point, 10, 12, 14, 15, 16
   division, 42–45, 46–49, 174–175
   equivalent, 28
   hundredth, 10, 12, 14, 20, 22
   in place-value charts, 11, 16
   modeling, 11, 12, 20, 23, 24, 28
   multiplication, 34–37, 174–175
   order, 18–21, 170–171
   patterns, 13, 15
   reading, 12, 13, 15, 16, 20, 77, 170–171
   subtraction, 26–29, 168–169
   tenth, 10, 12, 14, 20, 22
   writing, 12, 13, 77, 170–171

Distributive Property, 113, 117

198   iSucceed MATH

Division
  algorithm, 43, 163
  and fractions, 64–69
  checking, 43, 50–53
  decimal numbers, 42–45, 46–49
  dividend, 42, 46, 64, 66, 100, 102, 120
  divisor, 42, 46–49, 64, 66, 100, 102, 120
  fractions, 100–104
  integers, 146–149
  mixed numbers, 120–123
  modeling, 100–104
  quotient, 42, 46, 100, 102, 120, 146, 162
  rational numbers, 162–165
  reciprocals, 100, 103, 120, 122, 123
  using a number line, 122, 147, 148, 164
  whole numbers, 42–45
  zero in the quotient, 43

Equivalent fractions, 47, 65, 68–71, 85, 93, 110, 114, 178–179, 180–181

Error Alert, 43, 57, 61

Error Analysis, 23, 121

Estimate
  compatible numbers, 47, 50–52
  differences, 31, 32
  products, 36, 39–41
  quotients, 52, 53
  sums, 31, 32, 86
  using benchmarks, 86, 90

Fact families, 148, 164

Fractions
  adding, 84–87, 178–179, 180–181
  and decimal numbers, 15, 23, 76–79, 117, 118, 152, 156
  and division, 64–67
  and measurement, 69
  and money, 23, 77
  as a remainder, 65
  circle model, 61
  compare, 80–83, 176–177, 180–181
  defined, 56, 68
  denominator, 56, 57, 60, 64, 66, 72
  dividing, 100–103
  drawing, 61
  equivalent, 47, 65, 68–71, 85, 93, 110, 114, 178–179, 180–181
  factor, 72, 74
  fourth, 56, 59, 60
  greatest common factor (GCF), 72–75
  half, 56, 57, 60
  modeling, 62, 63, 66, 73, 78, 178–179
  multiplying, 92–96
  numerator, 56, 57, 60, 64, 66, 72
  on a number line, 65, 70
  order, 80–83, 176–177
  part of a set, 56–59
  parts of a whole, 57, 60–63
  reading, 57, 58, 176–177
  reciprocals, 96–99, 103, 123
  renaming, 85
  simplest form, 65, 69, 72–75, 77
  subtracting, 88–91
  third, 56, 59, 60
  unit fractions, 121
  writing, 176–177, 178–179

Greatest common factor (GCF), 72–75

Identity Property of Multiplication, 109

Improper fractions, 65

Inequality symbols (≠, < , >), 7

Integers
    absolute value, 131
    adding, 134–137
    and temperature, 132
    compare, 182–183
    defined, 131, 132
    dividing, 146–149
    multiplying, 142–145
    negative numbers, 130–133
    on a number line, 131–133
    opposites, 130–133, 138
    order, 182–183
    positive numbers, 130–133
    subtracting, 138–141

Inverse operations
    addition and subtraction, 31, 32
    multiplication and division, 43, 147, 163

Irrational numbers, 151

Journal, 7, 13, 17, 21, 25, 29, 33, 37, 41, 45, 49, 53, 59, 63, 67, 71, 75, 79, 83, 87, 91, 95, 99, 103, 107, 111, 115, 119, 123, 127, 133, 137, 141, 145, 149, 153, 157, 161, 165

Mental math, 48, 121, 124, 126, 169

Mixed numbers
    adding, 108–111
    and decimal numbers, 105, 156
    common denominators, 108, 109, 110, 112
    dividing, 120–123
    expanding, 110, 114
    multiplying, 116–119
    reading, 105, 106
    renaming, 65, 85, 105, 106, 108, 109, 110, 112
    subtracting, 112–115
    writing, 106

Money
    and decimals, 12, 14–17, 23, 48
    and problem solving, 25, 29, 33, 45, 49, 119, 127
    combinations, 17
    dollar sign ($), 14, 16

Multiplication
    algorithm, 163
    checking, 38–41
    decimal numbers, 34–37, 174–175
    factor, 34, 35, 92, 96, 116, 142, 144
    fractions, 92–96
    integers, 142–145
    mixed numbers, 116–119
    modeling, 92–96
    product, 34, 35, 92, 96, 116, 142, 144, 162
    rational numbers, 162–165
    using a number line, 93, 144, 164
    using the Distributive Property, 117
    whole numbers, 36

Number line, 21, 32, 40, 65, 66, 70, 82, 83, 86, 87, 90, 91, 93, 106, 110, 122, 136, 140, 144, 148, 152, 156, 160, 164

Odd numbers, 45

Opposites, 130, 138, 140, 152, 158, 160

Order
    decimals, 18–21, 170–171
    fractions, 80–83, 176–177
    integers, 182–183
    rational numbers, 154–157
    using a number line, 21, 82, 156

Order of operations, 125

Patterns, 13

Personal glossary, 6

Place value, 15, 47, 79, 155, 172–173, 174–175

Problem-solving strategies and skills
    Act It Out, 59
    Check for Reasonableness, 41, 53, 99, 111
    Choose an Estimate or Exact Amount, 25, 29, 83
    Combine Strategies, 95
    Draw a Diagram, 5, 99
    Draw a Picture, 21, 63, 71, 87, 91
    Find Information You Need, 7
    Guess, Check, and Revise, 149
    Is the Answer Reasonable? 33, 75, 79, 127
    Look for a Pattern, 13, 67, 103, 123, 153
    Make a List, 17
    Make a Plan, 161, 165
    More Than One Answer, 149
    Solve in More Than One Way, 45, 115, 141
    Solve Multi-Step Problems, 49, 53, 145, 157
    Use Logical Reasoning, 107, 133, 145
    Use Simpler Numbers, 119
    Write an Equation, 37, 137, 161, 165

Rational numbers
    adding, 158–161
    as fractions, 81
    compare, 154–157
    defined, 150, 151
    dividing, 162–165
    equivalent forms, 151, 168
    multiplying, 162–165
    on a number line, 152
    opposites, 152
    order, 154–157
    subtracting, 158–161

Reciprocals, 96–99, 100, 103, 120–123

Remainder, 65

Round
    decimals, 31, 32, 38, 39, 51
    to nearest whole number, 38, 39
    using a number line, 40

Skip counting, 66

Subtraction
   algorithm, 28, 112–115
   checking, 30–33
   decimal numbers, 26–29, 168–169
   difference, 26, 88, 90, 112, 138, 140, 158, 160
   fractions, 88–91, 168–169
   integers, 138–141
   missing addend, 88–90
   mixed numbers, 112–115
   rational numbers, 158–161
   regroup, 26, 27, 112, 113
   using a number line, 90, 140, 160
   using models, 28, 139
   using place value, 28

Word wall, 4, 10, 14, 18, 22, 26, 30, 34, 38, 42, 46, 50, 56, 60, 64, 68, 72, 76, 80, 84, 88, 92, 96, 100, 104, 108, 112, 116, 120, 124, 130, 134, 138, 142, 146, 150, 154, 158, 162

Zero, 130, 131